The Tortured Life of Scofield Thayer

UNIVERSITY PRESS OF FLORIDA

Florida A&M University, Tallahassee
Florida Atlantic University, Boca Raton
Florida Gulf Coast University, Ft. Myers
Florida International University, Miami
Florida State University, Tallahassee
New College of Florida, Sarasota
University of Central Florida, Orlando
University of Florida, Gainesville
University of North Florida, Jacksonville
University of South Florida, Tampa
University of West Florida, Pensacola

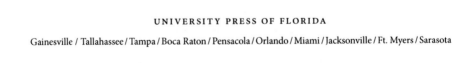
UNIVERSITY PRESS OF FLORIDA

Gainesville / Tallahassee / Tampa / Boca Raton / Pensacola / Orlando / Miami / Jacksonville / Ft. Myers / Sarasota

THE TORTURED LIFE OF

SCOFIELD THAYER

JAMES DEMPSEY

This book may be available in an electronic edition.

19 18 17 16 15 14   6 5 4 3 2 1

Dempsey, James, 1948– author.
The tortured life of Scofield Thayer / James Dempsey.
pages cm
Includes bibliographical references and index.
Summary: Scofield Thayer, as owner of The Dial during the 1920s, was the center of the
flow of cultural ideas between the United States and Europe, particularly those of the
various modernist movements. This is the first biography of Thayer.
ISBN 978-0-8130-4926-7
1. Thayer, Scofield, 1889–1982. 2. Poets, American—20th century—Biography.
3. Authors and publishers—United States—20th century—Biography. I. Title.
PS3539.H175Z57 2014
811'.52—dc23   [B]   2013034527

The University Press of Florida is the scholarly publishing agency for the State University
System of Florida, comprising Florida A&M University, Florida Atlantic University,
Florida Gulf Coast University, Florida International University, Florida State University,
New College of Florida, University of Central Florida, University of Florida, University
of North Florida, University of South Florida, and University of West Florida.

University Press of Florida
15 Northwest 15th Street
Gainesville, FL 32611-2079
http://www.upf.com

FOR GAIL

I have no home unless it be
The tortured excellence of the sea.

FROM SCOFIELD THAYER'S "ON AN OLD
PAINTING OF PORTSMOUTH HARBOR"

CONTENTS

PREFACE

Scofield Thayer's grave is a ten-minute walk from my office, and I visited it many times while writing this book. The three graves in the Thayer lot—his father and mother are also interred there—lie in the shadow of a monolithic lozenge of granite ten feet high. The monument is quite unlike the elaborate crypts and funerary décor in the graveyard, much of which radiates a genteel Victorianism. The Thayer stone is imposingly minimalistic, all the more so for so much work having gone into the smoothness of its upper surface and its flawlessness of form. It is inscribed with the names of the Thayers—Edward, Florence, and Scofield—and the circled pattée cross that Thayer referred to as looking like "a potato-chip or a Nabisco wafer." Thayer saw everything in terms of metaphor.

Scofield Thayer's mental eclipse came in the prime of his life. He was hospitalized in his late thirties and not long after declared to be, in the unsentimental language of the time, "an insane person." His madness, which was advertised annually in the local newspaper, as required by state law, ended a flaringly brief career that had powerfully influenced the art and literature of the twentieth century. As owner and editor of the *Dial*, Thayer published the writing and the art of a vast number of talents, both American and European, both avant-garde and traditional, and in doing so introduced the ideas of modernism to America and gave American artists a new audience in Europe.

But Thayer's story has never been fully told. His name appears in many of the books on the intellectual and cultural history of the period, and he shows up again and again in the biographies and correspondence of his contemporaries, where he is more often than not given a walk-on role as a wealthy, effete patron of the arts. With such little concrete information available, it is unsurprising that the image that comes down to us is largely a simplified and therefore distorted one. For instance, that he was cuckolded by his friend E. E. Cummings and that Hemingway famously referred to him as "Scofield Buggaring Thayer" has given rise to the perception of Thayer as homosexual. But we find from his papers that Thayer discovered soon after his first and only marriage that he could never be happy with one sexual partner and that he needed continuing novelty in his intimacies; it was he who decided that he and his wife would live separately. And as for Hemingway, the fact that his poems were turned down by Thayer is more than enough to provoke such a Hemingwayesque homophobic rant. Biographers, of course, can be somewhat conflicted about using their research skills to put people in bed with others, but with Thayer the endeavor is probably at least defensible (if not wholly honorable), and the record shows that while Thayer may have made an occasional foray into the homoerotic, he was also undeniably and indeed rampantly heterosexual. As his mental illness worsened, his passion for flawless young women apparently perverted itself into a lust for the inappropriately minor female.

Thayer saw himself as a philosopher and a poet. He was a student of the philosopher George Santayana, who would later use a Thayer-like character as the hero in his best-selling novel *The Last Puritan*. Thayer's verse was praised by Cummings, Marianne Moore, and others. Indeed, the epigraph to this book refers to a line from Thayer's poem "On an Old Painting of Portsmouth Harbor," which treats, among other things, of Thayer's discomfort in the world, his inability to find respite except while piloting his beloved sailboat: "I have no home, unless it be / The tortured excellence of the sea." Thayer, whose looks women described as Byronic, was a twentieth-century Childe Harold, a disillusioned wanderer, an eternal student of the world around him, one for whom the creations of art and literature brought an aesthetic ecstasy but who was never at peace in the world or with the people who generated those beautiful things.

Thayer's Oxford friend Valentine Farrar, who died of a bullet wound to the head in the trenches of the Great War, made the prescient remark that Thayer would be remembered for something other than his philosophy or his verse. "If you do any permanent work," he said, "I doubt if it will be in a genre which will appeal to you." And indeed, Thayer's greatest achievement must be the *Dial* of the 1920s. The importance of the little magazine in not only distributing but also formulating the art, literature, and criticism of the twentieth century has long been recognized by scholars, as has the importance of these publications in manifesting the social and aesthetic currents of the period. Further, the *Dial* has been singled out by scholars for its untold influence on the 1920s and the decades beyond. This was partly due to its relative longevity. Few little magazines outlasted the enthusiasm of their founders, and the rate of infant mortality among these earnest journals was high. *The Dial*, however, lasted the entire decade under Thayer and his partner, James Sibley Watson, thanks to not only the deep and generous pockets of its owners but also the choice of material for the magazine, which was exquisitely in touch with both traditional work and the avant-garde. Many of the writers and artists featured in the *Dial* would comprise a major portion of the canon of the century's culture. *The Dial* brought to the notice of American and European readers the work of Cummings, T. S. Eliot, Ezra Pound, Thomas Mann, William Carlos Williams, Marianne Moore, Bertrand Russell, Romain Roland, Edmund Wilson, Van Wyck Brooks, and many others. The artists whose work was seen (often for the first time) by readers included Picasso, Matisse, Chagall, Klimt, O'Keefe, Demuth, and Lachaise.

But to Thayer, the *Dial* was an albatross around his neck. It never in its almost ten years of existence turned a profit and, in fact, cost its owners as much as a hundred thousand dollars a year to keep going. Thayer complained that the magazine gave him no time to write, but the truth is that Thayer was deeply involved with microscopic details regarding the magazine, once pulping and reprinting an entire run because of a single grammatical error, as well as choosing, buying, and overseeing the reproduction of art in the magazine (his art collection, worth about $15 million at his death in 1982, was bequeathed to the Metropolitan Museum of Art in New York). With running a magazine, traveling, buying art, undergoing analysis, treating his many physical maladies, and conducting a complex set of personal relationships, Thayer had little time for anything else.

And yet, despite the magazine's impact in ushering modernism into America, Thayer himself rejected the label of modern. Indeed, he found much of the modernity celebrated by others—the city, technology, speed, mass-production—utterly horrific. He loathed the internal combustion engine, and many of his travels were not so much a search for adventure as an often desperate quest for peace and quiet. Since his vast fortune was created by his father's busily creative mind and the forces of the industrial and technological revolutions of the nineteenth century, Thayer must have seen the irony in his using that fortune to flee the factories and the cities that had created it.

Thayer found modernism more congenial in the form of art than of literature. He regarded Picasso as the greatest painter of his generation but was completely dismissive of Eliot's "disappointing" *The Waste Land* and

Ezra Pound's "silly" *Cantos*. He regarded James Joyce's later work as an unreadable failure. His championing of Cummings—the *Dial* just about made the poet's reputation—is perhaps understandable, considering how both men were highly visual in their tastes, Cummings as an artist and Thayer as a lover of art.

Thayer was also an early proponent of psychotherapy, and in 1921 he moved to Vienna for two years to become a patient of Freud's. For Thayer, psychoanalysis was very much an active, engaged practice. He challenged his therapists, including Freud, quizzing them on the very premises of their ideas and methods. Of course, this led to further inner conflict, for in challenging these ideas, Thayer was questioning what could potentially cure him. And if the analysand does not believe the process has any healing powers, what can be the outcome except failure? Indeed, one of his friends saw Thayer's eventual breakdown as an existential leap into insanity undertaken so as to demonstrate the superiority of his mind over the Freudian method. In this view, Thayer's mental eclipse was a tragedy of overweening coupled with an unshakeable disillusionment with life that, untouched by the ministrations of Freud and other analysts, sent Thayer plunging almost willingly into madness. There is romance in such a view, but the more banal fact is that the cause of his illness may well have been that form of schizophrenia that attacks the young up to the age of thirty. That Thayer was somewhat older than usual when the disease was noted may simply have been the cushioning effect of his wealth. Certainly, he manifested paranoid and schizophrenic behavior long before being diagnosed.

After his removal from public life in 1927, he became more and more a figure of mystery. The scholar Nicholas Joost hoped to write the biography, but Thayer was still alive, and his guardians refused to allow anything of a personal nature to be mentioned in Joost's books on the *Dial*. By the time he died in 1982, he was all but forgotten except by scholars of modernism.

My hope is that this book will set the figure of Scofield Thayer back where it belongs, at the center of that madding press of movements, talents, and personalities that has been subsumed, for better or worse, under the encrusting rubric of modernism. His correspondence and his personal writings show a man intensely involved in his time. He traveled frequently between America and Europe. His apartment at the Benedick in New York City was visited by artists and writers, and the monthly dinner at the offices of the *Dial* in Greenwich Village attracted artists, musicians, journalists, the literati, and celebrities. Thayer was one of the few Americans invited by Gerald and Sara

Murphy to the legendary champagne dinner party on the Seine to celebrate the 1923 opening of Igor Stravinsky's *Les noces*. Attending were Pablo Picasso, Darius Mulhaud, Jean Cocteau, Stravinsky, Sergei Diaghilev, Gontcharova, Mikhail Larionov, Marcelle Mayer, Ernest Ansermet (who conducted *Les noces*), and the poets Tristan Tzara and Blaise Cendrars. The gala itself, which featured hijinks by Picasso, Cocteau, and Stravinsky, has entered the lore of the period and become as much or more of a touchstone of modernism as the event it celebrated. Thayer's work as editor of the *Dial* and his voluminous correspondence with the writers and artists whose work he published gives us a sense of the frenetic and often contradictory intellectual and aesthetic currents that were then flowing, charging the era with a rare energy.

Thayer was a paradox—a millionaire who boasted of voting the Socialist ticket, a romantic who loved prostitutes, a man who would argue over a trifling tradesman's bill and yet who lavished money on artists and poets. With his curious blend of the Victorian and the libertine—social rudeness enraged him, yet he championed free love—Thayer was both a paradigm of propriety and a student of the crude. His taste was similarly far-reaching, and he enjoyed prizefights and burlesque as much as poetry readings and evenings at the opera. He was pugnacious regarding art and literature, and he rarely allowed a reputation to impress him. Of Pound and his exhortation that "Poetry should be at least as well written as prose," Thayer remarked, "Better, we hope, than his prose."

My trips to the hulking Thayer monolith were made with no real purpose other than to put myself into a space where Thayer, in life, had been. We know that he came to the site as a schoolboy when his father died suddenly in 1907. Probably, after being declared insane, he was here with his guardians when his mother died in 1936. And in July 1982, he made his final trip to the grave when his cremated remains were buried here.

Thayer spent much of his life seeking respite from the modern world through medicine, psychoanalysis, travel, and art. There is great irony, then, in his being perceived as the father of the *Dial*, the conduit through which passed so much of what would come to be called modernistic.

ACKNOWLEDGMENTS

It was Gerard Goggins, author and journalist, who first suggested Scofield Thayer to me as a project, and I thank him for what turned into a job that has pleasurably dominated my professional life for some years, even though I must say that it is fortunate that, at the tentative beginnings of my research, I was cheerfully ignorant of the vast amount of material I would need to view before this book took its final shape. My interest in the mysterious Thayer was also piqued by the work of three other journalists with whom it was my pleasure to work—Peter Donker, Gary Murray, and Daryl Perch.

I relied heavily on the work done by Nicholas Joost in his several books on Thayer and the *Dial* and also on his papers at Georgetown University Library. While Joost was unable to treat of Thayer's personal life, his precise descriptions of the daily workings of the magazine and its staff were endlessly useful. The Cummings scholar Michael Webster helped in filling in my knowledge of the poet and in transcribing Cummings's handwriting. Another Cummings expert and scholar, Bernard Stehle, was also generous with both his knowledge of and his material on Elaine Orr, Thayer's wife, and her daughter, Nancy. Dale Davis, literary executor for James Sibley Watson, welcomed me into her home and gave me access to material available nowhere else. My gratitude also goes out to the following individuals: Christopher Sinclair-Stevenson for permission to quote from the works and writing of Alyse Gregory; Sally Connely for permission to quote from the works of Llewelyn Powys; Craig Tenney for permission to quote from the works of Sherwood Anderson; Andy Lowe for permission to quote from the writing of Adolf Dehn; Stanley Ellis Cushing of the Boston Athenaeum for permission to quote from the papers of Stewart Mitchell; Anthony Burke for allowing me to quote from Kenneth Burke's correspondence; the Santayana Edition at Indiana University for allowing the use of quotes from

Santayana; Marianne and Tim Seldes for allowing me to quote from the work of Gilbert Seldes; Dale T. Davis for allowing me to quote from Dr. James Sibley Watson Jr. and Hildegarde Watson; and Mary Elizabeth Joost Lanigan for permitting me to quote from her father's writings.

I am also most grateful to Diane Ducharme of the Beinecke Rare Book and Manuscript Library at Yale University, who offered invaluable and unique help and insight into Thayer's life and his papers; to Katy Rawdon, formerly of the Barnes Foundation, whose warm hospitality and generosity were inversely proportional to the tiny office in which she and her colleagues labored before the Barnes moved to more spacious digs; and to Diane Pierce-Williams at Milton Academy and Lynn St. Germain from Bancroft School, who provided me with endlessly interesting and useful information about Thayer's early schooling.

I am particularly grateful to the librarians and archivists at all the institutions I visited during the research for this work, not only for their curating, preservation, and ordering of the material, without which literary researchers would be all but helpless, but also for their inherent intellectual generosity. I am particularly thankful and fortunate to have had the support and assistance of the entire staff of the George C. Gordon Library at Worcester Polytechnic Institute.

Many thanks to Professors David Dollenmayer and Ulrike Brisson of Worcester Polytechnic Institute for their translations from the German and also to Clark University's Alain Grenier for his translations from the French.

For the shuttling of my carcass to and from airports, for managing our home affairs during my many research absences, for her suggestions and support, and for allowing me to live for so long with half (or more) of my mind in the early part of the last century, love and thanks to my wife, Gail.

1

AN INTELLECTUAL SEWER

In the summer of 1924, a newspaper reporter from the *Worcester (Mass.) Sunday Telegram* conducted an interview with the portraitist John Christen Johansen, who had been hired by Worcester's Clark University to paint a full-length portrait of its president, Wallace A. Atwood. The college was young, having opened its doors only thirty-five years before, but it had already made a name for itself partly by hooking its star to the newly emerging field of psychology. A conference there in 1909 had drawn such luminaries of the growing discipline as Carl Jung and Sigmund Freud; it was to be, as the college still proudly points out, Freud's only visit to the United States.

Johansen was a successful, prize-winning artist and portraitist and an old-school and unapologetic representationalist who made a living painting the wealthy and powerful. He was in the mood to talk. The artist's first anecdote was intended to demonstrate that, as a craftsman, he would have no truck with the romantic or the mystical. He told of a young woman who had enthused inordinately over one of his portraits.

"Oh, you have got the spirit exactly," she gushed to Johansen. "You have seen through the veil."

"Madam," responded the crusty limner, "if there had been a veil there, I should have painted it."[1]

Johansen was just priming himself for an attack on his young contemporaries, who irritated him no end. For one thing, he was furious with what many were beginning to call modern art, which he felt was at best sloppy and at worst fraudulent. "There is no such thing as the modern or the new in art," he said. "There is good, or bad. The 'new' artists want to approach their drawings from an intellectual standpoint. Art comes from the heart. If it doesn't, it isn't art. They are not willing to spend any time on craft, in learning how to do things well. Even a plumber has apprentices who have to learn their jobs."

Warming to his subject, Johansen expanded his argument to include the so-called naturalists in both arts and letters.

"The naturalists in all the arts have carried things to such idiotic extremes that they have superimposed on their work the very thing they set out to destroy—self-consciousness," he said. "They were dreadfully opposed to the craftsmen in art and called them prudes. But when they themselves write or paint they do so desire not to be prudish that they swing to the other extreme and concentrate upon the obscene. You will find that to be true in the novel and in the 'new' painting. If there is no definite obscene subject, the lines themselves are obscene, and there is an obscene effect."

He also criticized the subject matter of the moderns. "Instead of taking the great point of view, they take the little one," he went on. "They look at a small thing until it becomes too large to them. All great artists have done epic things, with proportionate epic figures. Even Matisse is doing figures of a woman looking searchingly at a hairpin or looking at herself in the mirror."

Modernism was hardly new at the time. The movement, which, among other things, had caused artists of every type to reconsider everything—their subject matter, their methods, their materials, the very definitions and foundations of their art—had been building steadily since the middle of the nineteenth century. The word "modernism" had entered the popular vocabulary following the outcries against such works as Marcel Duchamp's painting *Nude Descending a Staircase* and Igor Stravinsky's opera *Le sacre du printemps*. Modernist works in general were scolded by critics and mocked by the popular press.[2] Of course, these reactions served only to feed the fires of the movement, since some of the disciples of the avant-garde largely saw a world separated into three groups—artists, those who appreciated artists, and philistines. For some members of the avant-garde, the ire of those who did not understand was both a badge of honor and even a proof that one had indeed created art.

Nor at this point did the steamroller of modernism show signs of slowing down. In literature alone, the 1910s and 1920s had produced T. S. Eliot's *The Waste Land* (the publication of which in the *Dial* was described by poet William Carlos Williams as an "atom bomb");[3] the serialization of James Joyce's *Ulysses*, which resulted in a celebrated court case; and Ezra Pound's *Cantos*, poems that were dense and unyielding of their meaning even by modernist standards. So many -isms proliferated—imagism, vorticism, futurism, Dadaism, surrealism, cubism—that a couple of wags were able to fool renowned editors, critics, and poets into supporting and championing the movement of spectrism, which was a hoax.[4] Each movement came with its own manifesto, strident and earnest, puffing and blowing itself into paroxysms of aesthetic self-righteousness.

Like other artists of his generation, Johansen feared what many saw in some versions of modernism—a force that seemed to want to overthrow the very rules of order that for him defined art. "The whole modern world has been mad for sensation and has cared nothing for ideas," he said.

> As soon as people have had one sensation, they hop from one thing to an-other until they are so frightfully extreme that it's paralyzing. . . . From this extreme there is beginning to be a reaction again from sensation. There should of course be feeling as well as thought but this search for sensation has been like a prairie fire, burning with no restraint. . . . Take a fire and put it under steamers and boilers, and it's good for industry. But subject it to no restraints and it does only damage.

The portraitist also gave some counsel to those trying to understand art. He again dragged from his store of cautionary anecdotes a hapless female. "I remember that a woman who had no taste asked my advice about buying pic-tures," he said.

> Any academic mind can discover what is really best in paintings or pic-tures. I told her to buy a $5 one, and live with it a while, then to buy a $10 picture, and live with it, and when she felt like it to buy another, a $15 picture, and when she had three she would begin to have a basis for comparison of values and she would begin to learn. . . . If people who go to exhibits would be honest and, instead of admiring things because it was the thing to do, would say, "I don't like that, I think it's awful," there would be some hope for art.

At one point during the interview, he trained his sights on an exhibit held earlier that year at the Worcester Art Museum entitled *Exhibition of the Dial Collection of Paintings, Engravings, and Drawings by Contemporary Artists.* The New York magazine the *Dial* was in many ways the premier avant-garde journal of its time, and one of its owners, Scofield Thayer, had amassed the works of art by a variety of modernist masters that comprised the exhibit.

Johansen was not impressed.

"The Dial," he said, "is an intellectual sewer."

The Dial, an international magazine of art, literature, and criticism that was published in New York City, was considered by many the leading magazine of the modern. There were other American magazines of the period that took greater risks, resulting in their being closed down and their editors fined and even imprisoned, but the *Dial* had learned just how close it could sail to the winds of censorship and had achieved a longevity unusual for a "little magazine." It also helped that the owners, Scofield Thayer and James Sibley Watson, were extremely wealthy and willing to run the magazine at a loss.

Johansen may have felt safe in criticizing this influential journal and its often modernist contents in the pages of a small provincial newspaper that was unlikely to be read by the sophisticates of New York. But, unfortunately for him, Worcester was Scofield Thayer's hometown, and although Thayer rarely returned to the busy, hardworking mill city that had afforded his family its great wealth, Thayer's mother, Florence, and other relatives and friends still lived in Worcester, and many were heavily involved in the city's society and arts scene. One way or another, Thayer was bound to hear about the article.

Hear about it he indeed did, and in August Thayer initiated a campaign to rebuff the forces of philistinism. He wrote to the newspaper asking for permission to reproduce the photograph from the Johansen interview for a piece he was writing in response for the *Dial*.[5] Margaret Brandenburg of the *Worcester Sunday Telegram* duly sent the photograph and also asked if she might interview Thayer. A few days later, Brandenburg wrote to Thayer again, this time more urgently and now evidently working on damage control. She had spoken with Johansen, she said, and the artist would rather Thayer not refer to the article because there were errors in it and his artistic viewpoint was not adequately represented. Thayer returned the picture, saying he didn't want to use anything from the newspaper after considering the article. Unless the newspaper apologized for having printed that the *Dial* was an "intellectual sewer," he said, he retained the right to criticize.

In February, Brandenburg wrote to Thayer again, offering to profile him in the newspaper's Sunday magazine. She would be happy to allow him to read the copy before publication, she said. Thayer was having none of it, and his response was coolly polite. "Thank you for your kind letter," he wrote. "I do not know I shall be going to Worcester this winter. Should I do so, I may be able to get in touch with you."[6] In the meantime, Thayer got busy drafting his response to the portrait painter's charges. He had ordered the Johansen article through a clipping service and began notating it. He underlined the headline phrase "Famous American Artist," which he would reproduce in his article, sarcastically capitalized and centered on the page. Of the college president who was sitting for the portrait, and whom Thayer disliked greatly, he wrote, "One trusts nothing of Atwood will be good." Overleaf, he tried out a few cutting lines and listed potential points of attack.

His response was published in the May 1925 "Comment" section of the *Dial*. It used as its epigraph Johansen's "intellectual sewer" remark and then proceeded to vivisect the four players in the matter—the city of Worcester, the local newspaper, university president Atwood, and, of course, Johansen himself. He began mildly enough, characterizing the city of his birth as "this wholesome and brimming receptacle of legitimate activity" and its newspaper as the city's "outstanding intellectual effort."[7] He even allowed himself to be in agreement with several of Johansen's points regarding art. But then Thayer went on to quote the painter verbatim and, point by point, to demolish his self-contradictory and often downright wrong positions. To Johansen's assertion that modern painters lacked skill, Thayer pointed out that artists such as Picasso and Matisse were quite able to paint in the classical style if they wished, but that they sought new methods of expression. Regarding the matter of painting to please oneself rather than the public, which Johansen had claimed to do, Thayer stated that it was Johansen, and not Picasso or Georgia O'Keefe, who was making good money painting flattering portraits of the powerful. As for Johansen's story about teaching a woman to appreciate art, Thayer admitted himself utterly baffled as to what five-dollar, ten-dollar, and fifteen-dollar pictures had to do with the real value of art, not to mention how such a view squared with a man who claimed to paint to please himself.

Finally, Thayer's article linked Clark University and the *Worcester Telegram* by referring to an incident when the Socialist Scott Nearing was prevented from speaking at Clark after Atwood ordered the janitor to put out the lecture room lights and so end the offending lecture. The newspaper had supported Atwood, Thayer pointed out:

And that same esteemed contemporary journal, after regretting, upon the part of the student body of Clark University, misplaced interest in Freedom of Speech, adventured the following pertinent editorial observation: "Perhaps it is unfortunate Clark college boys do not indulge themselves more extensively in baseball, football and other matters of such critical importance in the lives of ordinary collegians." That the natural interest of young manhood in athletic games and competition should be in America so hypertrophied as quite to expunge all moral, political, and intellectual interests from American university undergraduate life would appear to be not wholly insusceptible of explanation.

All in all, the two articles, one in a provincial newspaper, the other in an international highbrow magazine, comprise a classic exchange between the modernist and conventional views of art. Further, it showed that Thayer saw philistinism not only as an individual failing but also as a fault that ran through many levels of society, infecting both academia and the media; Clark University and the Worcester newspaper come off just as badly in the piece as does Johansen. The article also shows Thayer at his most supercilious and combative. He was a man who would always make his point, no matter what.

It follows from a reading of the "Comment" that Thayer had never been particularly fond of Worcester and what he later called its "Alpine village" cultural outlook.[8] The one institution he had admired was the Worcester Art Museum, but even there he had been required to withdraw from the 1924 exhibit from his collection two works, a large Braque oil and a Picasso drawing, because of fears of how the more conservative art lovers might react to the paintings.[9]

By this time, Thayer had already begun to place pieces from his collection on long-term loan at the museum, and after his mental breakdown in the late 1920s and the consequent determination of his inability to look after himself, his mother continued to offer her son's pieces to the grateful museum. Most of his collection ended up there, and many people believed that the works would stay at the museum after his death. But when he died in 1982, it was discovered that his will bequeathed the entire collection at Worcester to the Metropolitan Museum of Art in New York City. A lawsuit ensued, but the end result was that Thayer's multimillion-dollar collection was packed up and trucked off to New York sixty years after Thayer's exhibit there had been censored. On October 18, 1984, *Worcester Telegram* arts writer Peter P. Donker described the seventy-eight carefully packed cartons making their way south and leaving a huge hole in the heart of the Worcester museum's collection. All of the sculptures fit into the cartons except one. "Gaston Lachaise's 'Standing Woman' was too large," Donker wrote. "The life-size bronze was wrapped in several blankets before being tied down in the truck. One of the hands was peeking from under the protective cover, and to Sally R. Freitag, the Worcester Art Museum's Registrar, it looked as though the woman were waving goodbye."

The will had been drawn up and notarized soon after Thayer used the pages of the *Dial* to slam the *Sunday Telegram* article that started it all. From the grave, and after a lifetime of madness, Thayer forcefully made his point.

2

HOMES OF VIRTUE

Worcester's Rural Cemetery dates back to 1838, and its ornate crypts and plots hold the remains of many of the city's most prosperous nineteenth-century families. Scofield Thayer's ashes lie in the plot next to that of the Crompton family, the patriarch of which was once in business with Thayer's father. The Crompton crypt is a red-tinged edifice of sandstone and granite decorated with carved scrolls and ferns. Sculpted cherubim gaze glumly down from the eaves. The building looks more like a miniature Gothic chapel than a crypt, with stained glass, an oaken door, and a rose window at the back. The Thayer monument next door is minimalist in contrast, a ten-foot, smooth granite oval monolith standing on end and bearing the names of the three departed Thayers, parents Edward and Florence and son Scofield. The trio made up the last small family unit in their particular line of Thayers.

The Worcester of the late nineteenth century was an industrial power-house of a mill town that ground out massive wealth for the innovative and the fortunate. It had been a city for only half a century, but during those decades it had grown inordinately. Its success can be in part attributed to the Blackstone Canal. Financed by Rhode Island merchants, the Blackstone moved Worcester's manufacturing products by barge down to the port of Providence and thence to worldwide markets and carried foreign products back into the American hinterland. The canal was relatively successful for twenty years or so, but by midcentury the expanding railroads, which were faster by orders of magnitude than canal transportation and not susceptible to the seasonal problems of flooding, drought, and ice, brought about the demise of the ca-nal. Worcester, with the rude nimbleness of an adolescent, didn't miss a step. The canal had done its duty, giving the city important trade links to the outside world. Worcester's industries churned merrily on, producing false teeth, guns, boots and shoes, boxes, coffins, carriages, medicines, leather, metal goods, perfumes, barbed wire, books, dyes, tallow, corsets, carpets, and textiles. Worcester, the city boosters boasted, had the largest wire factory in the world and the largest card-clothing and envelope factories in the country.[1] The canal was all but forgotten. Eventually it would serve as a sewer for the city. It still does.

The hardworking, hard-nosed, pragmatic Worcester of this period also had a softer, more enlightened side. Its institutions of learning included three colleges, a state normal school, a military academy, several private schools, and a city-wide public school system. There were nine weekly and five daily newspapers. There was an art museum, a musical association, a horticultural society, a free public library, and a natural history society. Scholars pored over the historical manuscripts and friable volumes at the American Antiquarian Society, which was founded by the printer Isaiah Thomas, publisher of the first dictionary in the United States. It was also a city kind to Progressive thought, and Worcester boasted among other things the state's first insane asylum, a humane and forward-thinking institution for its time. But for all the accessories of culture and forward thinking, Worcester grew to maturity on its brute strength as a factory city, an old-fashioned mill town. Worcester *made* things. It was famous for breeding and attracting those who invented, who improved processes, who thought up new ways of doing things. Scofield's father, Edward D. Thayer, was one such. The Thayers had been textile magnates for three generations, and Edward had greatly expanded the already successful enterprises passed down to him, buying more mills and entering the business of manufacturing machines for the production of textiles. One of his inventions made the changing of shuttles so much more efficient that a weaver could run four looms at once rather than the typical two.[2]

The year before Thayer's birth, the burgeoning and successful municipality had built a new city hall from the local pink granite. The building's dedication, which coincided with Worcester's semi-centennial anniversary as a city, bristled with all the pomp and circumstance one would expect of a brash, confident city, with bands, hymns, scriptures, parades, and a regatta. At the ceremonial laying of the cornerstone, Masonic officials applied their "jewels" (the square, the level, and the plumb line), after which it was struck three times by the grandmaster's gavel, pronounced "true and trusty," and libations of corn, wine, and oil were made. A strong box was laid under the cornerstone containing books on the history of the city and its institutions; silver and copper coins minted by a local bank; copies of local newspapers, which included those serving the city's

French Canadian, German, and Scandinavian immigrants; a copy of the *New York Herald* from April 16, 1865, containing an account of Lincoln's death; and copies of the Bible, a book showing scenes of the city, the course catalogues of Holy Cross College and the Polytechnic Institute, and a report from the horticultural society. Such were the arrivé fetishes of this growing and diverse industrial city.[3]

Mayor Dodge's speech was peppered with references to the city's Puritan roots and the industrious character of a people who had hacked civilization from the wilderness: "The history of Worcester," he orated, "as town and city, is replete with incidents showing a community wise, conservative but progressive in business and public affairs, loyal to the traditions of its founders, patriotic toward national government, and beneficent in voluntary public benefits. Like other New England towns," he continued "it was founded on hardship and privation. To us can come no more inspiring thoughts than those aroused by contemplation of the works wrought by the pioneers. Surrounded by menaces threatening their families as well as their community, they met all situations as firm as the hills upon whose summits, or in whose valleys, were built homes of virtue and devout religion."[4]

The Thayers could trace their forebears back to the early 1600s, and Scofield was the ninth generation of the family in Massachusetts. Scofield's great-grandfather was the first in the family to enter the textile business, and the following two generations of Thayers greatly expanded and diversified the family holdings.[5] Every year, usually on January 1, Scofield's father, Edward Thayer, sat down with a small notebook and made a list of what he owned and what it was worth. He called this his "Inventory" from 1885 to 1903, when he changed the designation to "Assets." In 1885, his holdings included stock in his Worcester mills in the Cherry Valley and Tatnuck neighborhoods. In the years following, growth was even more rapid as Thayer opened more mills, bought stock in other companies, and speculated in real estate. The Thayer coffers swelled.

Florence Scofield, the future Mrs. Thayer, came from a more modestly successful background, her father having started a newspaper in Connecticut, the *Hartford Post*, before settling down as an insurance agent in Worcester.[6] After the wedding, Edward Thayer moved in with his bride, her widowed mother, and his new brother-in-law and business partner, William B. Scofield. At the time of the wedding in July 1884, Edward Thayer was on his way to becoming perhaps the largest individual manufacturer of woolen goods in the country.

Five years later, on December 12, 1889, Scofield Thayer was born into this family of great privilege and prosperity. The family home was still at the Scofield residence at 973 Main Street. Across the street was the relatively new Clark

University, the clock tower of which young Scofield could see from his room. On the north side of the house lay the green sward of University Park, with its pond and fountain. Beyond was a sandstone Baptist church and beyond that the Gothic façade of the Catholic church of St. Peter's. Today the neighborhood is heavily urban and working-class, but in the late nineteenth century it was leafy, well-to-do, and spacious. Indeed, Florence's father had wanted to keep it that way, and he lobbied the city to rule that any new houses built for a mile on either side of his home be set back one hundred feet from the road. He was unsuccessful in this bid. A public school was just to the south of the home, and Scofield could hear the pupils "like so many parrots screeching."[7] Noise would bother him his whole life. It was also in that year of Scofield's birth that the city's Catholic cathedral was finally finished, thirty years after ground had been broken for it; the Harrington & Richardson Arms Co., which was enjoying rapid growth, patented its .38 Special handgun; and Ernest L. Thayer, brother of Edward and future uncle of Scofield, produced what may be the most famous American poem ever written, "Casey at the Bat," the tale of a hapless baseball lug who failed to save his team. A little *annus mirabilis* for Worcester and the Thayers, indeed.

The house at 973 Main Street was fondly remembered by Ernest Thayer, Scofield's uncle, who said that his "most vivid and most pleasant memories" of Worcester were framed there. "I recall with a very tender feeling the many happy Sunday evenings which I spent there," he wrote, some years later. "On those occasions Ed always managed to be in the best of spirits, as carefree, seemingly, as a school boy, and he was then, I think, most himself, a big, strong, warm-hearted and affectionate man. When I visit Worcester it is my custom to go out and look at the Main St. house in order to intensify my recollections of the old days."[8]

Scofield's memories of the house and the period were less sanguine. "I was not brought up on the playroom-playground plan," he later wrote of his child-hood. "I was brought up on the attic-or-basement-vacant lot plan."[9] At the Main Street house, he also began to experience the anxiety that would become so paralyzing to him later in his life: "So tense in climbing cellar-stairs at 973," he remembered. "I could have heard a cat's intake of breath, had such a creature been even in that cellar's most remote coign."[10]

There is little physical description in Thayer's memories of the house. He does speak of the foliage between his room and the Clark University clock tower as "Heavy + rich + enormous, great bulging coils of green," and the oc-casional bluebirds he sees are like "envoys from another + chaster world,"[11] but these seem more like literary efforts than descriptive writing, and he notes less poetically that the curtains were "cocoa-brown" and that one of his mother's flower pieces belonged in the bedroom of a "classy Paris 19th cent[ury] house of prostitution."[12]

This is not to say that the young Thayer was unobservant. Indeed, he was a single child among adults, one who carefully watched and evaluated all that was going on around him. "At 973 there was no conversation: there was only conniving," he wrote. "Conniving between William and Ed[ward] toward financial gain; between W[illiam] and Flora toward social gain. There was absolutely no turning over of ideas or images either for pleasure in this turning or toward understanding or amelioration of any social condition in which they were not themselves competitively interested. Nothing was ever said which could have pleased or interested anybody not sympathetically interested in the worldly position of these three protagonists."[13]

It was also very much a traditional family arrangement. "At my father's table (at 973 as otherwise) the only person who sat above the salt was my father. Others proposed, he disposed."[14] Nor did he have any fond remembrances of his mother, recalling little but her obsession with the social scene: "Listing names for her dinner parties at Main Street my mother sat at her block, pencil in hand, like a book-maker at roulette. She was at the big game."[15] The one person he always retained warm memories of was his grandmother. "So exquisite was my grandmother's sympathy," he wrote, "that when a servant, in passing a dish about the table for the second time, offered it to her, her manner of declining was immediately apologetic, she instinctively feeling the servant might be abraded by her declining the proffered dish. 'O'—bending forward and, at the same time, turning her head toward the servant at her left—'I think I won't have any *more*, Delia'—with a sweet, almost pleadingly placating smile."[16] When she died some years later, he would record his distaste for the funerary decorations: "My grandmother's face, contrasting with the bland array of coffin flowers, of polished wood and silver . . . and marble, and of significanceless Japonaiserie."[17] His mother, he said, directed the undertaker on the placement of his grandmother's coffin "as though it had been a rather longish and odd shaped hamper of clothes."[18]

The early years of Thayer's schooling are something of a mystery. There is no mention of formal education until Thayer entered the Bancroft School in Worcester in 1900, when he was ten years old. He may have had schooling before this, either at private school or through tutors, but we cannot be sure. We do know that Thayer suffered from some kind of serious sickness or traumatic event in his fourth year, which perhaps affected his education. The Bancroft School had just opened its doors in 1900 when Thayer began attending. He played football there in 1903 and in 1904 took second place in the 100-yard dash and first in the "potato race." There is no record of any athletic prowess after this; indeed, he came to detest exercise, believing it to be harmful. His father, who was passionate about sports his whole life, must have been disappointed. An entry in Thayer's personal notebooks shows what may have been his parents' point of view on the matter: "Your father and mother don't want you to be *puny*, Scofield! We want you to play football and base-ball! I don't want *my* son to be a book-worm!"[19]

But the boy's interests were aesthetic rather than athletic, and it was at Bancroft that he made some of his early attempts at writing. One of his first stories is found in a notebook from his English IV class: "Once upon a time they live a boy, out in the woods and father was a hunter and one day he was out way off from his house. And he had taught his little boy to shot like him and he was out with him. And they saw a roaring tiger the little boy shot his big bow and arrow he shot to kill the tiger. And of course it killed the tiger! And the father took and cut the skin off of the tiger. They took skin to an uncle who was in woolen business. He made very nice blanket for the two-seated carriage. The End."[20] That the tiger skin should end up being processed in a textile mill is perhaps to be expected, given that the Thayer fortune, and no doubt the dinner-table conversation, revolved around the Thayer mills. Around this time he also produced, perhaps in imitation of the Worcester historian George Bancroft, after whom his school was named, his "American History in Three Volumes." Another of his stories about a father and mother who took in "a little man cub" suggests Kipling's tales of Mowgli, which were popular during this period. Another story, written in 1903, "Yeko: The Story of a Japanese Boy," has the hero's father dying prematurely, leaving the son and the mother to face the world without him.[21] The story may have been in response to the death of Thayer's grandfather, which occurred in May of that year. In 1904, just as he was turning fifteen, he published in the school magazine an essay entitled "Port Arthur." He kept two copies of the published piece, one clean and one in which he had written in corrections, changed wordings, and inserted punctuation, no doubt to return the work to its state of correctness before its having been mishandled by the magazine's editor.[22] His subjects at the Bancroft School included arithmetic, drawing, English, French, history, Latin, music, writing, and spelling.[23]

In 1905, the family moved into a house that Edward Thayer had long coveted, the Clark House on Elm Street. The house, an imposing pile of stone and dark wood, had been built by Jonas Clark, founder of Clark University. Also that year, the elder Thayer bought a 245-ton steam yacht named *Margaret*. The highly successful Thayer seemed to have decided to start enjoying the fortune he had amassed. His family, though, was not as thrilled with all of these purchases. His son recalled mostly how absurd his father was on board, comparing him sarcastically to a commander of the Trojan fleet. "On his yacht my father should have worn a gown: he was—uncharacteristically—like Thoas there."[24] The younger Thayer also remembered his father's splendid yachting cap, which was "new + starched, gleamed on top like the white frosting on an objectionably gilded cake."[25] The boy found repulsive even the food served aboard: "Bread and butter sandwiches at tea (on the yacht) with the crust cut off,—small naked things, finger nails removed."[26]

Florence Thayer was unsettled by what she saw as her husband's excessive fondness for the yacht, and she found a doctor who agreed with her that it was not a healthy pastime for Scofield. Edward Thayer sold the vessel.[27]

As for the Clark house, Florence seems to have settled in well, but Scofield found the house suffocating in its massiveness and more of a monument to the success of Edward Thayer than a home: "That orgulous pile—39."[28] Despite Edward Thayer's great material success, his son held low opinions of his father's sensitivity and intelligence. His father, he wrote, "ignored psychology, even the psychology of animals."[29] He was "singularly unencumbered."[30] And in his writings Thayer occasionally notes his father's dislike of him, perhaps because of the sensitive and at times sickly nature of his son: "My father's eyes showed *hatred + detestation* of me."[31] (Even Florence seems to have been dismayed at Thayer's lack of good health. One snippet of her conversation from Thayer's notebooks reads, "Both (of) his parents, both his father and I, have always had such splendid health.")[32]

Despite his disdain for his father's mind and tastes, Thayer also betrays a humorous fondness for the older man. He was "like a giant, somewhat stocky piston-rod."[33] And in comparing the personality of his father to food (Thayer compared almost everyone close to him to a comestible, often to more than one), Thayer chose a solid, somewhat unappetizing New England dish: "My father—like cold baked beans, coagulated and solid in a plain white bowl."[34]

In 1907, when Thayer was seventeen, his father died unexpectedly. He had been planning a family trip to Europe when he was brought down by appendicitis. Doctors operating on him "discovered his condition worse than thought," and he was taken back to the old house at 973 Main Street to be cared for by his mother-in-law, Thayer's beloved grandmother. He died within days. The newspaper said that he was reported to be the largest individual woolen manufacturer in the United States, and the front-page story of this locally important death carried interviews with the mayor, the former mayor, businessmen, an attorney, a bank president, a colonel, a general, the chief of police, and various captains of Worcester industry.[35]

Thayer remembered three things about his father's death—that his mother's behavior at the time "was *most unbecoming*,"[36] that his mother and her brother William "seem to have been more interested in my father's money than in his son,"[37] and that Edward Thayer was buried in a casket that seemed to the boy horribly appropriate: "My father's coffin was terrible; it was exactly like his Elm St. house."[38]

Thayer was at this time at Milton Academy, a preparatory school that had the reputation of being a feeder school for Harvard. He had entered as a rather elderly high school freshman of fifteen years. Whether this arrested education was occasioned by the mysterious event that befell him as a four-year-old, we do not know.

Outside of the liberal arts, the only required subjects at Milton were mathematics, biology, and physics. The school was heavily Eurocentric in its curriculum, with English, Roman, and Greek history being taught before that of the United States. Literature courses were similarly inclined. Students read the Bible, Shakespeare, Defoe, Bunyan, Milton, Pope, Swift, Scott, Byron, Browning, and Tennyson. American literature was represented by Washington Irving, Henry Wadsworth Longfellow, and Nathaniel Hawthorne. The Latin curriculum included Caesar, Nepos, Ovid, Virgil, Cicero, and Sallust, while the Greeks read were Xenophon, Homer, Herodotus, and Thucydides. Thayer may also have taken courses in German, which would become his favorite language, reading Schiller, Heine, Goethe, and others.

Thayer entered Milton the same year as a young man from Missouri named Thomas Stearns Eliot. The two would later say that they were aware of each other, both staying in the Forbes House dormitory, but no friendship seems to have developed at the school. Eliot was at Milton only a year before going on to Harvard. Thayer, still apparently catching up with the education he had missed because of childhood illness, was at the school through 1907.

Thayer was evidently a good student. A note to his parents from the headmaster remarked that he was doing good work in all subjects, but particularly English. He also won prizes in Latin. Indeed, Thayer did so well at Milton that he was able to leave after three rather than the usual four years, having already passed the exams he needed to enter Harvard.[39]

3

HARVARD

There was really no question as to whether or not Thayer would enter Harvard. His father had attended the college, as had his uncle William, and for a wealthy young man from Massachusetts, especially one with literary leanings, there was really nowhere else. "I consider Harvard the greatest university in the world, Scofield," he was told by one of his Milton masters.[1] His instructors at Harvard were not at first impressed. In an early essay, Thayer argued that some of the works of Alfred Noyes "deserve a place among the best poems of our language." "Come off your perch!" the instructor noted in the margin.[2] On another paper, he was advised to "shorten your sentences and try to refrain in future from making them salmagundies composed of everything in sight."[3] This was advice he would never take. Indeed, he always delighted in the sentence whose main idea was challenged and sometimes even overwhelmed by tangential material stuffed into parentheses and subordinate clauses. Another instructor tried to slap Thayer down with the remark, "Your punctuation is picturesque but without other merit."[4] None of this touched Thayer's sense of how he wanted to write. In a 1910 essay, which had received a grade of C, he carefully crossed out every one of his tutor's remarks, suggestions, and emendations.

As a budding writer, he no doubt was aware that his Milton Academy classmate, Tom Eliot, was also at Harvard, since Eliot was by this time publishing poetry fairly regularly in the *Harvard Advocate*. Eliot also read one of these poems, "Ode to Fair Harvard," at his graduation in 1910.[5] We may guess that the two did not see much of each other at Harvard, because Eliot was several years ahead of Thayer, and the period in which their time at Harvard overlapped as undergraduates was no more than eight months. Eliot, following a period at the Sorbonne, did return to Harvard as a graduate student, but there seems to have been little or no correspondence between the two. Neither makes mention of the other in correspondence from the period.

Thayer himself soon began publishing his own verse in the *Advocate* and in the *Harvard Monthly*, and in 1912 he became an editor of the latter.[6] He also received a Harvard scholarship for his final year for "marked excellence in his studies."[7]

Thayer took his work at Harvard seriously and had little respect for those of his classmates who didn't. "The role of gilded wastrel is so brilliantly + so ostentatiously cast at Harvard as to render all other earthly roles jejune, inferior, nugatory," he wrote.[8]

In May of his final year at Harvard, Thayer received this exquisitely polite letter from an underclassman:

> Dear Mr. Thayer,
>   I shall feel better when I have made trial of expressing, to you, my admiration of your poem. I shall be very proud and happy indeed when I can say the thing so completely, so purely, and with such a true and fine ring as you have said it:
>
>> "Her body is a reed, so slender
>> Whereon God's lips do blow,
>> And in each petty human motion
>> The great hymns come and go."
>
> If this letter needs an apology, it is that I love poetry.
>
> Yours sincerely,
> E. Estlin Cummings.[9]

Thayer invited Cummings to join the staff of the magazine, and the two soon became fast friends. That summer, Cummings visited the Thayer summer home on Martha's Vineyard.[10] One of their amorous adventures around Boston included an evening out with a couple of young ladies that Cummings recalled: "ST & I-2 gals, 1 healthy and attractive, other wicked and sicklooking take us to Hotel 'Richmond.'" Thayer knew what to do but Cummings, "afraid of disease, only went to a certain point, being satisfied with only what would make [him] go off."[11]

But evidently Thayer's love life in Cambridge was otherwise not all that successful. He later wrote, "My bad luck at the dice of love at Harvard + beyond was the result of a simple fact,—the dice were loaded. I had money and I hesitated to buy. They were all selling only, and I did not know."[12] What he learned at Harvard was the connection there was between money and sex. This connection, which he would come to see not as tawdry but as rational and even beautiful, he would eventually elevate into a personal philosophy of sex that approached Lawrentian proportions. As a hugely wealthy young man, Thayer quickly learned that the connection between money and love (or sex) was more complicated than the simple transaction between a prostitute and her john. Serial marriages comprised a form of prostitution (indeed, a less honest form) by which a woman could become wealthy in exchange for allowing her body to be enjoyed by more than one man: "American girls enjoy the distinction of being the only members of the animal kingdom which—thanks to the American system of frequent and advantageous divorces and remarriage—pull themselves up by the cunt."[13]

Other friends and coworkers on the school magazine at this time included Stewart Mitchell, J. Donald Adams, Cuthbert Wright, Gilbert Seldes, and Lincoln MacVeagh, all of whom would eventually be involved with the *Dial*.

At Harvard he also befriended the young poet Alan Seeger, who had spent part of his youth in Mexico and had a close relationship with George Santayana, the Madrid-born professor of philosophy of whom Thayer was also greatly fond. Thayer described Seeger in heroic and worshipful terms: his "face was an army with banners," and he "walked about Cambridge like a young *hidalgo*." Thayer noted that Seeger's hair was "extremely coarse, stiff and straight, like a horse's mane," and he wondered if his friend had "Indian blood."[14]

Seeger would join the French Foreign Legion so that he could fight in the Great War, and it was Santayana's response to this news, "It will make a man of him," that may have begun Thayer's eventual disillusionment with Santayana and his generally conservative and pragmatic philosophy. "To such an extent has the Philistine virtue of associating the aesthetic life with womanhood and the military life with manhood permeated even the essentially aesthetic and non-military mind,"[15] Thayer noted.

After Seeger's death in the trenches in 1916, Thayer would help arrange for the posthumous publication of his poems, including the well-known "I Have a Rendezvous with Death." Later still, he would be pleased to find a copy of the book in the home of a Chicago paramour: "Finding Seeger's verse chez la cocotte chicagoaise I knew it had indeed 'gone' (go in U.S.A!)."[16]

Thayer did not share Seeger's romantic view of war in general or of the Great

War in particular, but he was full of admiration for his friend's bravery and poetic achievement: "Seeger wooed beautiful moods, even in the cannon's mouth," he wrote.[17]

One of Thayer's frequent female companions during his time at Harvard was Hildegarde Lasell, whose family owned a textile machinery factory to the south of Worcester. He began calling on her in a chauffeur-driven car, bringing presents of books. He was, she said, one of those people "with magnetic looks and personality who, upon entering a room, will turn all heads in their direction." She remembered visiting the Elm Street house for a dinner-dance. The front parlor was lighted by heavily shaded lamps, and the atmosphere, as Thayer himself similarly described it, was "thick as night." She recalled:

> On a table was a reproduction of a drawing of William Butler Yeats as a young man by John Singer Sargent, oddly out of place in that Victorian atmosphere. Mrs. Thayer later sent me a photograph of this. I had admired it so because of the arresting likeness to her son, the similar flashing eyes and the expressive mouth. Mrs. Thayer, a little woman, was wearing a gown of black satin with much jet and a high-boned lace collar—to me, in a full, light evening dress, like something from another period. She seemed rather to fear her brilliant son.[18]

Thayer escorted Hildegarde to dances, operas, ballets, and symphonies, and his uncle William was quite fond of her, admiringly calling her "a crackerjack,"[19] but the only hint the relationship may have been other than Platonic is an unexplained note of Thayer's that reads, "Startled to note Hildegarde's honest legs. I had never expected to see so much of so small a person."[20] Thayer eventually introduced the young woman to his Harvard classmate and future business partner, James Sibley Watson. The two married a few years later.

Hildegarde was also one of the first to note a change in Thayer from the apparently outgoing, fun-loving youth to something darker. The occasion was some years later, when Thayer's friends had come to the Elm Street house to see the bronze bust of Thayer that had just been completed by the sculptor Gaston Lachaise. Thayer's mother had remarked, somewhat timidly, "You are better looking, Scofield." He angrily had the piece removed and shouted at his mother, "I will never let you see it again."

"An excessive gesture, we then began to realize," the young woman noted.[21]

4

OXFORD DURING THE WAR

Thayer had no intention of going into the business of running woolen mills. In all his prolific writings, the generations-old family business that provided him with such a great fortune is almost never mentioned. The lone mention of a mill of any kind is in a criticism of modern ecclesiastical architecture: "The mill in which my grandfather worked was more genteel than the churches are today hereabouts."[1]

After he was graduated from Harvard in 1913, Thayer decided on postgraduate work. For this, he chose England, which was still very much an intellectual and cultural mother country to the young Anglophile. His school of choice was Oxford, where he entered Magdalen College as a "commoner"—a student who has received no scholarships and so must foot the bill himself. The quarterly tuition at the time was just £8, although the cost of living at this socially and academically prestigious Oxford college was very high. He took rooms in the much-coveted cloisters that looked onto the grassy fifteenth-century quadrangle. Prince George of Teck and the Prince of Wales, later King Edward VIII, were among his well-to-do fellow residents. Two of his Harvard classmates were also at Oxford: Charles Gouverneur Hoffman ("Govvy") and Francis Butler-Thwing. A third, J. Brett Langstaff, would enter Magdalen the following year. Thayer was surprised to find that his old schoolmate from Milton and Harvard, Tom Eliot, was also studying at Oxford.

Thayer seemed in no hurry to choose a career. He began by reading Greats, the college's traditional course in the classics, but he chafed at his tutor's close supervision of what he read and the required two essays a week. "I get even less time than at Harvard to read and to think," he grumbled in a letter to his mother. "Ancient history" interested him "no more than gasoline engines," he said, and he had no wish to learn to write Latin prose, so after a year of studying literature, he switched to philosophy. "I have always hated doing what I'm told," he wrote.[2]

He had hoped to find in Oxford an unhurried idyll where he could ponder great literature and ideas, and he was to be disappointed. "To the sharp contrary," he wrote, "he finds himself jammed head foremost into a monstrous hugger-mugger of games, talk, drink, lectures and motor-cycles."[3]

The president of Magdalen at the time was Sir Herbert Warren, a minor poet whose heroes were Alfred Lord Tennyson and Robert Bridges and a scholar who wrote introductions to collections and anthologies of poetry. The Prince of Wales called him "an awful old man,"[4] but he was also remembered as being friendly if socially awkward with students.[5]

The period at Oxford was very much a time of change and growth for Thayer, but ironically his studies seem to have had little to do with this evolution. Indeed, after his first unsatisfactory year of studying literature, we find him becoming less and less interested in the idea of studying the past and more involved in the ideas of his own time. He flirted with religion, befriending the Catholic chaplain, Fr. Basil William Maturin, and was invited by him to High Masses and lectures at the Newman Society. His interest in Catholicism moved him so far as to arrange an audience with Pope Pius X in Rome during the winter break, but the experience proved less than epiphanic. "I wore my dress-coat in the morning (such is the custom)," he wrote, "waited two hours in a hot and stuffy antechamber and was in due course blessed by His Holiness." He found the pope "rather commonplace,"[6] however, and showed no further interest in the Catholic or any other religion.

Back at Magdalen after the break, Thayer's interest in his studies began to wane even further. He took golf lessons from "Count Bobinskey" but was not bitten by the golf bug.[7] "Playing golf you move, like the Romans, thro[ugh] a desert," he wrote. "All spontaneous spiritual life has been sacrificed to competition."[8] He helped organize a literary club at Magdalen that was known as the Pleiades, entertained visiting friends and family (his cousins Ellen and Lucy were living in London at the time),[9] and spent time with his old teacher and mentor George Santayana.[10] Santayana had left Harvard and moved to England, he told J. Brett Langstaff, because he was tired of "pushing men through a sieve of examination."[11]

In a letter to his mother complaining about his heavy workload at Magdalen, Thayer had suggested that he might not return to Oxford for a second year.[12] But return he did, after a summer at Edgartown, and although he was still reading philosophy at Magdalen College and filling much of his spare time reading contemporary literature, his extracurricular interests were also blossoming. He took up the sport of beagling, which entailed following on foot a pack of beagles in pursuit of hares. The sport is often referred to as poor man's hunting, but there was nothing impecunious about the Magdalen beaglers. Theirs was a "socially smart sport" that was prohibitively expensive for all but the wealthy, according to the Magdalene archivist Robin Darwall-Smith, in that one had to pay a subscription for the pack of beagles, purchase a hunting kit, and so on. At Thayer's time at the university, only the socially exclusive colleges such as Magdalen went in for the sport. Some colleges, like Magdalen, had their own packs of beagles. His taking part in such an exclusive sport meant that Thayer would have had to have moved in exalted circles, Darwall-Smith said; very few Americans were considered eligible to participate in the sport.[13]

Thayer's classmate and fellow American J. Brett Langstaff recalled one outing with the dogs:

The little hounds were let loose, and finally we struck a scent and all started running. While I was trudging over the rough fields I ate my sandwich. As a result my stomach was feeling a bit upset when after an hour or two we made a *kill*. The hare had taken to the water and was drowned. When they had cut off the *mask* and the *pads* they threw the carcass to the beagles. It was a miserably bloody sight and did not help settle my luncheon at all. They surprised me by pushing a bleeding foot of the hare into my hand because I was *in at the kill*.[14]

Thayer had taken up the sport with great enthusiasm, as he had his study of literature, but found that it soon palled. "The beagling, like all physical exertion, bores me to death; were I not a whip [in charge of the hounds] and thus to a certain extent landed with moral responsibility, I should give it up," he wrote his mother.[15]

Tom Eliot, with whom Thayer had been spending a good deal of his spare time, had already noted in Thayer this tendency to dabble, to pick things up in a flush of pleasure, only to eventually find them wanting and set them down, often with a sense of distaste and disappointment. Thayer, he told his friend Conrad Aiken, "has developed a good deal and promises to be a fine dilettante and talker if he loses all literary ambition."[16]

We may also infer from Eliot's biting remark the latent rivalry between the two men that would cause much misunderstanding and resentment some years later in the negotiations over the publication of *The Waste Land*, which was yet unwritten. To complicate the matter even further, the woman who some believe was responsible for the state of mind that gave birth to Eliot's modernist master-piece was about to enter the picture at Oxford and herself greatly intensify that rivalry. On March 27, 1915, after having tea with Eliot, Thayer went to dinner at his cousin's and there met Lucy's friend, the vivacious Vivien Haigh-Wood. Thayer was stricken. "Lucy's friend is a very attractive and intelligent girl," he wrote his mother.[17] The friendship quickly deepened. The two women began visiting Oxford, where Thayer entertained them with dinners, regattas, teas, picnics, and punting. They were occasionally joined by Eustace Robert Parr, a friend of Thayer's who would soon join the military and leave for Serbia. In a second letter to his mother, Thayer felt the need to again comment on the loveli-ness of Vivien. "Miss Haigh-Wood is very attractive," he said. "Thayer girls seem to have made some very pleasant friends. They and Miss Haigh-Wood and an-other girl have just taken a cottage in the country for the summer."[18] Thayer's appreciation of Haigh-Wood was returned by her. "Liked him very much," she noted in her diary after meeting the rich American.[19] At some point during this period, Thayer introduced his friend Tom Eliot to the young ladies. At this point, Thayer seems to have overcome the paucity of physical relationships he complained about at Harvard, describing the women of Oxford as being as "full of sex as a squirming cat."[20]

Haigh-Wood's letters to Thayer are filled with a strange mix of flirtatious-ness, condescension, wheedling, demanding, begging, and boasting. Consider this one, which she fired off after she and Lucy had been stood up for a week-end meeting with Thayer and Eliot. After berating the two men generally, she focuses on Thayer, speaking of the depression her doctor had warned her to avoid:

> Remember the specialist's words, Scofield, & do not be the instrument of
> pushing me more quickly than is necessary into an untimely melancholia,
> or else, as he also prophesied, an early grave. So will you . . . come to me in
> *London* on Saturday if we are *not* able to go to Oxford? There is no better
> way you could spend a wet Saturday than by coming to town & having a
> cheerful afternoon spent in looking at pictures or going to the Irish Play-
> ers, having tea at the Piccadilly & dinner . . . with little Vivien to jog along
> beside you & gaze lovingly upon you with her golden eyes.[21]

Since Thayer had broken the date because of a Sunday appointment (probably with his friend Valentine Farrar, who was stationed in army barracks in Epsom awaiting being sent to the front), Haigh-Wood suggests that the two meet (she and Thayer alone—"come to me in *London*"). Haigh-Wood seems to have her sights set quite firmly on Thayer at this point. Vivien goes on, referring to the fact that Thayer is due to return soon to the United States:

> And you are an *awful* fool—my dear. In two weeks you will go back to your savage land, & from that day—when, like a rat, you desert the sinking ship—from that day I do *solemnly promise* you I will never have speech, or correspondence with you, nor will I *ever* look upon your promising-much & fulfilling-little countenance again. Never. . . .
>
> . . . Well you ought to snatch *every hour* in these last days & try, try to burn just one of your fingers in the white flame—just for the experience you know.[22]

Haigh-Wood shows here her dramatic flair, begging Thayer in "these last days" (he was returning to America) to burn one of his fingers in her "white flame."

Her next letter was more sober and seems to be responding to Thayer's attempts to mollify her. She again makes the point that she is available for intimacies—though they may be only aesthetic intimacies—with Thayer. She points out that she has influenza "[in] spite of my exceeding radiance of countenance which you were kind enough to refer to." She responds to a compliment he makes about her beauty by making reference to the famous art theft of the *Mona Lisa*, which had occurred a few years before: "It's nice of you to compare me to the Mona Lisa! I wish she and I had anyhow one point in common, and that is that someone would cut me out of my frame too." (She would repeat to him this desire to be freed from her situation some years later, when Eliot was writing *The Waste Land*.) And there is this: "No, Scofield—you have never seen me 'divine' or 'exquisite' yet. I hope you may, one day. There is a key to that—you know?"[23]

Eliot was also at pains to direct Haigh-Wood's reading. He gave her a book by Dostoevsky, and Thayer found himself dismayed at her response to the work. "She said it took her out of herself, that it was an anodyne. I thought this a somewhat casual and superficial reason for liking a work of art." Later, he would come to understand the importance of a book when one is in "unsympathetic surroundings."[24]

The Great War, of course, was impossible to avoid even in the idyll of Oxford. The college's large examination halls were being used as military hospitals, and the wounded who were brought there were often welcomed by cheering crowds.[25] Recruits undertook drilling practice in nearby meadows, and Thayer was deeply aware of the fact that his friends and classmates, both English and American, were joining up to fight and shipping out.

Thayer managed to continue his studies, despite the distractions. "The war affects my work not at all," he wrote his mother. "The only difference that it makes in my studious leisure is that instead of reading verse and fiction in my spare moments I now read the paper and magazines. But this would be the case equally, were I in America or Timbuctoo. This war is at least worth understanding. Anyhow I have good precedent for this change of habit. Santayana, who never before looked at a journal, now cannot go on the street but he must buy an extra."[26] It was during this period that Santayana produced the book *Soliloquies in England*, which is startling for its avoidance of the subject of the war that raged during Santayana's stay in that country. Indeed, the philosopher felt it necessary to explain this absence in the prologue.

> Often over Port Meadow the whirr of aeroplanes sent an iron tremor through these reveries, and the daily casualty list, the constant sight of the wounded, the cadets strangely replacing the undergraduates, made the foreground to these distances. Yet nature and solitude continued to envelop me in their gentleness, and seemed to remain nearer to me than all that was so near.[27]

Only in the essay "Tipperary" does Santayana touch on the great conflict, and then only to dismiss it with a cool pragmatism:

> War is but resisted change; and change must needs be resisted so long as the organism it would destroy retains any vitality. Peace itself means discipline at home and invulnerability abroad—two forms of permanent virtual war; peace requires so vigorous an internal regimen that every germ of dissolution or infection shall be repelled before it reaches the public soul. This war has been a short one, and its ravages slight in comparison with what remains standing; a severe war is one in which the entire manhood of a nation is destroyed, its cities razed, and its women and children driven into slavery. In this instance the slaughter has been greater, perhaps, only because modern populations are so enormous; the disturbance has been acute only because the modern industrial system is so dangerously complex and unstable; and the expense seems prodigious because we were so extravagantly rich. . . . An ancient city would have thought this war, or one relatively as costly, only a normal incident; and certainly the Germans will not regard it otherwise.[28]

That final year at Oxford also saw the deepening of Thayer's friendship with Valentine Farrar, a classmate who had joined a regiment that was stationed for training at Epsom. None of the letters from Thayer to Farrar have been saved, which is a loss, since the two discussed art, philosophy, and religion a great deal, and the letters would have given us some insight into Thayer's thinking at the time. Further, Farrar notes that he is "hopelessly in your debt as to letters," suggesting that Thayer wrote a good deal more than did Farrar, whose correspondence is itself voluminous. However, the letters from Farrar to Thayer do give us a good sense of how Thayer's later career at Oxford proceeded, when he seems to have settled on a pleasant schedule of reading and study and gotten out of his system the beagling and other aristocratic pastimes: "I envy you your scholastic retirement there," Farrar wrote from his barracks at Epsom. "I should much enjoy being able to devote myself for a space to reading, in some quiet old place, without the intolerable shackles of varsity routine, and the society of sporting bloods and intellectual snobs. When this war is over, if I am not laid out to rest under the waving green of Belgian field (as I could be content to do) I shall go to the Scilly Isles."[29]

It is also evident from the letters that Thayer was thinking hard and passionately about his aesthetic philosophy and that Farrar was somewhat concerned that his friend was asking too much of art and literature, suggesting that Thayer was making a mistake in raising the aesthetic experience to the level of a religion.

> You and I disagree fundamentally on almost every subject. I sometimes wonder whether your creed—not your religion, but your aesthetic creed, will ever fail you. At least one half of all literature and art must be meaningless to you, and at least one half of life, because you demand piquancy and gusto from everything, and say, with Baudelaire,

> "Que n'importe que tu sois sage?
> Sois belle! Et sois triste!"

> You smile at anything that is homely, and at any man who is merely goodnatured and straightforward, n'est ce pas?[30]

Farrar obviously detected that Thayer had picked up that disdain for the philistine and the bourgeois that was not uncommon among some elements in the modernist and the avant-garde movement. Farrar himself had some difficulty understanding the modern. He enjoyed some of Ezra Pound's poems and his "Provencal lore," but he dismissed Pound's emphasis on "newness." He found *Ripostes* disappointing. "Pound seems to be hugging to himself some artificial little mystery of no significance, and teasing people to guess at it," he wrote.[31]

The two also disagreed over religion. "Christianity is another thing," Farrar wrote. "I really rather wonder that it should have no aesthetic appeal to you. People connect a lot of didactic morality with it, but it is surprising how little morality comes into what traditions tell us of this man's sayings and doings. 'His morality,' said Oscar Wilde in De Profundis, 'is all sympathy—exactly what morality should be.'"

In the same letter, Farrar wrote, "If you do any permanent work, I doubt if it will be in a genre which will appeal to you."[32] This is a highly prophetic remark. Thayer regarded his poetry as his most important literary output (he compared it with Longfellow's), but even an apologist must allow that it rarely rises to the sublime. If any parts of Thayer's literary achievements are lasting, they must include the *Dial* itself (which Thayer saw mostly as an irritating distraction from his own work), his often brilliant private notes, and the letters he wrote describing life in Vienna after the war.

Farrar also seemed to see that Thayer's exquisitely refined aesthetic sense was perhaps tied too closely to his great fortune, which enabled him to avoid many of the mundane and less than pleasant realities of life that Farrar and his fellow soldiers had to face daily. "Here one has no privacy and next to no leisure, and everything has to be done according to a prescribed formula," he wrote of life in the barracks. "It gives me soul-nausea sometimes. Here one has to believe in the eternal brotherhood of all men, since menial duties and the elements of life reduce all men to a common level. . . . I wager it would need all your faith in beauty, and all the favor of your aesthetic purity, to bear you through this weary and abstruse ritual of plate-washing and floor-scrubbing."[33]

Thayer was still unsure how to begin his career, whatever that career was going to be, and his letters show more than a little confusion about his future. In January, he wrote his mother that "Tuesday I go to London for the rest of the war. I look forward to seeing Farrar, Eliot, and Hoffman."[34] But just three days later, he had another idea: "[B]oth my old friends Tom Eliot and Santayana counsel me to eschew the life academic and to seek an asylum in Paris, the foster-mother of artists."[35] A month or so later, he seemed to have made up his mind to stay put. He preferred London to both Oxford and Cambridge, he said, and was greatly enjoying the company of Tom Eliot.

I now plan to pass the bulk of the spring war in London. After my visit to Cambridge I shall take a bedroom, study, and bath in some small London hotel. There I shall try to get on with my reading. The fact that my friend Tom Eliot also intends to be in the city is an added inducement. I find him most congenial. There is some irony in the history of our friendship.

He was with me in Forbes House at Milton and again at Harvard; then we scarcely knew each other. Now when I am come to the long desired and sacred cloisters of Oxford, I find here no one else so good company as my old neighbour [at Milton Academy].[36]

His time in London in early 1915 was busy. He bought a great many books ranging from the classics to contemporary literature but complained that his social life left him little time to read. He regularly saw his cousins, Lucy and Ellen, as well as Vivien Haigh-Wood. Weekends he sometimes took the train to Epsom to see Farrar. Eliot introduced him to Ezra Pound and other writers and artists, including Bertrand Russell and Raymond Mortimer. Thayer described Pound as "one of the most interesting of the young poets,"[37] an opinion that was to change drastically. He was intrigued by Pound's early verse and pronouncements, but he ended up being much put off by Pound's rigid dogmatism, as we see from his notes for an unpublished review of Pound's *Pavannes and Divagations*: "This book is a waste-basket chock-full of those diverse spit balls which this so par excellence small bad boy has been for years blowing at us. He now, to boot, assumes the chair of a master and we are expected to sit numb-chance and take his spit-balls in the eye."[38]

He returned to Oxford briefly to read a paper on Compton Mackenzie, a prolific and successful Scottish novelist of the time and a youthful favorite of his, to the literary club. Eliot and Santayana were in the audience.[39]

Thayer seemed to be settling down for a lengthy stay in London, despite the war. Even after the torpedoing of the *Lusitania* in May, he was looking at rooms in Soho, where Eliot lived. (He learned soon after the sinking of the ship that Fr. Basil William Maturin, the Catholic chaplain at Oxford, was among the dead.) But as summer approached and it became more and more obvious that America would enter the war, Thayer decided to return home. The very day, June 26, that Thayer passed through the Aliens Office in Liverpool before boarding a ship for New York, Tom Eliot and Vivien Haigh-Wood married hurriedly and without the knowledge of their families. We don't know if there was a farewell between Haigh-Wood and Thayer, but there is this snippet from Thayer's notebooks: "Eyes of cat-vitriol,—Vivien, after, her voice rising at end, she had screamed, 'I'm going to marry T.E!'"[40] The "after" is utterly intriguing.

There was undoubtedly a close relationship between Vivien and Thayer, and indeed the evidence seems to suggest that Thayer had indeed proposed or otherwise pledged his troth to Vivien, since he later was concerned about being sued for breach of promise (see chapter 5). From Thayer's notebooks we get an idea, if impressionistic, of how he viewed her: "Vivien lay spread out before me (all the time, spiritually) like a fish, white + naked. All she could do was to flop and hope to attract the custom of myself [or] some other man of means. She breathed."[41]

Their romance, if such it was, was greatly complicated, though, in Thayer's final summer in England, when he met the woman he would eventually marry, Elaine Orr. She was an eighteen-year-old of great beauty from a wealthy family from Troy, New York. She was vacationing in England, looking forward to her final year at Miss Bennett's, a finishing school in Millbrook, New York. The two had met at least three years earlier, when she was fifteen. Thayer doesn't mention Elaine in his letters, perhaps because he was somewhat embarrassed by the age difference between Elaine and himself, he being seven years her senior.

Apart from her physical beauty, what may also have attracted Thayer to the girl from Troy was her straightforwardness and stability. Her later letters show a woman who is determined and pragmatic. Thayer's companions in England—his cousin Lucy Thayer, Vivien Haigh Wood, and Tom Eliot—were, like him, fragile creatures whose psyches would all suffer greatly under the buffetings of life. All four would endure serious mental breakdowns, and three of them—all but Eliot—would end their lives under care.

5

THE CHICAGO EXPERIMENT

Thayer left Oxford without being awarded a degree and returned to Massachusetts. He continued to correspond with Farrar, who was training on Salisbury Plain in preparation for being sent to the front. Farrar wrote, "No; the army has not yet steam-rolled me into its orthodox pattern; it has only set my mind all of a jangle, and I have lost all harmony at present—'there is no direction.'"[1]

In August, Thayer received from Eliot a letter discussing Thayer's being "nettled"—the word used by Thayer, apparently (his letter is lost)—that Eliot had married Vivien. "I must confess," Eliot wrote, "that at the time I was surprised at the extent to which you were 'nettled.' You had never given me the impression that your interest in the lady was exclusive—or indeed in the slightest degree a pursuit; and as you did not give *her* this impression, I presumed that I had wounded your vanity rather than thwarted your passion. If I was in error, at least Time (let us say) is the anodyne of disappointment rather than the separation of friends."[2]

Teasing out the motivations here is difficult. Eliot may be showing some disingenuousness here, since the tenor of the correspondence between Thayer and Vivien suggests a romantic closeness. Furthermore, Thayer, it seems, had indeed proposed to Vivien, but evidently had had second thoughts about the wisdom of the union, especially after meeting and falling in love with Elaine. In his notes we find this: "I might have had a breach of promise suit as it was if it hadn't been for Eliot stepping into the breach. . . . But I really do think he put his foot in it this time."[3] One would not put it past Thayer that his claim of being "nettled" was a way of putting on record the fact that his proposal to Vivien, if there was one, had been superseded legally and romantically by her nuptials with Eliot.

Thayer's reading during the summer remained varied, including Tolstoy's *Youth*, Lawrence's *Sons and Lovers*, Oliver Onions's *In Accordance with the Evidence*, Algernon Blackwood's *The Centaur*, Galsworthy's *The Dark Flower*, Leonard Merrick's *Conrad in His Quest of Youth*, and his old favorite, Kipling.

One of the more curious of Thayer's exploits took place in early May 1916, immediately before his marriage to Elaine Orr. Thayer had spent the previous months preparing for the wedding and a life of union with Elaine, but before doing so he determined to spend time completely friendless in a strange city. Thayer moved to Chicago with just ten dollars in his pocket and without employment prospects and there set himself the task of earning his own living for a month. He even supposedly gave his gold watch en route to a Pullman porter. Once in Chicago he tramped the pavements until he found work, then put in fourteen-hour days until he had achieved a level of financial stability.[4] The adventure had been recommended to Thayer by an older friend, perhaps to help Thayer prove to himself that, despite his inheritance, he still had the inherent ability to make his own way in the world. It may also have served to mitigate the guilt felt by a wealthy young man who conscientiously voted the Socialist ticket; if one has the ability to be prosperous under any circumstances, perhaps one need not reproach oneself for being wealthy. Moreover, the war in Europe was forcing many young men to test their mettle, either by participating in the conflict or by refusing to serve on the grounds of conscientious objection, neither of which routes Thayer wanted to take.

The Chicago saga smells heavily of personal mythmaking in the mold of Horatio Alger Jr., but the evidence bears up the facts. In recounting the story, the art critic Henry McBride exaggerated Thayer's impecuniousness,[5] since he did indeed have a little money—ten dollars—when he arrived in Chicago. And the detail about his giving away a gold watch sounds utterly unlike Thayer, who, despite his wealth and his generosity, knew the value of everything and would haggle over small amounts.

But there is no doubt the story is true, and it would seem the adventure was carried out to prove to the lovely Elaine Orr that he was a worthy husband. "I want to show you . . . that I am not an idler," he announced. "Therefore I write you that if it would either help you the tiniest bit to make your decision [regarding marriage, probably], or, if not that, give you any pleasure at all, I should immediately, by the next boat, sail for France and like Mrs. Fiche take my honeymoon alone in a hospital in Paris or work at the front. . . . Or if," he continued, "with your deep interest in money-making, you'd rather I should support myself with my hands . . . here in the muddy stream of American industry I'll do it gladly. I have but to send my lawyer my check-book, lock up my rooms, and go forth to seek a job."[6] So it was, as one might expect from a romantic young man of the period, a proving of his mettle.

Thayer took lodgings in Chicago at 158 East Pearson Street for three dollars a week. "My room is clean, quiet, and pleasant," he wrote his mother, who seems to have been one of the few people who knew of the excursion. "I have two windows looking out to the lake and the sun all day."[7]

He registered at the YMCA, which offered programs to assist young men in finding work. It cost a precious five dollars, but Thayer thought it would be money well spent. Then, rather than wait for the YMCA to contact him, he spent three days by himself beating the bushes in search of employment. On the third day, he answered an advertisement and landed a job selling Automobile Blue Books, highly detailed trip guides and maps that helped drivers navigate America's growing road system. By the time he accepted the job, he was down to his last twelve cents. "The YMCA had nothing to do with getting me this job," he said, "and I regret my five dollars."[8]

Thayer had taken up the pseudonym Samuel Taylor for his undercover work and insisted that his mother address his letters in that way. "I continuously run into people I know, but so far no one has recognized me in my disguise," he wrote. (Samuel Taylor is one of two pseudonyms Thayer alternately assumed, the other being Nelson Taylor.) He had noticed the presence of Mrs. Washburn, a Worcester matriarch, on the train to Chicago, but she "suspects nothing unusual," he said. "Please remember not to speak of my 'business' in Chicago to your friends," he wrote.[9]

By lunchtime on his first day, Thayer had already made three dollars, which he said came "none too soon." The work involved a good deal of walking. Thayer found that his best markets were in the many high-rise towers in downtown Chicago, but since peddling was not allowed in these buildings, Thayer was forced to use the stairs to keep out of sight. This put a lot of stress on his feet, which had always troubled him.[10]

Thayer seems to have written quite frequently to his mother during this period, and her mind naturally was very much on the impending marriage of her only son. She wanted Thayer and his bride to be married in a church service, but he was dead set against the idea. "I am sorry you should be troubled that our marriage is not to be participated in by the church," he wrote her. "That would of course be quite impossible for me, being, as I am, entirely hostile to that institution." He turned then to the more immediate matter of his sore feet. "My feet are, what with killed toe-nails, blisters, and strained insteps pretty far gone, but these other boots appear to ease them somewhat. I now travel in and out of town on a trolley and so conserve my feet as much as possible."[11]

Soon, he was able to give up working in the evenings. "I can support myself easily selling the books in the office-buildings in the morning and afternoon," he wrote. "They sell for 2.50 and I get 75 cents commission on each copy I sell. I now figure I can sell about one an hour. This means trotting up and down 20 story buildings most of the day, but this is, I believe, good exercise. I have to avoid the elevators as I am in constant danger of being put out of the building for peddling. I was ejected once on Friday. I walk into town in the morning and back at night. Thus I get plenty of air. Of course I am thrown into contact with all sorts of people and the work is therefore not without interest."[12]

He noted one instance of being ejected from an office that he managed to turn into a small triumph: "A few days ago I had the rare experience of being put out of a building by the janitor," he wrote his mother. "But the following day I put a feather in my cap by selling a book in the very office of the building superintendent."[13]

The experience left Thayer with a distaste for Chicago, which is mentioned in his notebooks more than any other city, almost always disparagingly. He wrote entire lists of mostly maledictions of the metropolis:

> The river at Rush Street Bridge is a clot of valid reality in this city, which has all the hideous papier-mâché quality of a made-over human face.
> This galvanized city within its etoliated population. . . .
> The pastoral or idyllic note of Chicago is sounded by the locomotives in the yards.
> Western manners are as casual as their houses dropped down here and there on the flat expanse.[14]

Another such listing is of interest because of its mention of the magazine he would one day own.

> Chicago curls like a blue oyster in the expansive shell of night.
> Chicago, mother of the stock-yards and The Dial, quaint gourmand of freight-cars, linked like sausages and painted as though they were not real. . . .
> In Chicago they disapprove of anything old, even of old trees.
> It appears Titanic but life there lived in comfortable middle-class.
> Taxis like potato bugs.
> New York, if only a station is at least a full stop on the route to Europe; Chicago, also a station, is on the way to nowhere.
> Chicago is the small town gone wrong.

Bourgeois and ridiculous, monstrous and sinister, Chicago yet remains, willy-nilly, a capital of fate.

Chicago has no heart, but real guts, and they are the stockyards.

Cattle in pens have already reached the final steep declivity of that slide which is their life from birth to boots and mucilage.

In Chicago, there is wind, but no air.[15]

"Business jogs along and affords a bare livelihood," he wrote his mother. "Some days I sell nothing and others I have sold six books. Then my daily income ranges from 0 to $4.50. This uncertainty of success keeps the work from becoming humdrum; on the other hand to work all day until at night you are physically unable to stand on your own feet and not to have a thing to show for it is discouraging. The lodgers in this house [are] singularly stand-offish. I fancy they think me either a German dynamiter or a Mexican conspirator. Their suspicions may have been confirmed by a call the other evening from my friend Emerson of New York who took me out for a motor-ride. He was here a couple of days fixing up the Roosevelt pow-wow for next month." Theodore Roosevelt was to be involved in both the Republican and Progressive conventions that were held in Chicago that summer.

"The weather here is bad most of the time," he wrote. "This Sunday like last is cold and raining. I am confined to my room where I wear my winter overcoat and try to keep warm. My feet, however, are better than they have been."[16]

He gave a week's notice to his employer and landlady May 21, and looked forward to returning to New York at the end of the month, in time to attend his fiancée's graduation from Miss Bennett's School for Girls in Millbrook. The attractive Elaine had the leading parts in the school's two dramatic productions.

His mother again raised the issue of a religious ceremony, and again Thayer responded. "You force me to speak decidedly: I detest the Christian Church and will not have it meddling in my affairs," he fumed. "If you had any conception of the strength of my feeling on this point you certainly would not want a minister to marry me."[17]

Still, one Rev. Henry R. Freeman was present at the wedding in Troy, New York, the hometown of the Orr family, according to the *Troy Northern Budget* newspaper, as well as "the groom's pastor."[18] So it would seem that a compromise had been reached between mother and son, and that although the Thayers' was not a church wedding, Mama managed to insert a clerical presence. The ceremony was held in the house of an Orr relative, in the same room where Elaine's parents had married. The article noted, "The hour of high noon brought many handsome summer gowns and hats out among the guests."[19]

On May 31, on his way from Chicago to New York, Thayer had stayed at the Bellevue-Stratford Hotel Philadelphia. He stayed just one night, and his bill included laundry, automobiles, carriages, flowers, and a valet. He was treating himself to a little luxury, perhaps, after the relative rigors of the Chicago experiment.[20]

The adventure was, for Thayer, a triumph. In his notebook we find this: "Having proved conclusively to my own satisfaction that it is far easier to make dollars than phrases, I return to my more serious business."[21] And there is also this excessive and pompous description of his sojourn in the Midwest: "Fortuna is not less fickle in Chicago than she was in Rome and from pinnacles of golden triumph I have more than once been plunged into gulfs of penniless despair. Yet I am able to support myself, to eat well, and to sleep better. What more could a noble soul desire[?]"[22]

The lone, glancing mention of the *Dial* in the Chicago entries of Thayer's notebooks suggests that he was less than overwhelmed by the magazine during his stay in the city in May 1916. It may well have been that in the evenings in his YMCA bedroom, tired from selling guidebooks, Thayer would leaf through the *Dial*. The leading articles that month focused on literature. The Great War, now in its second year, was alluded to only in a single short essay discussing soldiers' slang. The letters from readers discussed the spelling of Shakespeare's name and identified a school in London that Poe may have attended. Other letters dismissed *Spoon River Anthology* as real verse and discussed the matter of palindromes in Japanese. It was a pleasant, interesting, but not overly highbrow journal that gave the sense of being utterly disengaged with the age and its events. The liveliest exchange of opinion in the magazine's pages had taken place the year before, when Harriet Monroe and a *Dial* reviewer disagreed at length over the merits of William Cullen Bryant and of the new poetry, during which give-and-take Monroe was described as a "bardess" and an "editress." In short, there was little in the pages of the *Dial* to suggest that in another four years the magazine, under Thayer, would bring modernism, the avant-garde, and new forms of criticism to the United States.

6

LADY OF THE SONNETS

One thing I know: I owe him [Scofield Thayer] everything, he
taught me the lesson of my life[,] gave me the shaking-up of my life.

I loved him, I really did.
"And yet you had a child by somebody else."
I know. But I loved him.

ELAINE, FROM NOTEBOOKS OF E. E. CUMMINGS

Ellen Thayer, Scofield Thayer's cousin, believed that Scofield first met Elaine
Orr en route from England to the United States in June 1915, following the
outbreak and escalation of the European war. "That year I was teaching at
Bryn Mawr and he came to see me there," she wrote. "He told me about
Elaine[,] whom he had met on the steamer returning from Europe. He was
evidently much interested in her. She was beautiful, well educated. He said he
called her 'the Lily Maid of Astolat.'"[1] The Lily Maid in question was the fair
Elaine of Arthurian legend, a virgin who died of unrequited love for Lancelot.
Thayer's courtship of Elaine was, naturally, a literary one.

In fact, Thayer had met Elaine Orr in the fall of 1912, when he wrote her
a letter teasing her about being "so very, very young."[2] It may well have been
Elaine's tender years—she was just fifteen—that caused Thayer to be so un-
forthcoming about their relationship and to keep its existence a secret even
from his family. A letter in December 1912 refers to their having met during a
sea voyage, so it is possible that the meeting actually took place when Thayer
was returning from one of his summer European trips.

The two had exchanged affectionate letters frequently during his stay at Oxford, and from England Thayer had sent the young Elaine books, including a copy of his friend Cuthbert Wright's volume of verse, *One Way of Love*. It was in some ways a curious romantic gift, in that many of the poems in the collection celebrated love between men, but then such "Uranian" verse was popular at the time among young Progressives and aesthetes like Thayer. The relationship deepened; the following spring Thayer ordered a four-thousand-dollar Marquise diamond ring from Dreicer & Co. on Fifth Avenue, New York City, and, not long after, the engagement was announced in the *New York Times*.[3] May F. Bennett, who founded the finishing school Elaine attended in Millbrook, New York, wrote Thayer on his "having won the love of our darling little Elaine" and congratulated him on the match. "My respect for her singular purity and beauty and truth are so great that I have had implicit confidence in her choice," the letter went on. The writer also mentioned that Elaine and her sister had been through much after losing both parents unexpectedly, first their father, then their mother. "No girls ever were left so alone as those children were after their mother's death," the letter noted. "They have been tried in life's furnace as many never are in a life time— and they are all coming out new gold."[4]

But the European war that Thayer had fled intruded rudely on his happiness. Less than a week after the announcement, Thayer received a letter from England in response to one he had sent to his Oxford friend Valentine Farrar. It was from Farrar's mother, Mary, explaining that her son was dead. "He was shot through the head in the trenches on the morning of the 15th, and lived 39 hours, but was never conscious, nor did he have any suffering," she wrote. "He had been out just seven weeks and when he was shot it was after seven days in the trenches."[5]

Thayer was dashed by the news. "He was the finest man I have known," he wrote Elaine. "He was so holy that I always hesitated to touch him. Knowing him made me understand how the Apostles felt toward Christ. The highest aim we have is to people the world with men and women like him. Life came through his soul more perfectly and finely than anywhere else. In him there was a balance, a harmony, an essential concentration of manhood, which is the end of all our being."[6]

Elaine Orr came from a prominent family in Troy, New York, that had prospered in the paper business. Her father had died of a stroke in 1908, when Elaine was twelve, and her mother died suddenly three years later after a brief second marriage. Perhaps this shared loss of parents at an early age made for the sympathetic resonance between her and Thayer.

Thayer was utterly smitten with Elaine. "A friendship which from the first has been edged with a delicate fire, has, since I last wrote you, bit by bit become wholly suffused and is now the intense flame of conscious love," he wrote in what was perhaps a draft of a letter to a friend. "Such strength as I have I exhaust in a desperate and constant attempt to be aware of what I feel. For some sensations are so profound as to inhibit the action of our intelligence. Yet, being human, we can but seek to comprehend them, however inadequately. . . . I cannot describe her to you. Anything that I might say would be only a foot-note, meaningless until you know herself, and afterward impertinent."[7] He also wrote, at a rare loss for words, "E.O. of an incommunicable loveliness."[8] Nor was it only Thayer who was struck by her beauty. John Dos Passos spoke of her as "the blessed Damozel, the fair, the lovable, the lily maid of Astol[a]t. . . . She seemed the poet's dream."[9] Thayer described her as a "changeling," a "fairy child," "not like a mortal woman, at all."[10] She had an "Astartee quality," he wrote. She was "a virgin of Ashtaroth" who "curled + smiled into the room."[11] Hildegarde Watson, wife of Thayer's part-ner, herself a beauty who would appear in her husband's avant-garde films, said she never saw anyone prettier.[12]

E. E. Cummings probably first met Elaine on May 20, 1916, at a Cambridge party Thayer hosted following a performance of Galsworthy's *Justice*, which was that spring enjoying successful runs in New York, Boston, and New Haven. Cummings fell harder than anyone. "I considered EO as a princess, something wonderful, unearthly, ethereal, the like of which I had never seen," he wrote.[13] (Cummings later wrote many love poems for Elaine, including his longest poem, the 290-line "Puella Mea.")

In May 1916, Thayer's old friend and rival T. S. Eliot wrote to wish him well on his imminent wedding, referring to the Thayer of their days in Magdalen College as "the connoisseur of puberty and lilies" (a phrase that interestingly brings together Thayer's interest in younger women and his aestheticism) and paraphrasing Oscar Wilde's Dorian Gray: "Only the soul can cure the senses, and only the senses can cure the soul." He hoped that "domestic felicity may not extinguish the amateur" and that "possession of beauty many not quench the ardor of curiosity and that passionate detachment which your friends admired and your admirers envied."[14] Eliot's wife, Vivien, also wrote to wish Thayer well: "How nice that you are going to be married! Nothing could be better! Try black silk sheets + pillow covers—they are extraordinarily effective—so long as you are willing to sacrifice *yourself*."[15] Having been close to Thayer, Vivien had no doubt sensed his inability or unwillingness to dedicate himself wholeheartedly to a relationship. Thayer would make many sacrifices for the causes of art and letters, but never for marriage. Cummings joined in the good wishes in June, sending along a poem beginning, "Oh friend, who has attained thyself in her," along with a note saying, "I am very afraid . . . that it tries to honor a thing so perfect as your marriage with Elaine." He signed off with the unwittingly prophetic salutation, "Wishing you happiness improbable."[16]

The war continued to thrum in the background of all this prenuptial joy. Conscription had been in force in England since February, and young men were being hurriedly trained and shipped across the Channel. Canadians were also already fighting and dying in the trenches. In April, President Wilson had warned Germany about its submarine activity. As the body count rose—the butchery that would be called the Battle of the Somme would begin that summer and extend into late fall—the pros and cons of entering the war were argued ferociously in American magazines and newspapers.

The wedding took place on June 21, 1916, in Elaine Orr's hometown of Troy, New York; afterward, the couple seems to have spent some nights at the Dakota in New York City and perhaps on the island of Nantucket, before leaving for Santa Barbara, California, where Thayer had a connection in the person of his uncle, Ernest Thayer. The honeymoon began well. "Entering the room at the Dakota E.O. was a singularly enticing creature,"[17] Thayer wrote. He was aware, he said, "of the peculiar definition and strangeness of a face ideally Romantic."[18]

The idyll continued in California, whence Thayer reported to a friend that he and Elaine spent most of the day swimming and basking. "At irregular intervals we sip tea and nibble cinnamon toast. Thanks to the omnipresence of Poland Water, I scrub along excellently and Elaine, despite the burden of honeymooning with a philosopher, bears up."[19]

In July, they stayed at the Hotel Coronado. "The hotel is in the middle of a ten mile long beach and we have thus had a wonderful place for walking," he wrote his mother. "The sea because of the stinging fish is not practicable on the ocean side, but back of us in [the] bay there are no fish and there we swim every morning and then walk across the strand to lie on the ocean beach facing the breakers."[20] They drove out to Point Loma, where Thayer so loved the "magnificent" view that he contemplated buying a home there, but he found that more difficult than he had imagined. "All the best land is owned by the Government and by the Theosophists, who have their headquarters in a group of domed buildings overlooking the Pacific," he wrote. At the thriving Theosophist school, Thayer and his wife heard a lecture and watched the children perform a dance.[21]

Later that summer, Thayer received notice of a second death in battle. This time it was his Harvard classmate Alan Seeger, whose poem "I Have a Rendezvous with Death" so eerily predicted how he would fall on the field of battle. This news, along with the still-fresh memory of Valentine Farrar's death, may have put him in the somber mood manifested in another note from California, perhaps the draft of a letter to a former classmate, in which he recalled his time at Oxford and the war that had begun during his time in England:

> Here, a mile or two from Santa Barbara, between the mountains and the sea, we have found what we sought—a hearth, a garden, a fountain, and from our window a patch of sea. We have taken refuge until this war shall be over. Natural beauty is the best anodyne and the unsullied Pacific is good to look upon. Even here I recall Oxford. My memory of her is darkened and her summer skies, heavy with calm, made almost sinister by this ever-gaining tide of death. Those are indeed gallant who still keep their post in that saddest of all cities. I like to think that you and I, though so irremediably far apart, yet in surroundings not unworthy her high nurture, still retain in our minds untarnished her grey buildings and her glittering streams.[22]

Cummings remained a regular correspondent. He had produced to Thayer's order "Epithalamion," a long poem crammed with classical allusions celebrating the marriage of his friend. Thayer was pleased with the result. "The poem is really corking and Elaine and I have to thank you from the bottom of our heart," Thayer wrote Cummings that September. "It is not to have lived in vain, thus to have occasioned beauty. 'Whose smiling is the swiftly singular adventure of one inadvertent star (With angels previously a loiterer)' is completely worthy of that smile which is now always with me."[23] It was perhaps fitting, considering the relationship that would bloom between Cummings and Thayer's wife, that Cummings began his poem with an image of sexual infidelity.

> Thou aged unreluctant earth who dost
> with quivering continual thighs invite
> the thrilling rain the slender paramour
> to toy with thy extraordinary lust,
> (the sinuous rain which rising from thy bed
> steals to his wife the sky and hour by hour
> wholly renews her pale flesh with delight)
> —immortally whence are the high gods fled?

There is no evidence that Thayer was reading the *Dial* during this period, but as a man of literary tastes who had spent time in Chicago, where the magazine was published, there is every reason to believe that he did. If so, he would have noticed a new byline in the December 28 issue, that of Randolph Bourne, whose leading article, "Seeing It Through," expressed disappointment at H. G. Wells's apparent acceptance of and resignation to the war. Bourne was patently talented. His passionate, trenchant prose contrasted sharply with the magazine's usual fare of academic, muted, and remote editorials. Bourne had already made a name for himself in other magazines and was now stamping his style on the *Dial*.

In August, the Thayers moved into a house in Santa Barbara that was large enough to accommodate a cook and a butler-chauffeur, who, Thayer pointed out, were respectively a "negress" and an "Indian."[24] There was also a garage for the Dodge Roadster he had bought at the El Camino Real Motor Car Co. The butler-chauffeur, Harry King, was fitted out for uniforms in Santa Barbara. The couple settled in and continued their life of ease, bathing in the sea, reading, and shopping, punctuated by dinners with Thayer's uncle and aunt and motoring along the coast. Their evenings out included plays, a visit to a circus, and attending a Rabindranath Tagore lecture entitled "The Cult of Nationalism," which Thayer found too long.[25] Thayer would later write of the popular poet and lecturer: "Among those who have not contributed to The Dial is Tagore. I like to look upon his wide-hooved nobility as upon that of the white cattle in the marshes about Risa with their great brown eyes like pregnant women waiting their time; but I should as soon think of inviting one of these cows to write for The Dial as to invite a contribution from Tagore."[26]

They visited Los Angeles to see a doctor after Elaine complained about trouble with her eyes. Thayer loathed the noisiness of the city.

The only out-of-the-ordinary incidents were two unexplained hospitalizations. In September, "Master M. Maruyama of Montecito" was admitted to Santa Barbara Cottage Hospital ("c/o Mr. Scofield Thayer").[27] His physician was a Dr. Campbell, and he was released six days later. The following month Harry King, the butler-chauffeur, was admitted to the same hospital under the same doctor.[28]

In the fall, the couple returned briefly to the East Coast, perhaps for Thanksgiving with their families, and on their journey back to California they stopped off in Chicago to meet James Sibley Watson, a Harvard friend of Thayer's, and Watson's new wife, Hildegarde. The Watsons had been married in October in Massachusetts. Their wedding had been attended by Cummings, who was also a friend of Watson's. The Thayers were back on the West Coast at least by early December, according to a Santa Barbara drugstore shopping receipt.

Their purchases are listed as Douche Can Complete, K.Y. Jelly, a thermometer, breath tablets, and two packages of sanitary napkins. By the New Year they had resumed their sybaritic honeymoon, riding, swimming, and reading. Thayer read *Why Men Fight* by Bertrand Russell, and the couple read Henry James's *Portrait of a Lady* together. He had also bought Hugh Walpole's *The Dark Forest* and Prince C. Hopkins's *Ethics of Murder*. In March, they visited San Francisco, where they stayed at the Hotel St. Francis. (Later that year at the same hotel, the movie star and comedian Fatty Arbuckle would throw the notorious party at which a young woman died, a case that would fascinate Thayer.)

Cummings continued to keep in touch, and by early 1917 his friendship with Elaine had deepened to the point that he could write letters addressed only to her. "A jolly New year unto thy lord and his master (you), the wheels of whose dodge roll in the thunder (Longfellow)," he wrote. "He sent me a poembook by one seeger, who evidently inherited the fashionable talent of dying. Do you know his work?" He then proceeded to produce several brutal parodies of Seeger's work, which indeed sounded not unlike that of one of the more ornate Victorian disciples of Keats and Shelley.

Of interest here is the fact that Cummings is so disdainful of Seeger, who was a Harvard friend of Thayer's and whose poems Thayer, as Seeger's literary executor, had helped into publication. Moreover, Thayer's own verse was not unlike that of Seeger, highly Romantic in form, diction, syntax, and subject matter. One can speculate that Cummings did not expect Elaine to share the contents of this letter with her husband. Cummings concluded by asking Elaine to tell "Scof." that he was leaving that morning for New York, where he had found a job with a book distributor on West Thirteenth Street.[29]

In a March letter to Thayer, Cummings writes, "Am so glad Elaine remembers me sometimes; it is mutual."[30] It would seem that Thayer was unaware that Cummings was writing directly to Elaine.

In April 1917, the United States finally entered the Great War. Thayer began clipping articles from the *New York Times* about the draft, including those that listed the names of the draft board members in New York. This was the beginning of what would be a careful campaign to avoid conscription. Meanwhile, he and his wife continued their honeymoon, visiting Los Angeles to dine and dance and, in Santa Barbara, indulging in their favorite pastimes of swimming, riding, and reading. They read James's *The Ambassadors* together.

It's difficult to pinpoint exactly when the Thayers' marriage started to fall apart. One of Thayer's notes from the honeymoon reads, "We bask upon yellow sands and swim in blue waters and bask upon yellow sands," and penciled in at a later date are the words, "Flagrant idealisation."[31] Things definitely began to unravel on the California honeymoon, and perhaps even before that. Thayer mentions a sudden moment of disillusionment, possibly in Nantucket.

> E.O. at Nant. in stocking feet suddenly apperceived as *banal*. From a "spright" to a perfectly *banal* girl. As if a magic glass had been removed from before my eyes, a transforming glass. A magic cap doffed. An intoxication *suddenly* removed. Therefore rather an incantation or bewichery [sic] suddenly off. Cf. Midsummer Night's Dream. As though she had doffed something that had endowed her with a magic charm.[32]

During the honeymoon the couple stayed for a while at the palatial Potter Hotel in Santa Barbara, where Thayer described in his notes what seems like a moment of horror and desperation experienced by his bride. "E.O.'s cry at the Potter was not only the cry of the broken virgin," he wrote, "it was also the cry of the lost soul when, driven backwards, without the strength of backbone to withstand the Devil's push—when it feels the earth give way and only air beneath it." He went on to describe her vulnerability thus: "The eyes opened wide like windows to break (E.O. at Potter)."[33] Thayer's writing was often impressionistic rather than journalistic, and while one cannot surmise the specifics of what he is describing here, it was obviously a moment of shock, pain, and fear for Elaine, one that drained her. "E.O. at Montecito like a snake that's had its back broken," Thayer noted.[34] Another note perhaps suggests it was during the honeymoon, traditionally a time of love and intimacy, that Thayer told his wife he wanted nothing more to do with the marriage and that they were to live separately: "E.O. pausing in her breakfast at Montecito looked half-sick of her evil bargain."[35]

On the surface, things continued to seem ideal. The two were a good-looking, wealthy couple spending a year traveling, sightseeing, enjoying their prosperity and each other. But after what Thayer later called "the fatal spring,"[36] he experienced a "neurotic turning away"[37] from Elaine. What Thayer saw himself rejecting was not just Elaine but the institution of marriage itself, whose interminable familiarity bred contempt. "Long girls in bed in coition are like warm snakes," he wrote. "They taste—after a year of marriage—like baked banana."[38] (Again, we see Thayer comparing those close to him with foodstuffs. Was this a form of metaphorical cannibalism?) He came to believe that cohabitation simply killed sexual attraction. "In so far as a man marry for sexual pleasure," he wrote, "he kills the golden goose."[39]

One speculation is that in California Thayer convinced his wife that they should enjoy physical relationships with others. This is certainly one reading of an affectionate and unself-conscious letter from Thayer written in April 1917: "O yes, I'm coming down to L.A. Saturday too, yes, and I've engaged another single room with bath for myself. I wish one could do certain things by mail, no pun intended!"[40] In the same letter, he made this request of Elaine: "I want you to cut your hair as you did before. I really couldn't see it and I want to very much. . . . Of course, you suit yourself; only if you will, you will give me very great pleasure." There are other tantalizingly unedifying references in Thayer's notebooks to a situation between the two in a bedroom involving the cutting of the young bride's hair. "E.O. ran upstairs like a defeated angel," he wrote, "I having walked into—almost through her—like a dragoon. (After her hair-cut.) Later I turned her over as I had one time turned over the bodies of dead snakes, white beneath. She was equally limp absolutely defunct."[41] He tried another time to record what had happened: "E.O. turned over on bed after haircut weeping was like a dead horseshoe-crab so turned over on back, neither wet nor dry."[42] And then this: "Commemorative bells signalling the decisive step of my proposal; + the decisive end by her hair-cutting. Extreme psychic potency."[43] And this: "E.O. lay like a dry + oil-wrung shark on her face (after hair-cut)."[44]

His aphorisms on marriage are many: marriage was "wholesale," whereas prostitution was "retail."[45] Marriage was like a diving suit worn for protection against "those sharks which infest the glaucous waters of sexual adventure."[46] Monogamy was the "reductio ad absurdum" of marriage.[47] To marry was "to enter a lobster-trap."[48]

As his marriage failed—or perhaps because of that failure—Thayer became an advocate of free love, a philosophy of sexual liberation that was enjoying something of a revival at the time among some intellectual groups. "Marriage occupies [the] same relation to love as the forced activities of sinners in Inferno do to their activities in this world," he wrote. "Marriage is as if a profound and penetrating punishment for love."[49] Free love, on the other hand, "suits those in whom the nerves and intelligence predominates [*sic*]. For it gives novelty and curiosity has free way."[50] His devotion to these ideas he would later share with Alyse Gregory, who would become Thayer's best friend. After marrying the chronically ill Llewelyn Powys in order that she might more easily care for him, Gregory wrote a letter to Thayer begging that he understand what she had done and not disdain her for stooping to the act of marriage.[51]

Whatever the reason, physical, philosophical, or both, Thayer was finished and done with his beautiful wife just a year after marrying her. He noted, "Co-ition with a girl is like a bath in sensuality: with Elaine it was as though the water were only three inches deep."[52] And more metaphorically, "On top E.O. looks good milk," he wrote, "but having drunk + in vain awaited nourishment one opines the good, the strength, the native vigor . . . [has] been withdrawn, drawn off, sucked out. A congenitally sucked egg."[53]

Thayer decided to cut short the extended honeymoon in California and return to the East. In a letter to his mother, Thayer blamed the couple's abrupt decision on the appearance of sewage in the waters off Santa Barbara in which he and Elaine swam daily.[54] Others, including his uncle Ernest, who had lived in the area since 1912, disagreed that this was the case, saying that any discoloration or smell could have been related to the harvesting of kelp, benign microorganisms, or even brush fires. Thayer, however, was obdurate. The couple headed east in June 1917, stopping in Chicago to have lunch at the Blackstone Hotel with the Watsons. Hildegarde Watson was struck by the sorry state of the Thayers' marriage, which she connected to the troubled and uncertain feelings about the war that roiled the country. "But what an unsettled luncheon that appeared to me, full of unrest," she remembered. "The Thayers were, before long to separate, there was the prospect of war, and all were confused by patriotic and pacifist feelings."[55] The Thayers returned to New York to live in separate apartments, Elaine in a spacious first-floor apartment at 3 Washington Square North and Thayer at the Benedick, an apartment for bachelors at 80 Washington Square East. There were evidently still physical relations between the two, as suggested by Thayer's rather clinical note after a visit from Elaine: "E.O.'s face the colour of yellowish toilet-paper (taking douche, nose running, after coition in tears at 80)."[56] Another note suggests dramatic and emotional scenes between the couple: "After my mother at Elm St. and after Elaine at Wash Sq, I ached equally after cleanliness," he wrote, "a washing of this weeping, accusing, embracing filthiness, this thing called clinging womanhood."[57] We also see here Thayer conflating the person of Elaine with his mother.

When Thayer philosophizes about sex—which he does a great deal in his notebooks, almost never in his correspondence—he almost always sees the relationship between man and woman as a power struggle, and sex itself as a kind of currency:

> The male of great possessions *incorporates* for the female those possessions more than does such a female for the male. To him she is, after all, a physical and animal object; to her he is primarily a power, a force, a something capable of increase, actually of multiplication, through the worldly power there inherent. He can enjoy his knowledge of acquiring money with or through her; but he cannot emotionally and intellectu-

ally synthesise this pleasure with his lust for her quite distinct and cir-cumscribed person. She can thus largely synthesise her satisfaction in the worldly gain by association with him with her sexual satisfaction in pos-session of him, he being for her then primarily an indicted and relatively uncircumscribed vital force, a something capable of being jumped ahead, almost incommensurably, in power.[58]

But while Thayer tried hard to be dismissive of Elaine ("I would no more feel like shooting E.O. than like shooting a mess of shit"),[59] he was also obsessed by his former wife, referring to her in his personal notes hundreds of times. At times these references are to her physicality; she has "breasts like skinned pears,"[60] inner thighs like "Banana-flesh."[61] She was "exquisite and clinging—the very best lingerie."[62] Once, when she entered a room at 3 Washington Square, Thayer remembered, he was sexually excited by her "illuminating eyes."[63]

He occasionally loved also her wit and perception. When she once said to Thayer, "You ought to have to work under someone sometime," Thayer won-dered, perhaps admiringly, if she was making a "*double entente*," perhaps mean-ing "double entendre."[64] When she remarked to Thayer, "You *have* no small talk,"[65] he felt she was, in a way, showing her respect for and pride in him. And at times her remarks were squirreled away into his notebook, perhaps for future literary use: "Occasionally E.O. stepped out of her role and, like an author (Cf. Pirandello), made a straight remark. 'They talk about emotion; they mean sex.'"[66]

But the obsession also showed his hatred of Elaine. She was like a "hairless Mexican dog," "a meal-worm, or maggot." During sex she was like a "white, hairless wolf,"[67] her head sideways "like a floun[der's]."[68]

In June, he registered for the draft in New York.[69] For some time he had been clipping newspaper articles on the draft from the *New York Times*, in-cluding those that listed the names of the members of his local draft board. Despite his draft registration, however, Thayer had no intention of joining the armed services. His response to his mother's suggestion that he invest in Lib-erty loans carried echoes of the pacifist sentiments of Randolph Bourne: "No one understanding this war as I do can voluntarily contribute in any way to its continuance, least of all can he loan money and receive interest which to him appears blood-money in the most crass sense. There is only one possible course: to endeavour to reform the institution of our government and to stop the war. I cannot see how anyone who sympathized with Russell's Why Men Fight can contribute to this so-called liberty loan. 'O liberty! What crimes are committed in thy name!'"[70]

He and Elaine settled comfortably into their respective new digs, keeping up for a while the appearance of domestic felicity; Thayer explained to friends that his separate apartment was necessary for his work. In the fall, Thayer asked his lawyers to secure leases on his and his wife's separate apartments. Elaine initially may not have been so sanguine about the situation, a fact that Thayer seems to recognize. "E.O. was made to go on acting her heart-lacerating role until the harvest of lyric grief was in," he wrote some time later. "Only then was permitted to fall the heart-relieving—and what would have been . . . ruining—rain of truth, of sights of the real Elaine, of the real Lady of the Sonnets."[71]

Why "Lady of the Sonnets"? Partly, perhaps, because Elaine Thayer would eventually become the lover of poet Cummings, who wrote sheaves of idolatrous love poems and sonnets to and about Elaine. But what then was the "heart-lacerating role" she was forced to play? Was it that she was forced to maintain in society the fiction of her marriage to Thayer? Was it that she had to lie to Thayer's family for so long about who was the father of the child she would eventually have with Cummings? We know that soon after that birth, Thayer's uncle Ernest had excitedly congratulated Thayer on becoming a father, thrilled that the Thayer line was not to end with his nephew. And the child, Nancy, would be three years old when Elaine finally broke the news to Florence Thayer that the girl was in fact not her granddaughter.

There must also have been hurt for Elaine in the fact that both her husband and the father of her child voiced their opinion that the problems that would eventuate from the pregnancy could be easily averted by an abortion. This "Lady of the Sonnets" was not only a puzzle to others but perhaps also a puzzle to herself. She was a wife and a mother, but her husband had rejected her, and the father of her child would be poor, feckless, and unready for fatherhood. Neither man would want the child in her womb. Hers was indeed to be a "harvest of lyric grief."

7

DEATH OF THE PROPHET

Randolph Bourne came from modest beginnings in a small town in New Jersey, where he was one of four children. When the family business failed and the father turned to drinking, his mother expelled him from the family and raised her children alone. Bourne won admittance to Princeton but couldn't afford the tuition fees, and he eventually entered Columbia University on a full scholarship. A further scholarship enabled him to tour Europe after graduation. Despite periodic bouts of depression, Bourne had high aspirations and great energy. He was just five feet tall, facially disfigured from a botched forceps birth, hunchbacked from a childhood bout of spinal tuberculosis, and often sick. He was avoided by some and stared at by others. On first seeing Bourne, Theodore Dreiser called him "as frightening a dwarf" as he had ever seen.[1] In Greenwich Village, he was often seen wearing a cape, a not uncommon bohemian accessory at the time, but one that must have emphasized the sense of otherworldliness about this figure, so deformed of face and body but with such an incisive and cultured mind. John Dos Passos called him a "tiny twisted unscared ghost in a black cloak / hopping along the grimy old brick and brownstone streets."[2] His writings were his sole means of support.

Bourne is known today mostly by scholars of the Progressive movement in the United States, but during the second decade of the twentieth century he achieved great influence and even fame as an intellectual and seemed destined to become one of the great thinkers and writers of the century. His early interest was in the field of education, then an important issue to the Progressives, but with the onset of the Great War, he turned his attention more toward war, pacifism, and critiques of the state.

Bourne and Thayer met in the winter of 1917–18 at the home of Merrill C. Rogers, who had been the business manager of the radical magazine the *Masses*.[3] Thayer was delighted to finally meet Bourne, whose writing he admired, and he had at this point made up his mind either to buy or to start a magazine. Bourne would be his political editor. Also present at that meeting was Martyn Johnson, publisher of the *Dial*, who was seeking financial support to help, among other things, move the magazine to New York. Soon thereafter, Thayer began financing the *Dial*, signed on as contributing editor, and started lobbying on behalf of Bourne, a member of the staff whose work he greatly admired.

But Bourne, a pacifist, was then locked in an escalating disagreement with his colleague at the *Dial* and former mentor, John Dewey, by whom he felt betrayed over the latter's support for America's entry into the war. By the spring of 1918, patriotism was running high, and the anti-Bourne sentiment at the magazine was strong. The writers and editors of the *Dial* were acutely aware of the fact that in April of the previous year Bourne's article "The Intellectuals and the War" had brought about the demise of another magazine, the *Seven Arts*, after its nervous patron withdrew financial support. *The Masses* was also struggling under sharply increased postage rates and charges of obstructing conscription. Some saw the *Dial* as likely to suffer the same kind of fate if Bourne's radicalism went unchecked.

The treatment of Bourne by the staff of the *Dial* did nothing to dampen Thayer's support for him, and he continued to champion Bourne's unpopular political point of view, even though that stance could have jeopardized the considerable investment—it would eventually amount to thirty thousand dollars in stock and loans—he had made in the magazine.

Despite his largesse, Thayer was continually frustrated in his attempts to increase Bourne's power at the magazine. Bourne was not invited to sit in on editorial conferences, and the prestigious leading articles were written by others; Bourne's pieces, meanwhile, often merely book reviews (one was aptly headlined "Clipped Wings"),[4] were usually buried in the back pages. His name was eventually removed from the masthead. The best Thayer could do in protecting his friend was to ensure that his salary continued to be paid. This was crucial, because Bourne was a working journalist who already had been blacklisted by many magazines, a fact that his friend Alyse Gregory and others blamed on his unyieldingly antiwar articles. "He had never had any trouble in placing his work," wrote Gregory after the collapse of the *Seven Arts*, "but now every editor's door was closed against him."[5]

Thayer's patronage was a lifeline for Bourne. On November 4, 1918, Bourne wrote to his sister:

On the Dial there has been some fuss about my being an editor, owing to my radical views, but I am paid just the same as if I were one, and only have to write two articles a month. I seem to be in very strong with the young man who is giving most of the money to back the Dial this year. He says he gave his $25,000 on the strength of my contributions, and he was angry at their not wanting me as a regular associate editor. So I need not worry, apparently, as long as the money lasts.[6]

There has been some question among scholars as to whether Thayer's interest in working at the magazine arose at least partly from his reluctance to join the armed services. Herman Riccius, a loyal friend of the Thayer family, claimed that Thayer had fallen arches and had been classified as 4F, physically unable to serve. And indeed, in the summer of 1917 Thayer had received from the War Department a Certificate of Discharge Because Physically Deficient.[7] The notice does not detail the deficiency.

But further records show a more complicated chain of events as the country was drawn deeper into the war. In January 1918, the War Department informed Thayer that he was classified 2B.[8] This was a "Married man, without children, whose wife, although the registrant is engaged in a useful occupation, is not mainly dependent upon his labor and support, for the reason that the wife is skilled in some special class of work which she is physically able to perform and in which she is employed, or in which there is an immediate opening for her under conditions that will enable her to support herself decently and without suffering or hardship." This classification meant, of course, that Thayer could be called up.

While there is little to suggest that Thayer shared Bourne's high-minded pacifism, he did show a profound disdain for the war. In his private notes, Thayer referred to World War I as "The *first* Great War" (my emphasis), apparently believing, quite correctly, that the conflict would do little to settle the seemingly eternal disagreements among the European nations. When he and his new bride settled in Santa Barbara, California, in June 1916, Thayer had written that they had "taken refuge" there "until this war shall be over."[9] (Bourne used a strikingly similar phrase in a letter to Alyse Gregory, saying he wanted to go to some quiet place "where I can go and stay until the war is all over.") An undated note in Thayer's papers calls England's entrance into the war "brutal, dishonest, stupid."[10] Another says: "The war of 1914 [was] the most disgraceful of European history. Disgracefully muddled into, disgracefully muddled through, disgracefully muddled out of."[11]

Merrill Rogers was certainly of the mind that Thayer was nervous about being drafted, and that the wealthy young man thought he might be exempt from conscription if he were the editor of an established magazine. This point of view is greatly bolstered by a letter from Martyn Johnson to Thayer that summer from the New York offices of the magazine.

My Dear Scofield,

I have your letter by the morning post and am writing you direct since this letter is better for you and myself alone.

You did quite right in forwarding my letter to your Draft Board. Probably they will make inquiries of me—but until they do so I would not think of taking any steps. You are right in thinking that over-protestation is unwise.

When they approach me I shall give them the facts straight as they are: to make the Dial a weekly published here—I was looking around for the men I would require—when I met you I knew you were interested in writing and on the occasion of our first meeting I asked you to show me some of your work. On subsequent meetings developed the fact that you had intended acting as one of the American Editors of a journal to be started in England—knowing that and having seen one of your articles and sounded you out on the lines of your literary taste and viewpoint I decided to try you out as editorial timber. You accepted my proposition that you go to Chicago for the purpose of getting what experience was possible during the two June issues the understanding being that when the New York corporation was formed you were to become a member of our regular staff on a salary of $30 a week. You are now doing your work at Edgartown in order to get sufficiently rested for the strenuous work of the weekly publication.[12]

This would certainly seem to settle the matter once and for all. Yes, Thayer was antiwar, and yes, his history as editor of the *Harvard Monthly* suggested he was sincerely interested in a career in magazine publishing. But conscientious objection to the conflict was possible, though requiring a certain amount of moral courage. And many of his contemporaries who didn't want to fight in the war served as ambulance drivers in France, a choice generally considered honorable. Perhaps the kindest we can say of Thayer's actions at this time is that his managing to remain a civilian, find congenial work, and keep his public image largely free from stain demonstrated an astute and pragmatic approach to ethical challenges. Still, that October he received in the mail an anonymous letter containing a single white feather, the emblem of cowardice. He noted only that the stationery was "queer paper."[13]

Bourne introduced Thayer to several of his friends, including Alyse Gregory. Gregory was a young Progressive who had given up a promising career as

a singer to move to New York and work for women's suffrage and other issues. Her apartment at Patchin Place—then the focal point of the bohemia
of Greenwich Village—quickly became a salon for Bourne. "My rooms were
for a time a center for stormy discussion," she wrote. "Randolph would keep
bringing new acquaintances with him—journalists, artists, young revolution-
aries, university professors—some of them lately arrived from Europe. He was
for his generation in America, in the matter of the war, what Bertrand Russell
was for his in England and Romain Rolland for his in France."[14]

These gatherings of radicals and intellectuals quickly drew the attention and
curiosity of the authorities. A detective was seen watching whoever came in and
out of Patchin Place. "Most of my friends fell under suspicion, and Randolph,
who combined irrepressible impudence with a supercautious alarm, went to
stay with his friend Van Wyck Brooks in the country," Gregory wrote. "We had
some argument, just before he left that promoted me in a moment of injudi-
cious playfulness to send him a telegram containing the one word: PERFIDE.
This was a cause of extreme agitation to him, as it was suspected by the postal
authorities—whose knowledge of French was as scanty as their wits were slow
and their heads hot—of being a code word. He had the greatest difficulty in
quieting their suspicions."[15]

Thayer had moved to Chicago in May 1918 and joined the *Dial* at a salary of
thirty dollars a week. In June, he was elevated to the position of director and
vice president of the New York corporation of the journal. He immediately set
about trying to get his friend Cummings's work into the pages of the magazine.
The astonishing syntax and typographic experiments of Cummings did not go
down well with the other editors. "[W]e went through the stuff Estlin Cummings had let me have," he wrote his mother. "We intend to publish some of the
less astounding, and so we hope to the public, more digestible pieces. With the
possible exceptions of Sandburg and Amy Lowell, no one else in the country at
present can write any verse comparable in strength to Cummings."[16]

Cummings himself was not hopeful of seeing his work in the magazine. Writing to his father, he described Johnson's "Georgian anatomy" as being troubled
by anything new or different. "Another man dead—if not from the neck up, at
least downward," he wrote.[17]

The poet was prescient. Cummings's verse would not appear in the *Dial* that
year or the next. Only when Thayer and his partner, James Sibley Watson, were
fully in charge of the magazine would Cummings's ground-breaking "Seven
Poems" appear in the pages of the *Dial*.

Thayer stayed in Chicago for a couple of months to master the methods and
policies of the *Dial*, then moved to his summer home in Edgartown to write

and edit. He wrote an amusing letter to Elaine—the two were good friends, despite their separation—describing a day in the provincial and unexciting life of the *Dial*.

> My Wilde is not appearing in the next issue, and judging from the very civil lack of interest in my little verbal quickie I doubt if they will ever publish anything so futile, except at the repeated command of the more sympathetic [owner Martyn] Johnson. As to writing about the South Wind [a 1917 novel by Norman Douglas], I really have too much delicacy to parade the intimacies of that book before people who care only for what I have so frequently called "the sordid world of truth." Would that I were in Nepenthe [Thayer's review of *South Wind* appeared in the issue of August 15, 1918].
>
> After our collocation we trooped back to the office where nothing was done or so far as I can recall even said. Then we fought our way into an electric and went two blocks beyond Pearson Street and to a home not dissimilar from the one I [illegible] occupied. There we found [Willard] Kitchel [the magazine's secretary-treasurer] on the top floor. His rooms, formerly shared by Johnson whose room [Harold] Stearns [associate editor] now occupied are charming—quite the lair of heirlooms Mr Wilde expected of Cathay."[18]

In this letter, he also asked Elaine what had happened to her "Mongolian lover," suggesting again that the two were quite comfortable in speaking of each other's relationships.

Thayer also invited T. S. Eliot to write for the magazine. "*I* should be delighted to write for your paper—or rather for any paper with which you are connected," Eliot responded. He enthusiastically suggested that he be given the position of London correspondent. "I think that if I composed something in the hope of your printing it I ought to exploit my geographical position rather than send you my projected series on the Jacobean dramatists," he said. "Studies in European Literature, by one on the SPOT!"[19]

In the meantime, Bourne's difficulties at the magazine grew. Knowing that Thayer's coffers leant him some weight at the magazine, Bourne was keen to keep his patron and protector abreast of events in the office. In a letter to Thayer, after applauding one of Thayer's book reviews, Bourne gets down to some juicy gossip about the magazine staff.

> I was at the new Dial office yesterday, and discovered some interesting developments. It seems that a rivalry is developing between the two boards. The new board is said to feel alarmed at the risk of us irresponsible ones

misinterpreting the social and economic principles they are to promulgate and are rather inclined to wish to act as censor. [John] Dewey has discovered that, as editor, he will be held responsible for what appears, so that I am afraid under the new regime, clipped wings will be the order of the day. I think it most unfortunate that Dewey and [Thorstein] Veblen were not made "contributing editors," responsible only for what they wrote themselves, and privileged to say anything they liked. It is not as if they were both to be present, doing active editorial work. Dewey will be in California, all the year, and Veblen will not be regular. The idea seems to be that Miss [Helen] Marot shall act as the vice-regent, interpreting the will of the absentee rulers. I am sure that this will be most unsatisfactory. I think it should be a recognized principle that editors must be active participants in the work of the magazine, present on the job. Absentee editorship is as bad as absentee landlordism. If editors are not to be present, they should serve as contributing editors, without responsibility except for what they write. Unless the men present in the work, have both the authority and the responsibility, there is sure to be friction and misunderstanding. . . . The indubitable fact remains that the respective jurisdictions of the two boards are still quite undetermined. And that seems a most important question to be determined before the new regime begins. Of course, [Martyn] Johnson mustn't think I'm complaining, or revolting. I write you only the facts, and my sense of the principles that should obtain. I hope you will be back in September when I plan to return to town. I am very anxious to see the Dial take advantage of this opportunity.[20]

Writing to Alyse Gregory of the same situation, Bourne was less discreet: "I found Harold [Stearns] in revolt against Johnson, Dewey and Marot, and of course fanned the flames," he wrote.[21]

By September 1918, Thayer had given the Dial twenty thousand dollars, taking half in notes and half in stock. This did nothing to make the publisher, Martyn Johnson, any more willing to respond to Thayer's suggestion that Bourne's writing be published more frequently in the magazine, and in October, Bourne was removed as editor.

That September the Spanish Influenza was first brought to New York City, reportedly by merchant seamen. As the number of cases grew and the death toll rose, public buildings were closed and businesses were ordered to stagger their times of opening and closing so as to lessen the throngs in the streets and using public transportation. "To avoid the influenza we go about not at all," Thayer wrote his mother.[22]

At the same time, excitement was building as the brutal and exhausting war in Europe continued to wind down, and people began to see the possibility of a peaceful future. This resulted in "false armistices," premature celebrations by people eager for the war to retreat into history. *Dial* editor Harold Stearns remembers one such on November 9. He and publisher Horace Liveright were walking up Broadway toward Forty-Second Street "when, suddenly, all the whistles and sirens either of ships in the harbor or on the two rivers, as well as all the factory whistles in and around Manhattan Island, let loose a roar that must have thrilled every one of the millions of people—no need to ask about it, either. It was peace." He went on: "From every doorway of every skyscraper and office building and department store and hotel people began to pour forth. . . . In those days, the old Knickerbocker Hotel stood on the Southeast corner of 42nd Street and Broadway, and high up, from a small balcony that jutted out from his apartment, Enrico Caruso appeared with baskets of roses and other flowers, which he began throwing out over the crowd in what seemed to me, even that soon after the news, delirious happy excitement."[23]

The true armistice came two days later, on November 11. We don't know whether Thayer joined in the celebrations, but we do know that his mounting frustrations with the trajectory of the *Dial* were becoming intolerable. When he learned that the magazine planned to publish an almost entirely political issue, he resigned. "The Dial is too political for the taste of one who is not interested in how this world wags," he wrote.[24]

The issue in question, published December 14, 1918, included an editorial calling for the withdrawal of American forces from Russia, a piece on Russia and the American press, an essay entitled "The Soviet at Work," and a listing of the original decrees of the Soviet government. It wasn't so much the political content of the articles that offended Thayer but rather that Martyn Johnson had promised that the magazine would be a critical magazine in various spheres beyond politics, and Thayer saw the *Dial* devolving into just another cheerleading propaganda organ, of which there were already more than enough, he felt. Bourne's only contribution to that issue of the *Dial* was a review of fiction, and the only mention of Thayer was a short item on the back page noting his resignation.

Bourne fell sick during the influenza epidemic and contracted pneumonia. On December 17, he wrote his sister that he would be unable to come home for Christmas and that he would buy her a Christmas gift at another time. He also asked that his mother not be told of his condition. At the time, Bourne was staying at the home of Agnes de Lima, a friend.

Gregory was one of Bourne's closest friends at the time, and when she heard he was ill, she hurried to see him. "He looked strangely pitiful in bed," she wrote. "'I don't want to die,' he said, speaking with difficulty; but the words were imbued with his wonted irony, and so deeply involved was I in my love that I could not realize how serious was the threat to his life." Gregory, an attractive and distinguished-looking woman with light-colored hair, green-gray eyes, a high forehead, and a "bee-stung" upper lip,[25] was at the time in the middle of passionate love affair with a Frenchman.

A day or so later, there was a telephone call at Gregory's apartment. "It was during our love-making that the telephone began to ring," she wrote. "I thought, at first, I would disregard it, but it became so disturbing that I at last took down the receiver. It was a message to tell me that Randolph had died. I put back the receiver and returned to the arms of my lover. My dearest friend was lying dead on one bed and I was making love on another."[26]

Bourne died six weeks after the Armistice. "When he died," said Paul Rosenfeld, who was present at Bourne's death, "we knew that perhaps the strongest mind in the entire younger generation in America had gone."[27] Thayer was also in mourning. "Since my return to town this autumn I have been seeing more of him than of anyone else," he wrote his mother. "Indeed the last afternoon and evening before I started to feel off colour were passed in his company. I fancy we both got the same infection. Now that he is gone there seems much less to keep me in America. But I suppose I should think of my country's loss before my own. Bourne's death is a more serious blow to America than any other it could have sustained." In the same letter, he spoke of his leaving the *Dial*. "It had chiefly been Bourne's connection with The Dial that had interested me in it," he said, "and now that he is gone I have no reason to associate myself longer with what has become an uncongenial undertaking."[28] That same day he gave to Martyn Johnson five thousand dollars, the final installment of money he had promised the magazine. Johnson had absolved Thayer of this installment, considering the events that led to his resignation, but Thayer was determined to keep the contract.[29]

Thayer later wrote that he saw in Bourne "a rich, earthly, generative force"[30] and called him "O wise and venerable child!"[31] As for Bourne's physical deformities, Thayer dismissed them and probably would have disliked the figure of the Romantic, be-caped, aesthetic dwarf created by Dos Passos. When once asked, Thayer replied that he thought Bourne "very distinguished in appearance."[32] In his personal notes, he wrote: "His hump no more remarkable in this world than his truth. For he had set his course by other stars."[33]

8

TO THE CENTER OF THINGS

The Dial moved from Chicago to New York in 1918, probably to share in the cachet provided by an address in what had become the publishing capital of America. However, the late teens of the new century were trying times for New York City's magazines. The Lusk Committee was crusading vigorously against radical publications suspected of seditious activity, and grand juries were weighing evidence against publishers and writers. Those interviewed by the committee were barred by the Peace and Safety Act even from disclosing the contents of those interviews. Nor was it only the radical left-of-center journals that were being eyed by Senator Clayton R. Lusk. Even the staff of the *Dial*, who had largely avoided controversy in their pages, were "hauled before the Lusk Committee and examined under strict oath of secrecy about the activities of the paper," according to Lewis Mumford.[1]

By February 1919, publisher Martyn Johnson was beginning to feel the pinch as the *Dial* continued to lose money, and he now appealed for financial help to the formidable Albert C. Barnes of Philadelphia. Barnes, an irascible and wealthy collector of art, had had dealings with the *Dial* before. The magazine had rejected his article "The Psychology of Courage" in November 1918. (In the rejection letter, editor Helen Marot brassily asked for financial assistance. Barnes declined.)[2] The following month, Barnes's "Democracy, Watch Your Step" was published. In February, he sent Robert Morss Lovett, another *Dial* editor, a note introducing Laurence Buermeyer, who, he said, "can both think and write."[3] Buermeyer was a professor of philosophy whom Barnes had hired as his tutor and as a kind of scholarly mouthpiece for his ideas. The editors evidently were not impressed and did not ask to see any of Buermeyer's work. Johnson did, however, see Barnes as a potential patron of the magazine and made his pitch, putting the best possible spin on the condition of the journal.

For some time I have been negotiating with an individual concerning the sale of a large block of stock in the Dial Publishing Company. This last week it developed that he is interested only in financing THE DIAL on condition that he be allowed to obtain control of its editorial policy, with the ultimate intention of making it his personal organ.

I am unwilling to sell THE DIAL to an individual whom I know to be fundamentally antagonistic to Mr. Dewey and Mr. Veblen. It has been their vision and that of Miss Marot which has enabled THE DIAL to take its honest and fearless stand in the face of propaganda and hysteria. And because of this editorial policy THE DIAL had made its extraordinary success these past three months.

Since the first of November we have had to treble our editions in order to meet the increase in subscriptions and newsstand distribution. We are now publishing editions of 18,500 copies. This rapid growth is more than we are able to handle with our limited capital, since we do not get the returns from the newsstand sales until two months afterwards.

Unless we are able to raise $10,000 as working capital between now and the first of March among those who are sufficiently in sympathy with the policy which has so far characterized THE DIAL to allow us editorial freedom to develop along the same lines in the future, it will be necessary definitely to sell out.[4]

The identity of the "individual" mentioned by Johnson is unclear. Johnson may be referring to Thayer, but Thayer had stepped away from the magazine at this point because of its political turn and anyway bore no ill-will toward the editors. His only desire had been to see more of Bourne's work published. It is likely that Johnson was aware that Thayer's loan would be coming due within the year and that another source of finance needed to be tapped and made ready.

Albert Coombs Barnes was born in 1872 in The Neck, a poor area of Philadelphia. As a boy, he taught himself to box for his own protection. His ambition and his talents were prodigious, and after training in medicine, he formulated and produced an antiseptic by the name of Argyrol, which made his fortune. He then began collecting art and educating himself in psychology. Barnes's temperament could be sympathetically described as ireful, less benignly as brutish and vindictive. It is not known whether or not in this instance Barnes offered a helping hand to the *Dial*. In May, he submitted an article on "the Polish situation," which was rejected. He did not renew his subscription.[5] Barnes would eventually cause much trouble at the *Dial* and play a leading if unwitting role in Thayer's decline into madness.

Thayer and his wife had settled in their respective apartments. Elaine was at 3 Washington Square, while Thayer roomed at the Benedick, an apartment building for bachelors. There he had had the entire apartment remodeled, deepening the bookshelves, refinishing the floors, and replacing the doors. The long work-order list shows Thayer's signature attention to detail, requesting a variety of particular light bulbs, oxidized silver switch plates, and window-seat cushions made from the same black satin used for the curtains. He also had all the locks changed and installed a "floor stop with lead shield" to protect his belongings. Thayer's chambers greatly impressed visitors. "He lived on the top floor of an apartment house on Washington square, where he had his bookshelves filled with rare first editions and Aubrey Beardsley drawings on his walls," remembered Alyse Gregory. "Opposite an antique Chinese cabinet was a high, narrow window seat, covered with shabby leather, on which one perched as on one of these benches provided for lepers in medieval churches. The monk and the aesthete joined hands. He had an intellectual Japanese man-servant, a subscriber to the Nation, who, to salve his outraged pride, would sometimes enter the room backwards." (Thayer's interest in Japan stretched back to his boyhood, as reflected in one of his first stories, "Yeko: The Story of a Japanese Boy.")

Hildegarde Lasell Watson, his old family friend from Massachusetts, was another visitor. "The drawing room was papered in a gold tea paper and completely furnished with old Red-lacquer Chinese furniture," she recalled. "We sat, I believe, or really kneeled, on brocaded cushions, drinking Lapsang Souchong tea from rice-patterned cups. Hanging on all the walls was his newly acquired set of Aubrey Beardsley drawings. In this room, Scofield, then still in his twenties, entertained many important literary men and artists—anyone, in fact, he chose to invite; just before me it had been William Butler Yeats."[6]

Marianne Moore was also a guest at the Benedick. "A coon took me up in the elevator and a butler let me in," she wrote in a letter.

> There is a roomy hall carpeted with a yellow and blue Chinese rug—and at one end a library opens from it and at the other end a "lounge" opens from it with a blue gauze curtain hanging across the door way and a large iron candlestick stands by the door. Scofield has a gorgeous library, about 3 walls full of light calf bindings or blue bindings, a grate full of ashes a foot deep and a yellow desk like yours, not quite so large. He is very quiet friendly polished and amusing. . . . He showed me his art treasures (on request), a large black marble, nude, some Beardsley pen drawings—a "cubist" painting and some drawings of dancers. He has in his art room, a set of real red lacquer, a red lacquer cabinet three little benches and a

smoking stand in front of the fireplace. He doesn't smoke and has no chairs—one I think at his desk but that is all.[7]

All in all, these seem to be the rooms of a young man of both wealth and taste who was not afraid to show either. Elaine's residence was a spacious, first-floor apartment large enough for her soirees, which Thayer himself occasionally attended. There is little evidence that Elaine felt any bitterness toward Thayer. Indeed, many of her later letters to him are affectionate and concerned.

E. E. Cummings had had his eye on Elaine from the moment he first saw her. They must have met at the beginning of April 1916 or even earlier, certainly before her engagement to Thayer. Cummings wasted little time sending her one of his charming letters, which he decorated with a sketch of an elephant. She replied on April 16 from Millbrook, where she was still at finishing school.

Dear Mr. Cummings,

Thanks awfully for the compliment however, there was no opportunity for dancing. Sorry it took me three weeks to say this.

I greatly admire the elephant and would like to take lessons in drawing sometime from you.[8]

By 1919, Cummings had already produced two poems celebrating Thayer's marriage to Elaine, "Epithalamion" and "S.T.," both of which gave the poet the opportunity to rhapsodize on Elaine Orr Thayer's stunning beauty. The latter speaks of "Thy wife, the almost woman whose tresses are / / The stranger part of sunlight, in the far / Nearness of whose frail eyes instantly stir // Unchristian perfumes more remote than myrrh, / Whose smiling is the swiftly singular / Adventure of one inadvertent star / With angels previously a loiterer."

Cummings had begun escorting his friend's wife (the Thayers would not be legally divorced for several more years) early in 1918, when Thayer sent a check to Cummings "for the time, energy and other things you have expended upon Elaine."[9] Thayer and Cummings no doubt enjoyed the double entendre of this little note. The relationship between Cummings and Elaine Orr would become one of the great literary love affairs of the twentieth century. Cummings obsessed over Elaine, filling pages of his notebooks with his feelings toward her and producing many passionate love poems. By February 1919, Cummings had been demobilized after a short stateside stint in the army and had returned to New York, where he was living the bohemian life with his friend William Slater Brown. One morning, having no coal to heat the apartment, he tried but was unable to contact any coal merchants, and so threw himself upon Elaine's largesse. He describes the adventure in a letter to his mother:

In the morning I undressed and visited coal people. Nobody in. At length I rang at Elaine's. She wasn't up. Her maid came to the door. "Bergét"—she's great! "Give me a lump of coal" I said. She was slightly surprised, but did up 5 huge lumps (a foot-cube each) which I carried from Washington Square to 14th St. Nor did they ever break out of the paper! Nor did the string break!

Now we have (all night) an open fire to undress and dress by, & gas for cold weather, cooking, etc.

All sorts of things (tea-things, extra-army blankets; draperies etc etc) are en route from Wanamakers. Elaine Thayer came up this morning as we were drinking our first cup of coffee—best I ever tasted—and left, threatening innumerable luxuries for us, same to arrive in some hours.[10]

By at least spring, Cummings and Elaine Orr were lovers, and she was soon pregnant. Thayer viewed the relationship with a sanguine, though no doubt jaundiced, eye. He perhaps knew that Cummings was no match for Elaine Orr.

Thayer began a relationship with Alyse Gregory that year.[11] Much of his energy, though, went into reading. That spring he took the magazines the *Egoist* and the *Dial*, and he continued his reading of contemporary authors such as D. H. Lawrence and James Joyce. But he was also reading authors from the previous generation such as Rudyard Kipling, as well as Oscar Wilde, Keats, Dostoevsky, Tennyson, and a great deal of Henry James. His summer reading on Martha's Vineyard included Joseph Conrad, Thomas Hardy, George Moore, Theodore Dreiser, Ambrose Bierce, and Robert Hichens.

He was also consumed with interest in the burgeoning field of psychology, buying books by such early pioneers as Wilfrid Lay, Ernest Jones, A. A. Brill, Sándor Ferenczi, and, of course, Freud. Freud had visited Thayer's hometown of Worcester in the fall of 1909 for a conference on psychoanalysis at Clark University. Thayer probably didn't attend—he had just entered Harvard—but surely had heard of the greatly publicized event. Thayer probably first entered analysis in 1919, with Dr. L. Pierce Clark.[12]

That summer Thayer was approached by the writers Padraic and Mary Colum, who asked him for help in supporting James Joyce. Thayer wrote a check for seven hundred dollars, which the New York publisher B. W. Huebsch forwarded to Joyce along with a note saying, "Please don't imagine that America is full of rich young men of that kind!"[13]

Thayer knew Joyce's work well. The year before, during his stint at the *Dial*, he had written the first American critical survey of the writer's work, beginning with *Chamber Music* and moving through *Dubliners* and *Portrait of the Artist as a Young Man* to *Ulysses*, then being serialized in the magazine the *Little Review*. The phrase "stream of consciousness" had recently crossed from the field of psychology to literary criticism, and in his survey Thayer shows himself to be abreast of the idea: "He gives us, especially in 'Ulysses,' the streaming impressions, often only subconsciously cognate to one another, of our habitual life—that vague, tepid river of consciousness to which only our ephemeral moment of real will or appetite can give coherence."[14]

Thayer praised the "singular, spare, athletic phraseology" he found in Joyce, reserving his highest praise for *Dubliners*.

Meanwhile, things were not going well at the *Dial*. Johnson had burned through what was left of Thayer's investment in the magazine and had been unable to raise money elsewhere. When, in October, Thayer's note came due, Johnson had no option but to sell his remaining stock. It was bought, at a generous price, by Thayer and his friend and business partner, Dr. James Sibley Watson Jr.

Cummings was delighted, writing to his mother, "You will be glad to know that Sibley Watson and Scofield Thayer are now respectively (1) owner and publisher, and (2) editor, of The Dial; which will change its format, drop political and take on literary characteristics."[15]

In December, Elaine gave birth to Nancy, her child by Cummings. Thayer took the matter in his stride, caring for Elaine at the hospital while Cummings, the baby's father, watched sullenly from the sidelines. He "bitterly resented" the child. "Now Nancy becomes my rival," he wrote. He complained that he could no longer love Elaine "as a prostitute," and that she "has less sexual appeal." He partially admitted to his own callousness but fell back on the excuse that his relative poverty prevented him from doing the right thing. He compared himself to Thayer: "I-inferior, playing up to him i-poor he:rich AGGRESSIVE i:passive." As for Thayer's graciousness in supporting the new mother and child, Cummings could only grumble, "ST could do it:wealth i:nothing, only my art."[16] It was not Cummings's noblest moment, though he would eventually warm to his daughter.

Thayer and Watson, in the meantime, began preparing their first issue of the *Dial* as its new owners. The magazine's "Casual Comment" section on November 29, the last issue under Martyn Johnson, announced the new order: Watson was named president of the Dial Publishing Company, Thayer was named secretary-treasurer and editor, and Stewart Mitchell, who had worked with Thayer on the *Harvard Monthly*, was named managing editor. The announcement also mentioned that the magazine would in future also publish fiction and drawings. "We can assure all concerned that our choice of material will be independent of the conventional considerations, independent, that is, 'jusque au feu *exclusive*.' But for fear this become the occasion of a manifesto, we leave our readers to form their opinion of us from what we shall do rather than from what we say at present."[17] The French phrase is from Rabelais, meaning "to any point short of the stake." It is a reference to the wise adage that one should cling to one's convictions only so long as doing so doesn't lead to martyrdom, an editorial policy that Thayer would follow scrupulously.

Following Nancy's birth, Thayer received a letter of congratulation from his uncle in Santa Barbara. "The birth of your daughter has given more satisfaction to your Thayer relatives than you probably imagine," Ernest wrote. "My father's line, though he himself was one of ten or twelve children and had four of his own, seemed fated to end in the third generation. The arrival of your daughter encourages the hope that it will take a fresh start and definitely shed the onus of nature's curse."[18] Thayer, in his private notes, made a wry and crude pun on the matter about Elaine "expelling 'heir' from vagina at Wash. Sq."[19]

Ernest lived until 1940, and we don't know if he ever learned the truth about the Thayer line that was so important to him.

9

STARTING WITH A BANG

The knives were being sharpened for the *Dial* even before it appeared in its new incarnation. "You will be amused when you get the full story of Thayer & the Dial," Sherwood Anderson wrote to Waldo Frank in December 1919. "Poor man, he intended to be such a nice, rich man, a true English gentleman, bringing culture to America. It was vicious to step on his toes. I wired Sandburg to charge a minimum of $25 per page for poems. For my stories I shall get $200, or they will be sent free to someone else. If you send them a story and they want to print it, please stand out for that price. . . . One has to meet this sort of thing on these terms. All Thayer has is money, & [if] he does not surrender the money, he is N.G. to anyone. Will you also write something of the sort to [Van Wyck] Brooks? I feel like a labor leader, but if you have ever been in the presence of Thayer's interior decorator's soul, you'll understand, Brother."[1]

The first issue of the *Dial* put together by the new owners came out in January 1920, and the literati were eager to see it fail. The poet and critic Robert Hillyer, for one, was not impressed. "They published a perfect sheaf of awful unnameables by Estlin (Cummings) and some line drawings by him of trollops with their limbs spread wide apart," he wrote. "Then they had the Boom! Boom! Boom! of several foreign greatnesses such as Gilbert Cannan and other writers of a costly nature. Shades of *The Seven Arts!*"[2]

Even after several successful issues of the *Dial* had appeared, critics remained largely unmoved. Conrad Aiken wrote his impressions of the March issue to associate editor Clarence Britten, the lone carryover from the old regime who would soon resign from the magazine:

A pink thread of juvenility runs through it, and, with one or two exceptions, the articles strike me as selfconscious, carelessly written, mediocre in thought. In other words, forgive me for saying it, I find the issue somewhat dull. Mere "modernity," mere passion for the dernier cri is hardly sufficient basis for an intelligent review. I have, myself, those passions, and to that extent I am profoundly in sympathy with what Thayer is trying to do. But I fear he is engaged in collecting what is only the froth of the modern, and has little conception of the depth of the stream itself, or its direction. For the Lord's sake persuade him to sail a little more windward of the Little Review![3]

How strange it is to see the *Little Review* singled out as a magazine that did not understand "the modern" and didn't take risks, especially considering that it would soon publish the "Nausicaa" chapter from Joyce's *Ulysses*, resulting in a trial, the fining of the publishers, and the banning of the novel.

The reception in London by a rising literary American expatriate was also lukewarm. "I have just received a copy of the (New York) *Dial* in its new form," T. S. Eliot wrote to his mother.

It is very dull—just an imitation of The Atlantic Monthly, with a few atrocious drawings reproduced. It is owned and run by Scofield Thayer, who was with me at Milton and at Oxford, and who is enormously rich. He has sent me a message asking me to get contributions from certain writers here (Pound, Lewis Yeats, Russell, Strachey, and several others), but I am not going to complicate my personal relations with these people by asking them for writings unless I have a definite promise to accept what is sent.[4]

Ezra Pound described it as "one of those other mortuaries for the entombment of dead fecal mentality."[5] Pound was, of course, himself involved with many magazines over the years, and there may have been more than a touch of professional jealousy in his denunciation. We see Thayer having a similar reaction to the *London Mercury*, a new British magazine. "London Mercury smells not only like plush chair, but like such after a cat has lain ther[e and] left a spot and a smell," he wrote. "One imagines all the contributors as having drooping moustaches and bad breaths."[6]

Of advice there was plenty. John Dos Passos wrote to the managing editor of the *Dial*, Stewart Mitchell: "To get away with a literary magazine at this moment in America, *The Seven Arts* will have to be gone one better. . . . You are certainly a vivider person and have greater intelligence than any of the seven artists. For

God's sake, impose yourself—forget your nice manners, take off your coat, and be willing to make an ass of yourself. . . . We who have worshipped freedom and writing as God—shall we be annihilated by destiny filling up the precious printed pages with spacefillers?"[7]

One of the friendliest notes came, ironically, from the person who would become Thayer's archenemy and tormentor, Albert C. Barnes. "You set a mighty high standard in that January number," he wrote, "with, I think, only one exception [he disliked Paul Rosenfeld's musical criticism] and if you maintain it, or even near it, it is a safe bet that you can view the scene from Olympus with confidence as to the future of the journal."[8]

Despite all the criticism, the pages of the *Dial* rapidly became prestigious literary real estate, and many writers, when they weren't complaining about the magazine, were eagerly trying to get their work into it. Hillyer, Pound, Aiken, Eliot, and Anderson all appeared in the new magazine in its first year.

If there was one person who benefited from the *Dial*, it was Cummings. The first issue of 1920 contained his "Seven Poems," which included the seminal "Buffalo Bill's." His poems startled readers with their paucity of punctuation, unorthodox use of upper- and lowercase letters, the anomalous usage of parts of speech, and their curious mixing of abstract with concrete and of the modern with the archaic. The magazine also printed four of his drawings of the National Winter Garden Burlesque, which included the akimboed "trollops" sneered at by Hillyer. Both Thayer and his partner Watson were great promoters of Cummings's work, a fact of which the young poet/artist was well aware and for which he was grateful. He wrote to his father that year: "I need not say that I am extraordinarily that is as usual lucky in having what amounts to my own printing-press in Thayer and Watson—by which I refer to the attention which such minutiae as commas and small i's, in which minutiae my Firstness thrives, get at the hands of these utterly unique gentlemen."[9]

Thayer's distaste for what he saw as mere novelty was severe. He detested inventions such as the internal combustion engine and the gramophone for the unwanted noise they introduced into his world, and he distrusted even musical instruments of relatively recent vintage, calling the piano "the most vulgar of all God's instruments" and the saxophone "obscene" and "a degraded, degenerate bagpipe."[10] Considering this curmudgeonly dismissal of inventiveness, his long and strong support of Cummings may seem odd, in that Cummings was superficially at least the most astonishingly innovative of the experimental poets of the period. That Cummings is more of a traditionalist than his typography would suggest is axiomatic today. In his endless work in the sonnet and in his themes of romantic love, childish innocence, human brutality, and the redemptive power of nature, one finds much that echoes the more orthodox Romantic literary conventions. But in the early 1920s, Thayer was perforce the champion of Cummings taking up arms against a sea of disapprobation and ridicule.

One clue to the understanding that existed between the two men may be in their shared love of art that began at Harvard when Thayer gave Cummings a copy of Willard Huntington Wright's *Modern Painting,* the ideas of which the two discussed intensely. The ocular nature of much of Cummings's work was quite comprehensible to Thayer, whose understanding of poetry, indeed of much literature, was often perceived and explained through visual metaphors. Emily Dickinson's poems, he wrote, were like "glass knobs on old New England white-painted chamber-doors."[11] (The simile perhaps does not do justice to Thayer's high opinion of Dickinson, whom he also thought "a genius of the first water" and the "New England Sappho."[12] He planned a book of essays entitled *Hommage á Emily.*)[13] Robert Frost was "dry stone on hillside, but occasionally agreeably warmed by New England sun."[14] Of Virginia Woolf, he remarked that she has an "attractively furnished" and "agreeably ventilated" mind, but he added that "some of us find the atmosphere somewhat mild."[15] Writing of D. H. Lawrence, he said, "I find that through the dark [v]ale of this world of his those squishing carthorses are not seldom seen to emerge upon the embracing sky-line."[16] Marianne Moore was "a wooden doll painted in primary colours. An autochthonous and tough plant,"[17] and Oswald Spengler was "this tragedy queen who weeps and wrings her hands with such dry gusto."[18]

Nor did Cummings's capitalization of words he wished to emphasize seem at all erratic to Thayer, who was used to such distinguishing of nouns in German, in which he was near fluent.[19] But this understanding did not blind Thayer to the fact that Cummings's idiosyncratic capitalization was also a useful extratextural attention-getter. "The small I's of Cumming [sic] are not, as he wills them, merely negative or unpicked-out," Thayer wrote. "One infringes upon convention at one's peril. This I suggests a poet very minute, very hard, very Cockney, yet very American, and having a little penetrating stink all his own."[20]

His criticism of Cummings is sometimes insightful and sometimes nothing more than snobbery. His note that "[t]here is in Cummings a large admixture of Yahoo"[21] is more helpful in understanding the mind of Thayer than that of Cummings, as are Thayer's descents into vulgarity regarding the work of Cummings and others: "If Joyce gives out the smell of a refinement upon . . . an elixir of urine, Cummings exudes the mixed and less refined odour of a urinal."[22] (Thayer was fond of this urine metaphor: "When Dr Longfellow took occasion to relieve his bladder," he wrote, "there issued very nice camomile tea."[23] Interestingly, he thought his own verse closest to that of Longfellow.) At times, however, these literary digs are illuminating. A snide-sounding remark such as "Cummings is a soft-shoe poet"[24] is not unuseful in explaining a poet for whom burlesque and popular song provided so much inspiration.

Thayer was dismissive, and perhaps jealous, of his friend's prolific output: "Mr. Cummings goes off too often and too easily; there is a loss of dignity."[25]

Thayer struggled with Cummings's metaphors, which he found excessively coruscating in that they were at first striking but, after consideration, inappropriate in their application: "The agreeable excitement one has from them is thus impaired as by grit."[26] He came, however, to an understanding that both Cummings and Eliot shared with the metaphysical poets a trait that Samuel Johnson had remarked upon, the forced and violent connecting of unlike ideas: "E.E.C. + T.S.E. a little like Donne. . . . 'Patient . . . upon a table.'"[27]

It is only in Thayer's private writings that we find his criticisms of Cummings. His public support, in the *Dial* and elsewhere, was unwavering. Among his papers is a sheet of lined notepaper upon which Thayer memorialized, in his own hand, a wager he made with Amy Lowell as to the future place Cummings would reach in the American canon.

> Miss Amy Lowell and Scofield Thayer bet each other one hundred dollars that Edward Estlin Cummings will have achieved a position in English or American literature equal to that of Edwin Arlington Robinson, Robert Frost, or Carl Sandburg in fifteen years from this June, 1920. Judgement to be given and payment made June 2nd, 1935. In case of the death of either signatory, this is void.[28]

Thayer's view of Cummings must also have been colored by the fact that he had been cuckolded by the poet, and some of Thayer's remarks on his friend are a blend of literary criticism and sexual umbrage. Thayer was more aware than anyone of the passion Cummings felt for Elaine Orr, an awareness that is perhaps reflected in this note: "Cummings—a sentimentalist with protective cubist coloration. C. does not distinguish between the beautiful and the sexually to him attractive; so parallelly not between the beautiful and the egoistically to him attractive."[29]

Ezra Pound did well by the *Dial*, too. The September 1920 issue featured an early version of Pound's masterpiece "Hugh Selwyn Mauberley." Pound also saw published in the *Dial* "Dust for Sparrows," his translations of the maxims of the French writer Remy de Gourmont. Pound turned this work into something of a jobs program for himself, sending the *Dial* one installment after another. (Thayer eventually took to calling the series "Shit for Sparrows,"[30] and D. H. Lawrence told Thayer that he was glad when it finally came to an end and that it was "rubbish.")[31] And although Thayer disliked Pound's frenetic pushing of material that was too experimental for the *Dial* (Thayer called Pound "that agitated agitator"),[32] he greatly approved of Pound's ability to extract good material from his friends. He published "Canto IV" in the June 1920 issue and in September hired Pound as the Paris correspondent of the magazine.

The magazine made an undoubted splash. A list of the writers and artists featured in that first year of the *Dial* under its new owners demonstrates the astonishing breadth of work it published. There was verse by Cummings, Pound, Carl Sandburg, Marianne Moore, Amy Lowell, Edna St. Vincent Millay, A.E., Louis Untermeyer, William Carlos Williams, William Butler Yeats, H.D., and James Joyce. The fiction came from the pens of D. H. Lawrence, Marcel Proust, Arthur Schnitzler, Sherwood Anderson, Mina Loy, and Djuna Barnes. Artists whose work was reproduced included Charles Demuth, Charles Burchfield, John Marin, Gaston Lachaise, Khalil Gibran, Rockwell Kent, and Wyndham Lewis. As importantly, the *Dial* in its first year also gave a forum for reviewing and criticism that was taken advantage of by T. S. Eliot, Walter Pach, Edmund Wilson, S. Foster Damon, Van Wyck Brooks, Malcolm Cowley, Kenneth Burke, Henry McBride, Emory Holloway, and Gilbert Seldes. Philosophical writings came from Bertrand Russell, Romain Rolland, John Dewey, and Edward Sapir.

The success of the journal came not only from its judicious selection of talent but also from its careful tempering of the avant-garde with the traditional. Of course, it was precisely this moderation that infuriated its detractors. "The dial will never print 'Ulysses,'" Pound wrote prophetically to James Joyce. "The Dial will never be any real fun."[33]

But there were also plenty of those who thought the magazine went too far. Even Watson's mother was shocked at the risqué contents, as Cummings gleefully informed his father: "Allow me to inform you that Mrs. Watson (senior)—High church Episcopal—or is it something else?—raised such a cry over the 'Jesus' in Buffalo Bill that J. S. [Watson] Junior arrived in New York the day after he left it for Rochester!"[34]

In the "Comment" section of the March issue, Thayer published an essay on the mission of the magazine, still carefully avoiding anything like a manifesto but trying to articulate the editorial philosophy:

> If a magazine isn't to be simply a waste of good white paper it ought to print, with some regularity, either such work as would otherwise have to wait years for publication, or such as would not be acceptable elsewhere. The inevitable and the "impossible" pieces of work give the special tone to a magazine which must, in the interest of completeness, publish a number of other things which are, in any case, predestined for publication. So we thank our critics for the rebuke that "you are printing things no other magazine would print" as well as words of praise that "you are bringing into the light work any publication would be proud of." THE DIAL hopes always to deserve both comments.[35]

However, the more modernist and sexually explicit material continued to offend. It was not only outraged readers that worried Thayer but also the postal authorities, who had the power to censor material deemed obscene, and since magazines relied on the postal service for their distribution, not being able to use the mails was a de facto death sentence. The New York Society for the Suppression of Vice, which was at this time training its virtuous sights on art and literature, was also a concern. The society's tentacles reached into any venue where it considered there were dangers to the morality of the American public, confiscating and destroying smutty postcards, ribald books, saloon paintings of nudes, sex toys, and the pills and powders used in abortions. With the rapid expansion of the magazine market in the early part of the twentieth century, the society turned its attention more and more toward the printed page.

Steering a contemporary magazine of literature and the arts through these shoals of righteousness was no easy task, and credit must be given to Thayer and to Watson for doing this over the *Dial's* nine years of existence, a longevity rare in the world of such magazines. But it took work. We can get some idea of the delicacy Thayer needed as editor from a letter he wrote to managing editor Stewart Mitchell regarding a Waldo Frank story (probably "Under the Dome") that described sexual acts. "I want you to have [Gilbert] Seldes read it and then confer with him as to whether we dare publish in present form," he wrote.

> If you and he feel we can, please notify Frank (he should have sent in his address: I don't have it) from me that I liked the story much, that we accept and that I trust he will send in *the other of which he spoke to me.* If

you and G.S. decide the sex is too thick (I'm inclined to think we might swallow it), please write Frank as from The Dial in general that we like his story much, but don't know what to do, that we have already had trouble from the smut-hounds, that our expenses are appalling and do not permit us to chance trouble with the P.O., that we therefore hesitate. Does he prefer us to print it anyhow? If so say we will. Or does he prefer to cut one or two words. (Please do *not* specify the words). And does he prefer to send me some other story not less good and not as dangerous.[36]

In the same letter, Thayer told Mitchell to accept a D. H. Lawrence story ("Adolf") in which Lawrence described a rabbit's droppings as "pills." "Leave 'pills' in Lawrence!" he exhorted Mitchell.

In May 1920, Thayer also shared his difficulties, both financial and editorial, with Ezra Pound. "It seems wise that I should speak to you rather frankly about the difficulties of publishing THE DIAL," he wrote.

Of course it is most important to keep up an appearance of prosperity before the world and therefore what I am about to say is said in all confidence. Although you are in a position to have some conception of conditions over here, I really believe the public's attitude toward our rather too harmless journal would astonish you. It certainly has astonished Watson and myself. We are attacked most violently on every occasion, in the press and by mail and in personal conversation, for publishing verse that does not rhyme and pictures that are not lifelike. For some reason that is quite impossible of analysis, to publish a reproduction of a painting by Cezanne is discovered to be an attack, more terrible because in[sid]ious, upon the very heart of patriotism, Christianity and morality in general. THE DIAL has been characterized in a letter written by a gentleman of some position in artistic circles hereabouts as a dastardly attack upon "all that the good and wise of every generation have lived and died for." You get the authentic note, hey? I myself was recently characterized at a dinner dance as a degenerate. We should never have thought of undertaking this job had we anticipated one-tenth of the difficulties we have encountered. Newsstands even refuse to carry THE DIAL and only day before yesterday the American News company, after months of deliberation, decided that they could not undertake to circulate our paper. . . .

Mr. Watson and myself have, since we took over control of the paper in the latter part of November, expended upon it about sixty thousand dollars. It is going to cost us another forty to finish up the current year.

He went on to tell Pound that the *Dial* was forced to create a separate section of the magazine, "Modern Forms," devoted to unconventional verse, prose, and art, and asked that Pound resubmit for this section three Cantos that Thayer had rejected a few weeks earlier. He concluded: "with many apologies for your country and mine."[37]

For all the criticism Thayer suffered for not taking more risks with the material he used in the *Dial*, he was quite willing to stand behind the work he felt deserved an audience. An early champion of Thomas Mann (the *Dial* was the first English-language magazine to translate and publish "Death in Venice"), in one letter to Watson he argued forcefully for publishing Mann's story "Loulou." "I consider Mann's story the best thing we've had and am violently opposed to returning it," Thayer wrote. "I consider it less objectionable than [illegible] and 10 times as good. Also I want The Dial to be international. . . . The Mann is so good that I believe even the offended will understand our reason for publishing it and so not be offended against *us*."[38]

In April 1921, Ernest Boyd wrote in the *Dial* on censorship in the United States, mentioning the case of the *Little Review* and characterizing organizations such as the New York Society for the Suppression of Vice as "literary lynching parties."[39] This of course, got the attention of John S. Sumner, who was the leader of that antivice organization, and in the July issue of that year Thayer allowed Sumner to respond to Boyd. It was astonishing, really, to see the byline of the nemesis of the avant-garde and the risqué in such a progressive journal of culture. Sumner's piece, "The Truth about 'Literary Lynchings,'"[40] unsurprisingly defended the work of the society. But Sumner was out of his depth, and, rather than make a good case for his activities, he damned himself with his own language. "There are a great many people in this country who like to bring forward something 'foreign' and hold it forth as an example of the way things should be done over here," he wrote, exhibiting that very fear of the foreign against which the *Dial* and other journals were trying to militate. Thayer allowed Boyd a single paragraph of rebuttal, which ended thus: "I can only conclude that plain English is as incomprehensible to Mr Sumner as art, which he confounds with dirty post cards."

Giving the bumbling Sumner a few pages in the journal to make his case for crusading against vice was a shrewd move on Thayer's part. For Sumner to prosecute the *Dial* at any future time on the grounds of indecency would be at the very least uncomfortable for one who had himself been published therein. But Thayer wasn't satisfied with merely giving Sumner enough rope to hang himself. He sandwiched Sumner's article between a couple of pieces that must have been chosen for the express purpose of mocking the antivice crusader. Directly before Sumner's article was a sonnet by George Moore in French that mocked the distrust Sumner expressed with the "foreign," and facing the last page of this article by the man who fought against even mildly erotic saloon paintings was a drawing by Gaston Lachaise of a zaftig, big-eyed, big-bosomed, voluptuous, and naked woman.

10

MANHATTAN LOVE STORIES

Toward the end of Thayer's first full year running the *Dial*, his mother, who was not yet aware that the marriage with Elaine had broken down, scolded him for neglecting his wife and advised him that "a good wife is more precious than many dials."[1]

Thayer was certainly working hard on the magazine, but that was not taking up all of his time. Living separately from his wife allowed Thayer to live the life of a rich bachelor, and he threw himself into the role with gusto. He admitted in a private note to going somewhat overboard in his sexual activity, which he blamed on a lack of physical intimacy before getting married: "I felt after E.O. the need to be in my sexual life messy because of my overlong virginity," he wrote.[2]

He often pondered in his writing the problem of marriage, and how the familiarity that naturally grew between man and wife was for him a passion killer of the first order. He required excitement in his physical relationships, and this lessened as soon as the novelty of a newly taken lover wore off. He had not so much recoiled from lovemaking with his wife as he had simply grown tired of it. "A man's loving (sexually) his own wife is rather like a dog chasing its own tail," he wrote." The more intelligent the dog, the less exciting this particular form of combat is."[3]

His description of sex as "combat" is also significant, in that he would come to require in a sexual partner not only novelty but also resistance. True, some of his writings on the subject demonstrate a reverence for and a gentleness toward female sexuality, as in this observation: "In the female flirting even genteely, sex is exposed as never in the male except by actual coition (even *then* its visibility is not so great): it is natural and appropriate the male should hover about her and feel and show respect and tenderness toward this exposed sex. As one appropriately kneels before the elevated host."[4] But, for the most part, it would seem that whatever pleasure and excitement Thayer found in sex was in the idea of the male attacking, breaking down, and ravishing a mate. "The sexual act upon the part of the male is an aggressive act. The female is (to take a figure from football practice) a dummy."[5]

There is a thuggishness here that stands in sharp contrast to the refined, aesthetic figure that Thayer showed to the world. But Thayer himself had no difficulty reconciling these two very different attitudes and, indeed, believed that these opposites in a man were actually sought out by women. "In woman her sex desires to feel the male as brutal; her heart desires to feel him as pure," he wrote. "There is thus an opposition which results in permitting women in general to feel the male about as he is. The male, on the other hand, *qua* heart, desires to feel the woman as pure; *qua* animal, he again desires to feel her as pure, for she is the more provocative and attractive to his aggressive sexual instinct."[6] In these last sentences we begin to see what appears to be a desire to bespoil purity, and from here it is not very far to his darker urge to ravish the virgin.

It is curious, then, to read the words of those women who seem to have been most intimate with him and to see in them few signs of the violent misogynistic brute we find in his writings. Certainly, he seems to have been capable of cruelty, and his later relationships with women prior to his breakdown were confused and dysfunctional. However, in the words of two women who were deeply involved with Thayer, one over many years—Alyse Gregory—and one for a brief, passionate summer—Louise Bryant—Thayer seems to have been generous, charming, and gentle.

Alyse Gregory had met Thayer in 1918 through their mutual friend Randolph Bourne. Gregory was a writer and a Progressive activist who lived in Greenwich Village's Patchin Place and ran a small tea shop. She would eventually become the managing editor of the *Dial*. "When Randolph had first mentioned Scofield Thayer to me, it was with warnings that I must curb any irrelevant witticisms," she wrote.

> I came later to believe that he was one of those men the key to whose nature is so obscurely hidden that they alienate people because they remain outside their understanding. He was sensitive to noise as Proust and paid a monthly sum to the family living under him to turn off their gramophone at his will. In his summer home, at Cape Cod, he made a bargain with the owners of motor boats to muffle their engines. Alas! What for-

tune today could be vast enough to protect the most princely of the senses against the cunning torture of the machine? Scofield was himself a daring yachtsman and would, like Guy de Maupassant, exult in steering his adventurous cutter through turbulent seas.[7]

There is no doubt that Gregory, who would be Thayer's most loyal and lasting female friend, understood him more profoundly than anyone. She was of a nervous nature herself and soon came to see how Thayer's mental anguish, which to others appeared as standoffishness, often made the simple daily living of life an onerous task.

Gregory's descriptions of Thayer are both loving and incisive:

Slender of build, swift of movement, always strikingly pale, with coal-black hair, black eyes veiled and flashing, and lips that curved like those of Lord Byron, he seemed to many the embodiment of the aesthete with overrefined tastes and sensibilities. This was far from the case. Arts and letters he pursued, but it was with a purpose so elevated and so impassioned that he remained insulated from the ironical comments about him. He suspected, however, the whole world, and it was perhaps this general distrust as betrayed by the carriage of his head and timbre of his voice, that created about him an attitude of strain. He had, as Freud confirmed in speaking to me of him much later, a most gentle heart. He administered his wealth largely as a trust, supporting or helping to support many young writers and artists. He dressed with considerable simplicity, pleased to be seen in a suit of clothes he had worn since his university days. What were taken for affectations were mannerisms indigenous to his character. His irony, though as swift as Randolph's, was seldom as light. He was ice on the surface and molten lava underneath.[8]

When she first met Thayer, Gregory was in a passionate relationship with a Frenchman. After this lover returned to France, sometime after the death of Randolph Bourne in late 1918, she and Thayer became closer and perhaps intimate.[9] She found his company all the more exciting for its unpredictability. "The hours I spent with him were never dull, though they might on occasion be nervous," she wrote. "Like most people of distinction he was often egocentric, though not egotistical; his courtesy could be exquisite and he was touchingly susceptible to the words of the people he valued. His mind was inflammable and satirical, and it was at the same time sober and sad. He defended himself with his wit, the best way of banishing fear. Like Diderot, he would rather be impatient than bored, and he alternated between the tempest and the frozen lake."[10]

The two exchanged frequent visits, though Gregory seems to have preferred meeting at Thayer's apartment, where she could escape the noise and sordidness she found in bohemian Patchin Place.

Gregory eventually married the British writer Llewelyn Powys. She did this somewhat reluctantly, being philosophically opposed to the idea of marriage, but Powys desired it, and she could not deny him. She also realized that—Powys being as sick as he was (he suffered from tuberculosis all his life)—their marriage would on many levels simplify the task of looking after him. Thayer wrote back mocking the institutional union she was about to enter, and she chided him for his ironic remarks and unwillingness to understand her reasoning. "Please do not mistake," he responded with gentle humor. "I am not so doctrinaire as not to understand. And it is not irony, really; it is only the playfulness appropriate—by established usage—to nuptial occasions."[11]

Even after Powys had moved in with Gregory, she continued to see Thayer. Once, when Powys was out giving a lecture, Thayer arrived at Patchin Place with his manservant, who cooked and served lunch for the couple. Gregory found herself comparing the two men in her life. "He [Thayer] talks with me more intimately than with anyone in his life so desperate, so little understood," she wrote.

> No two people could be more different than he and L. S.T.'s mind is like the swinging tail of an aroused lynx. All is ferment, intellect, observation collected for battle. He is jealous of L. and L. lacks address with him and I am ill at ease with them together. S.T. belongs to an old American tradition and at the same time is cosmopolitan in a way that L. is not. His distinction is of a different kind from L's. His haughty, suspicious head and flashing expression, his manner both arrogant and civil, and the fertility of his tormented mind make him a nervous and exciting companion. Waiters rush to serve him, girls turn around to look at him.[12]

While Thayer's relationship with Gregory endured over many years, up to and after the breakdown that would remove him from public life, his romantic involvement with the strikingly lovely and sensual Louise Bryant was more meteoric in its intensity and brevity, burning through the summer of 1920. Bryant and her husband, John Reed, were both journalists. Reed was a fervent Communist who had reported on the Russian Revolution and was at the time living in Russia. Bryant was planning to join him, and she seems to have met Thayer just a month or so before sailing. Her first letter refers to the loss of her beloved grandfather at the age of fifteen. "You were still in my thoughts and through you the loss of my grandfather became somehow near again," she wrote. "I felt caught in a sudden grief about it after all these years."[13] Thayer had been about the same age when his father died, and the shared loss of a central family figure seems to have brought the two closer together, perhaps as the shared trauma of losing a parent at an early age had at first created a romantic resonance between Thayer and Elaine Orr. Bryant was an attractive woman who had herself married early—she left her husband for Reed—and had begun a life of traveling and writing. In her letter—written from 72 Washington Square, just a few hundred feet from Thayer's apartment—Bryant enclosed some poems. She insisted that they were not sent with the intent of being considered for the *Dial*, but she also remarked that should such an event transpire, she would not complain. "I want you never to consider publishing what I send you unless some fragment particularly strikes you," she wrote. "I like to write you poems instead of letters of the orthodox sort and I would be shy and embarrassed if I imagined you thought I was trying to get them into print. I really would not mind if I never published another poem for at least ten years. I hope you are happy—and send you my blessing 'with both hands' as the Russians say."[14] (Thayer responded enigmatically, "Dear Lady Bountiful, It is not only your blessing that you give with both hands.")[15] Bryant sent Thayer more of her verse in subsequent letters. These were also "not to print," she said. One, titled simply "Night," suggests nocturnal lovemaking:

> In the room
> Was her slimness
> And darkness very velvet.
>
> There was also laughter
> Kisses . . . sounds . . .
> And even little struggles,
> Entirely hypocritical.

A second poem, "Invitation," may refer to an evening of unrequited passion.

> In her dream
> She penned a letter:
>   Don't condemn my garden
>   Because of that sad circumstance
>   On a night in June . . .

> There is fruit so golden
> ... if you would but search!
> Lilies white as fireflies,
> Scarlet zinnias,
> Fragrance caught between cool leaves,
> Poppies all along the paths
> In attitudes of ecstacy ...
> Will you come again?[16]

Just what constituted the "sad circumstance," and how this prevented the poem's addressee from enjoying the sights and sensations of this fecund garden presented in the verse, is a mystery.

In yet another letter to Thayer containing her verse, Bryant confessed that she had not included all she had written: "I wrote five others but when I read them again I decided to destroy them. Three were for you."[17]

The next month, Bryant revealed to Thayer how much she enjoyed his company. "I'm not sure that I don't like you better than anyone,"[18] she wrote. Indeed, as the date of her sailing grew closer, her letters become more wistful: "I have only a few days more at 72—less than a week. I can afford to be extravagant and write you often. I may not ever come back again. There is always Bessarabia with its deserts—but there is also the quiet of Edgartown with ragged sailor pinks and the formal sweet Williams—and I think that has the strongest hold upon you. Be that as it may."[19]

In her final letter before sailing, Bryant shows an excitement at the adventure ahead of her, a fear of failing in her work of reporting on the new order of Soviet Russia, and a sadness at leaving Thayer.

> Now it is dawn—and the last day at 72—and I have just burned your letters—and shed a tear at that. You are very dear to me. I'm even serious about you—too serious to be amusing—and I know that is a grave fault [probably because of Thayer's opinions on free love and closed relationships]. . . .
>
> A vagrant thought recurred to me at the idea of failure—something sub-conscious bubbling through—I kept thinking that if I failed—I would see you again—soon. But I *will*—in any case.
>
> I will write you from Sweden—and tell you my plans—and give you addresses. If you go across this Fall I'll meet you anywhere you say. It will be delightful! I really want to—

... I'm an extravagant person I give you all I have, dear, this little book or my nicest poem or what ever you need of me—This I do because you are altogether charming and because I feel as lonely as Lancelot—now that I must put the seas between us and the curve of the earth. I carry along with me thoughts of you—and I do not crave any freedom from them. And I will look for you again—as one looks for the end of a rainbow.

The square is deserted now—your windows stare at my windows— whistles from the harbor reach me as I write—there is a grey fog which this morning has not yet dissipated. The ships are afraid of the fog and call out continually. The arch looks very ghostly (like the Statue of Liberty did the night we were in Brooklyn.) The trees drip cold tears on the blue coat of a sleeping policeman—and I think of you—I send you my love, Scofield—I send it you—with everything—Louise.[20]

Thayer's response was more measured, but still flirtatious. He spoke of his work at the *Dial*, and the art he was choosing for it. He thanked her for giving him a copy of her book, *Six Red Months in Russia*, which he had begun reading. "I already see I've got to look out sharply or I'll be in love with the heroine," he wrote. He ended the letter thus: "Really, I can't imagine anything lovelier than you in the sea—not fresh water, but the rich, hard, salt sea. . . . You're a divine girl."[21]

The year 1920 seemed a good one for Thayer, busy as he was with his work at the magazine and enjoying a full social life. But not all was well. Always something of a hypochondriac, Thayer had been visiting doctors and specialists who administered a variety of tests. In 1919 alone, he had his urine tested six times by doctors in Boston and New York City. There were also tests of his blood and stool. His largest medical bill from the period was paid to Dr. L. Pierce Clark, a psychoanalyst. In July 1920, Thayer wrote him a check for $4,700 to cover the previous nine months of sessions.[22] But Thayer felt he was making no progress with Clark and determined to become a patient of Sigmund Freud, whose works he was reading voraciously. In Freud, he saw not just a doctor but also a sage of the mind who could guide him through the journey of psychoanalysis he felt bound to take. "I am extremely eager to lay before him my troubles,"[23] he told his partner James Sibley Watson.

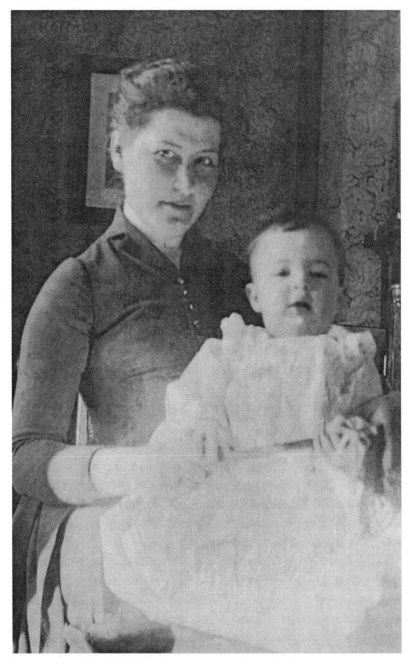

"The painful and thorny weaning from my mother." Scofield Thayer with his mother, Florence, probably 1890–91, at the family's Main Street home in Worcester, Massachusetts. Yale Collection of American Literature, Beinecke Rare Book and Manuscript Library.

Undated picture of Thayer as a boy. Yale Collection of American Literature, Beinecke Rare Book and Manuscript Library.

Thayer at Milton Academy, ca. 1905. Thayer is third from the right, first row. T. S. Eliot is second from the right, back row. Courtesy of Milton Academy.

A portrait of Thayer taken in Munich, probably during his visit there in 1922 to buy art. Yale Collection of American Literature, Beinecke Rare Book and Manuscript Library.

Thayer with the beagle pack at Oxford, 1913 or 1914. The picture seems to have been created by adding Thayer's face to a stock picture. Yale Collection of American Literature, Beinecke Rare Book and Manuscript Library.

"The Lily Maid of Astolat." A photograph of Elaine Orr ca. 1916, probably around the time she was graduated from finishing school and married Scofield Thayer in Troy, New York, in June 1916. Yale Collection of American Literature, Beinecke Rare Book and Manuscript Library.

A rare photograph of Marianne Moore and Alyse Gregory together at the *Dial*, perhaps during the transition in editorship in the spring of 1925. Yale Collection of American Literature, Beinecke Rare Book and Manuscript Library.

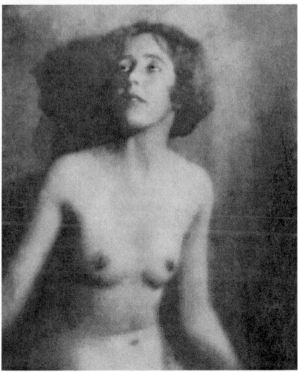

A photograph of Louise Bryant that Thayer kept in his personal papers. Bryant was a journalist, the wife of Communist John Reed, and, like Thayer, a champion of sexual freedom. She may have given Thayer the picture during the summer of 1920, when the two had a relationship before she left for Russia. Yale Collection of American Literature, Beinecke Rare Book and Manuscript Library.

Adolf Dehn's 1924 caricature of Thayer as the satirist Byron, drawn during Thayer's feud with Leo Stein. *The Dial* 80 (June 1926): 484.

LE BYRON DE NOS JOURS. BY ADOLF DEHN

Albert C. Barnes in 1942, about ten years after Thayer had been declared insane. Photograph by Pinto Studios. Photograph Collection, Barnes Foundation Archives, © 2013 The Barnes Foundation.

11

ANTI-EPITHALAMION

On February 13, 1921, Marianne Moore wrote a chatty letter to her brother about the comings and goings of writers in her New York circle. She spoke of the arrival of Hilda Doolittle (who went by the pen name H.D.) and "Winifred Bryher," who was the daughter of the wealthy and powerful shipping magnate Sir John Ellerman ("Bryher" was also a pen name); they were all going to tea with Thayer and Watson the next day. Bryher, despite being in a relationship with Doolittle, had attracted the attentions of a bohemian writer by the name of Robert McAlmon, a dashing figure who had served in the air force and served as a nude model for Greenwich Village artists.[1]

Moore mentioned in the letter that Sir John Ellerman was planning to "come after" his daughter and her partner from England; it was not considered appropriate for young women to travel together without a male escort. Bryher chafed greatly at this and other constraints placed upon her by her parents and by London society. Robert McAlmon—"Piggy"—was a writer who had just started the magazine *Contact* with William Carlos Williams. A handsome midwesterner, McAlmon had quickly won over the Greenwich Village crowd. "McAlmon was not tall," wrote Sylvia Beach, "and, except for his eyes, which were a bright blue, not exactly good-looking, yet, as a rule, he attracted people, and I know few who did so as much. He was certainly the most popular member of 'the Crowd,' as he called it. Somehow he dominated whatever group he was in. Whatever café or bar McAlmon patronized at the moment was the one where you saw everybody."[2]

McAlmon was eager to see Europe and was especially keen to meet his hero, James Joyce. So when Bryher proposed a marriage of convenience between them, which would have the happy effects of both enriching McAlmon and ensuring that Bryher's family would leave her alone, it must have seemed a good idea. "We neither of us felt the slightest attraction to each other, but remained perfectly friendly," Bryher wrote.[3]

Just one week after her previous gossipy letter, Moore wrote her brother again with the news, astounding to her conservative nature, that McAlmon and Bryher were married. "The worst event is Piggy McAlmon's being married at City hall on Monday, (an hour or two before our tea), to Winifred 'Bryher,'" she wrote. "The girls arrived at about a quarter past five, Scofield Thayer and Mr. Watson at about twenty minutes past. Hilda just had time before the men came to say that W[inifred]. had been married to 'Robert' a little while before and that had made them late. The girls looked lovely and the men were graciousness and responsiveness itself, but what an earthquake."[4]

The Valentine's Day marriage between the fabulously wealthy young woman and the struggling writer was immediately the talk of not only Greenwich Village but all New York society. The March 12 morning edition of the *New York Times* carried the full story:

'HEIRESS' WRITER
WEDS VILLAGE POET

———

Greenwich circles stirred by
The Romance of Robert
Menzies McAlmon

———

GIRL PROPOSED, IS REPORT

———

Bride Exploited as Daughter of Sir
John Ellerman, to whom Burke's
Peerage Credits Only a Son

Greenwich Village had a fresh topic of conversation yesterday: the marriage of one of its best known characters, Robert Menzies McAlmon, "editor and poet," of 351 West Fifteenth Street, and an English girl writer who indited a book of self-revelation under the nom de plume of Winifred Bryher.

But the Village talk veered sharply away from the official records of the Marriage License Bureau, which told briefly that McAlmon and Miss Winifred Ellerman—that is said to be her real name—on Feb. 14 obtained a license to wed.

Greenwich Village gossip was that the bride was wealthy in her own name and that she was related to Sir John Reeves Ellerman, the British ship owner, and some of this gossip went even so far as to say that the author of the revelations was the daughter of Sir John. According to *Who's Who* 1920 and *Burke's Peerage* 1921, however, Sir John was married only in 1903 and has only one child, a boy 11 years old. Face to face with romance, Greenwich Village was willing to admit that this took a little of the tang out of the romance, but it was still romance nevertheless, because—

The woman writer is reported to have proposed to the "poet and editor" because she became enthralled and entranced with a poem that appeared in one of the Greenwich Village publications. According to the villagers, she then met the poet at a party given by one of her friends. He whispered a line or two of the poetry and there was nothing to do but call a minister.

Captive and captor having sailed away for England two weeks ago on a White Star liner, the imagination of the village could take full wing on this new romance without regard for any of the facts. It is reported that many more new poems and satires are under way on the subject. And the villagers are only too glad to point out that all their literary efforts lack is appreciation—"just see how this romance turned out on a single poem."

McAlmon was a halfback on the University of Minnesota football team several years ago, and then became an expert on aviation, serving in the air services during the war. Then he saw one of the Greenwich Village publications—so the villagers say—and decided to come to this city to become a Bohemian. Poetry was a last resort, and the village publications have had many of his flings. His parents live in the West.

The girl writer came to this country from England last August and has been living in the village. She wrote her book there, and had decided to remain in this country. Then she met McAlmon and—still according to the villagers—she proposed and won. All of which has enough fact to suit the village imagination.[5]

It's hard to know where to begin criticizing what is, even by tabloid standards, such a tremendously poor piece of journalism. It's the kind of article in which the many errors of fact—McAlmon's career with the recently created air force only involved editing the camp newspaper in San Diego; McAlmon's father was dead; and the poetry-whispering line is an utter fabrication—are the least of its shabbinesses. The author refers to "village gossip" or simply "the village" as the sources of the story. The epithets are typically patronizing; the bride is a "girl writer," and the groom is referred to once as "editor and poet" and once as "poet and editor," the quotation marks serving to suggest that the titles are worthless and probably self-conferred. The subheadline's reference to the fact that *Burke's Peerage* (a guide to royal and titled British families) mentions only a son in the family is a not-so-subtle reference to the somewhat open secret that Bryher was born four years before her parents married. It is, in short, a good old-fashioned journalistic hatchet job.

The marriage shocked even the bohemians of Greenwich Village, but the two people most personally affected by it were, perhaps, Marianne Moore and William Carlos Williams. Moore, who always maintained her independence, was shaken by this "earthquake" into writing her longest and arguably most feminist poem, the dense, shifting, inconclusive "On Marriage." Williams and McAlmon had just set up shop in the form of their magazine *Contact*. The two were also good friends, and Williams had great hopes for the American-centered literature he championed and that he felt they could produce and publish together. To see McAlmon sail off for Europe, whose literary values Williams rejected, was a bitter blow. "Bryher's sudden wedding must have surprised you," he wrote to Amy Lowell.

> I say nothing of McAlmon. I wish I had the boy back with me and not lost there abroad, to no good purpose I feel sure. My God, have we not had enough Pounds and Eliots? *The Sacred Wood* is full of them and their air rifles. But perhaps Bob will do better. He will do better only on condition that he comes back to America soon.
>
> I must confess that I am heartbroken.[6]

For all the excesses of the newspaper story on the marriage, in at least one thing it was correct: other poems and satires were indeed under way on the matter. The author of one such would be Thayer, who was positively gleeful about the marriage.

Marianne Moore was scandalized when Thayer shared his intentions with her, perhaps more so than by the marriage itself. When Thayer showed Moore the above "nauseous" clipping from the *Times*, she responded forcefully. "I told Scofield how it was not funny to me," she wrote to her brother, "and he said, 'Yes, it's all very well for me to be amused looking at it from the point of view of an outsider.' I said it was an outrage for anyone to marry Winifred Bryher in such style so unromantic—and he said, 'You think it was unromantic to be married on Valentine's Day?'"[7]

She was also worried that Thayer intended to use for his piece humorous remarks that Moore had made to him in confidence about the situation. He agreed to leave them out, as well as a reference to Bryher's father as "the old rooster."

The first reference to the marriage in the *Dial* appeared as a long footnote in the May issue's "Comment" section. The main article treats of the founding of *Broom*, an international magazine of the arts, by Alfred Kreymborg and Harold Loeb. The main piece itself is altogether too long, too excessive in its endless and tiresome wordplay and allusions, and too twee. A sample:

> Alfred and Harold, kings, were exemplary and Saxon: their names have long been (among those capable of appreciating good things) conjured with. But Messrs, Alfred Kreymborg and Harold Loeb, contrarily enough, plump, in temperament and in taste, for the Norman. I hope no one will overshoot my meaning: I never saw, I never expect to see, Alfred Kreymborg (a real pepper-and-salt American, a live lecture-platform poet) toying with or trying on any Tooting coronet. He is, simply, not that kind of boy. But to show in his cap, as did Geoffrey the Handsome, a sprig of the popular and golden plant known as Broom, to put on (I speak vulgarly) *golden dog*—this has continued through several days the acute ambition of a heart at tassel arrantly, nay, flauntingly, Norman."

The kindest thing that can be said of this paragraph is that the writer wears his learning neither well nor lightly.

The whole point of publishing the article (which continues in a similar vein for four pages), however, seems to be the footnote on the third page, which is eventuated by the mention of McAlmon in the text. The footnote reads:

> The four ciphers of our 10000 readers not in on this aesthetic know must permit me to remind them (*vide* Dr Samuel Johnson) that Dr Williams and Mr McAlmon together publish a local magazine, that Mr McAlmon recently took to wife a young British woman, that he recently conceived— it is not yet established, I am in honour bound to state, whether or no this conception actually did (as I imply in the text) antedate matrimony—the notion of buying print-paper in her country cheap, that he forthwith dispatched himself and her to the British capital, and that by now he is in a position to know the price of paper in his wife's home-town. It is, not surprisingly, the same as it is here.

Note the placement of "conceived," the parenthesizing dashes distancing it from its subject to extend the ambiguity of the word, which could mean either "thought of" or "impregnated." Note that the parenthesis itself raises the embarrassing question of out-of-wedlock pregnancy, which applied to Bryher. Note that McAlmon is here shown as an opportunist eager to use the marriage to further his publishing ambitions. The reference to Samuel Johnson may be simply a noticing of the parallel relationships—Dr. Johnson and Boswell equals Dr. Williams and McAlmon—or it may be an echo ("permit me to remind") from a speech by the poet Richard Glover reported in *The Lives of the Poets*, in which Glover stresses his lack of interest in "lucrative reward" and "private emolument."

This "prancing" piece (I steal the adjective from the book reviewer Richard Poirier) was not enough to satisfy Thayer's desire to ridicule the marriage, and he further recounted the entire saga in the July "Comment." Here he tossed his barbs not only at McAlmon but also at McAlmon's good friend Williams, who had a medical practice in New Jersey. *Contact* had been founded on the belief that American literature should grow out of its natural environment rather than echo European and other models, and its motto was, "We seek only contact with the local conditions which confront us." Thayer scoffed: "Robert MacAlmon [*sic*] has gone to London; Contact is going to London; 'local conditions' have gone to pot; and there is no joy in Jersey."

Taken together, the pieces constitute a kind of anti-epithalamion, a thorough scorning of the institution of marriage. But if one chastises Thayer, one should also remember the journey from romantic to cynic that Thayer had traveled since falling in love with his "Lily Maid of Astolat," Elaine Orr, five years earlier. Their marriage, which had been celebrated in Cummings's impossibly romantic and heroically gaseous "Epithalamion," had failed on an epic scale, embittering Thayer toward the institution and to the ulterior motives he saw in those who approached him romantically. His own marriage to Elaine had long been hollow, and earlier that year he must have reacted sardonically but with some pain to the delighted letters from his family congratulating him on the birth of Nancy, who was of course the child of Cummings. Close friends knew or suspected this, but Thayer had so far kept his family in the dark. He also had to know that he himself was the subject of much whispering and gossip, on the one hand that he was walking out with women other than his wife, and on the other that he was, as his enemy Albert Barnes would put it, "a grass widower." Perhaps he just couldn't resist the opportunity of focusing the prurient interests of Greenwich Village gossips somewhere other than on himself.

Pound, evidently laboring under the mistaken belief that Ellerman was Jewish, wrote Thayer, "Report from London that Lloyds (in person of father Ellerman) likes his son in law but that McA. is not favorably impressed by the splendours of S. Audley St. [where the Ellermans lived]. . . . after all it is something to have a Christian in the family . . . the butler of Hebrew families 'ave been known to appreciate even those who come but to dine."[8] It's interesting that two decades later, during World War II, when Pound was fulminating for the fascists on Italian radio, William Joyce ("Lord Haw-Haw") made the same assumption about Ellerman's son, John, who donated to Jewish causes.

McAlmon, evidently affected by Thayer's article, shared his concerns with T. S. Eliot, who responded: "I should not worry at all about what Thayer says. I thought his witticisms in the May number very tasteless and pointless. Why do our compatriots try so hard to be clever? Furthermore, his language is so opaque, through his cleverness, that it is unintelligible gibberish. Cummings has the same exasperating vice."[9]

To his credit, Eliot said as much to Thayer himself in a later letter, saying that he found the "Comment" mystifying.

What on earth does it all mean? I have ventured to tell McAlmon that it means nothing. I have found him a very charming young man of lively intelligence and amiable personality. But why on earth do you devote so much space and so much obscure vaticination to a young writer who might just as well, and who would willingly, remain in privacy until he has performed some notable feat? . . . [W]hy make an international event out of a matrimonial union which is only interesting for the parties concerned?[10]

Thayer believed that marriage, in general, was a relationship of power rather than love, and he saw more authenticity in the transaction between a prostitute and her john than between man and wife. "The prostitute does not sell herself; only in marriage does a woman do that," he wrote. "The prostitute merely rents out the use of her person."[11] To Thayer, the Bryher-McAlmon marriage was grimly amusing in the way it aped the institution exactly as he himself saw it, as a "romantic" public avowal that served only to paper over what was very much a commercial contract. This marriage of convenience was well-intentioned, perhaps, and honest in its way, but still utterly cynical. There was no thalamus, so there could be no true epithalamion.

Bryher and McAlmon were divorced in 1927.

12

TO THE GREAT MASTER

A neurosis is a kind of embarrassment, a perpetual unconscious
embarrassment. And as under ordinary embarrassments so here
too we act spasmodically and emphatically.

SCOFIELD THAYER

The January issue of the *Dial* in 1921 featured a self-complimentary "Comment" by Thayer on the successes the magazine had enjoyed during the first year under its new owners. The self-congratulation was perhaps understandable, in that the magazine had indeed quickly established itself as unusually discerning in its choice of work by both established and rising writers and artists.

The "Comment" was not wholly smug, however. It made mention of one notable failure from that first year, the implementation of the section "Modern Forms." This was an attempt by the editors to make more palatable the avant-garde material by segregating it from the more orthodox offerings. Thayer admitted that the experiment was not a success and noted the absurdity of supposing that older but active and important writers such as W. B. Yeats and Joseph Conrad were somehow not "modern," and he regretted the decision to "cage off" one group from the other.[1]

The January issue was a classic *Dial* mixture of work by traditional and experimental writers, including Ford Madox Hueffer, George Moore, Jean Cocteau, William Carlos Williams, Ezra Pound, Marianne Moore, Aleksei Remizov, and Malcolm Cowley. Art was provided by Wyndham Lewis, C.R.W. Nevinson, and James Earle Fraser.

Cummings was also well represented in the issue, which featured four of his line drawings and the poem "Puella Mea," an extended love poem to, of course, Elaine. Thayer and his wife were at this time going about the work of legally dismantling their relationship. They had agreed that Thayer would create that year a one-hundred-thousand-dollar trust fund "for the support, maintenance and education of Nancy Thayer."[2] Thayer must also have at this time started planning for divorce. He eventually decided on a so-called French divorce, which offered the advantages of the quickness of the procedure and the lack of attendant publicity, not to mention what Thayer saw as a more enlightened attitude toward legal separation. "To oppose divorce is like opposing funerals, the death in each case has already taken place," he wrote.[3]

Thayer's family was still ignorant of his separation from Elaine, although his mother may have had her suspicions; after noting that Thayer had hardly seen Elaine the previous summer, she had scolded him for neglect. Thayer immediately wrote to Cummings, who was already in Paris with Elaine and their daughter, to arrange for the divorce. He told Cummings that Elaine should correspond with his mother more frequently, no doubt so as to not raise her suspicions any further.[4]

In February, Thayer appeared with the novelist John Cowper Powys (brother of Llewelyn) and the playwright Philip Moeller as expert witnesses to testify at the Court of Special Sessions as to the literary quality of "Nausicaa," the thirteenth episode of James Joyce's *Ulysses*, for the publication of which Margaret Anderson and Jane Heap of the *Little Review* were being prosecuted. How useful Thayer's testimony was is questionable, in that he allowed on the stand that he would not have published the chapter in the *Dial*.[5] This angered Anderson, but the position was, of course, perfectly in line with the policy that Thayer always followed in not publishing anything that could threaten the continued existence of the *Dial*. Anderson and Heap were found guilty and fined one hundred dollars.

Thayer maintained an active social life. He was often seen with Marianne Moore, who had first visited him in the fall of 1920 at his Benedick apartment, which greatly impressed her.[6] Thayer also continued to spend time with Alyse Gregory. He pressured her greatly to become his secretary, but she resisted, valuing her independence too much. Eventually she would agree to become the managing editor of the *Dial*. Thayer also greatly enjoyed the company of Sophia Wittenberg, a strikingly beautiful dark-haired stenographer at the *Dial* who eventually married Lewis Mumford.

In May, Louise Bryant, with whom Thayer had enjoyed a brief but intense few weeks the year before, wrote him from Riga, Latvia, where she was waiting for the State Department to allow her back into the United States following her travels in Russia.

> Some days ago I wrote you a very long letter. I've no notion what about— so I very much hope you got it. I'm still stuck in this funny little border town waiting the august decision of the state department. If they really want to make an exile of me they ought to announce it. If not, I shall be back soon. Riga has had the effect of a very good sanitorium on me. I feel better and weigh more and have acquired sunburn. I have written a lot of poetry watching the lilacs and the yellow roses that overwhelm this land. I am sending one. If you do not like it perhaps Max Eastman will. Personally, I always feel that poetry has no place in the Liberator.
>
> Oh, Scoffield [*sic*], I am absolutely perishing to talk to someone. I don't know anyone here except government officials and, merciless God! How lonely it is . . .
>
> I hope everything goes well with you.
>
> Louise Bryant[7]

Thayer's response was friendly, flirtatious, and typically noncommittal.

> Dear Louise,
>
> It is good to hear from you again and to know first-hand that you are alive. No, I have not yet got the long letter. Doubtless I shall directly and can then write you with lengthy and appropriate comment upon each and every detail thereof! But perhaps, instead of the letter, you yourself will turn up in town? Such an event would also receive from me an appropriate comment. Not, however, editorial.

He matter-of-factly rejected her poem. "For tiresome reasons we found we couldn't ourselves make room for it," he wrote.[8]

Thayer also began in 1921 a relationship with Doris Beck, about whom we know little except that she seems to have been considerably younger than Thayer. "I suppose you were convinced you have a 'school-girl' fascinated but you are wrong and the only tragic part of my knowing you was my utter disappointment in you, damn it," she wrote in one letter.[9] Thayer sent the girl some issues of the magazine, to which she responded,

> I received the three Dials and read a good deal of them, some of the things I enjoyed but as for some of the things I need an interpreter (Is that the way

you spell it? Looks funny) as the point goes by me without stopping. As for Ezra Pound's "Three Cantos" ??? Whew! Words, words, help me. Don't tell me it takes intelligence to appreciate those sort of things, I know it.

As for the [illegible] I think with her conceited mouth and her mercy-what-a-fool-but-you're-amusing expression she is more like you in spite of the eyes and difference in sex.

Write me some news about where you are + what you're doing as your letter was a temporary relief from boredom

. . .

What did you think of Hamsun's "Shallow Soil"? can't make up my mind I know I am foolish don't rub it in.[10]

Thayer sailed for France in July aboard the *Aquitania*. "We have had an easy trip across and the porpoises have played decoratively about our incisive bow," he wrote his friend Demuth. "The Barengaria, appearing somewhat heavy with the intellectuals of Mr Harold Stearns in the waist, we slowly but conclusively overtook and passed on our port beam yesterday."[11]

Eastbound transatlantic liners were indeed "heavy with intellectuals" that summer, as this letter from Malcolm Cowley to Kenneth Burke demonstrates:

Djuna Barnes	is going abroad.			
Harold Stearns	"	"	"	
Ivan Opffer	"	"	"	
Bill Brown	"	"	"	
Estlin Cummins	"	"	"	
Dos Passos	"	"	"	
Dorothy Day	"	"	"	
Mary Reynolds	"	"	"	and oh God

I can't continue this list for weariness.[12]

Psychoanalysis was also very much on Thayer's mind at this time. He had been analyzed since at least 1919 by Dr. L. Pierce Clark, who would go on to do pioneering work in psychobiography. Thayer had also written to Sigmund Freud asking whether analysis could be beneficial to artists and poets, and Freud had referred him to the book *The Artist* by Dr. Otto Rank. At the end of the letter, Freud made a heavy-handed joke to the effect that Leonardo da Vinci had not undergone analysis.[13] Thayer had hoped that, after the divorce in Paris was settled, he could move on to Vienna to undergo analysis with Freud, whom he called the "Great Magician" and the "Great Master." He was delighted, therefore, soon after arriving in Paris, to receive from Freud a letter accepting him as a patient beginning in September. Freud wrote that he was sorry that Thayer had already been subjected to the "incompetency" of a previous analyst and that he, Freud, was unable to get Thayer "fresh." He sympathized with Thayer's determination to heal his psyche. "The man who suffers deeply has a good chance to recover by analysis," he wrote.[14]

Soon after arriving in Paris, Thayer bumped into his old mentor Santayana, and the two spent an evening together. "He entertained me at dinner and we talked until midnight, or rather he did, for conversation with him is always listening to a monologue," he wrote his mother. "He has a novel projected and rehearsed the plot which is about a Puritan, born in Springfield and dead in France."[15] This was, of course, Santayana's only novel, the best-selling *The Last Puritan*, whose hero, Oliver Alden, would be based on a young American like Thayer, whom Santayana saw as a kind of anachronistic puritan. After the book was published in 1936, almost a decade after Thayer had left public life, Santayana would correspond with Llewelyn Powys and describe Thayer as "very self-conscious and affected,"[16] a charge to which Alyse Gregory took offense and complained about in a letter back to Santayana. Santayana was somewhat conciliatory, writing to Gregory that Thayer "didn't seem spontaneous and natural; he found life difficult, and wasn't at home in this world."[17]

Santayana also wrote later that he had considered having his hero born in Thayer's hometown of Worcester,[18] and perhaps he told Thayer during their meeting in Paris that Alden's birthplace was Springfield, Massachusetts, so as not to tip Thayer off that he was in fact a model for the character. In any case, Thayer seemed not to recognize himself at all in Santayana's description. And Alyse Gregory, who knew Thayer better than anyone, read the book and did not see anything of Thayer in it.[19]

The Thayers' initial divorce decree was issued on July 28, 1921, and almost immediately we see a greater sense of lightness and enjoyment in Thayer's letters. Here he describes Pound to Alyse Gregory:

> Ezra Pound, of whom I have been seeing more rather than less, is a queer duck. One has observed him so awkward as unintentionally to knock over a waiter and then so self-conscious as to be unable to say he is sorry. But like most other people he means well and unlike most other people he has a fine imagination. At close quarters he is much more fair in his judgments than his correspondence and his books would warrant one to believe.[20]

He also described Gertrude Stein, whom he visited with Pound, as being five feet high and two feet wide and has a dark brown face and small, wise, old Jewess eyes. She curls up in the corner of a divan and falls over like a doll in trying to receive editors. She possesses the homely finish of a brown buckram bean bag. In conversation she put it all over Ezra, who got back by saying all sorts of things on the way home.[21]

By the end of August, Thayer was on the island of Westerland in the North Sea, one of the most northerly parts of Germany. Here he took the time to answer an earlier letter from his young admirer Doris Beck. "Hello Yourself!" he wrote, echoing her usual salutation. "I am sitting in a dining-room with great shop-windows built just above the North Sea. The way I'm looking I could see Iceland if it hadn't taken it into its head to lie so far away. The sun has just set and the breakers rolling in are a cold hard gray green."

In his letters to younger women—especially to those who might seem inappropriately young by some standards—Thayer's prose becomes calmer, less convoluted, less eager to impress. One wonders, as his interest in young girls seems to increase over the years, if he found himself more able to relax with them because of their relative lack of sophistication. "But Sylt is an island and I am so far as I know, the only Anglo-Saxon on it," he went on.

There are twenty or forty thousand Germans loose here, but they do not [sneer?] at me or otherwise molest. On the contrary they . . . feed me pancakes and have relatives in Iowa (which they pronounce in such a way that you guess every other state, city, and molehill before you get it straight). . . . Sylt—as I'm sure all young ladies who frequent convent-schools are aware—is one of that group of islands called Frisians, which stretches from Denmark to Holland.

All in all, it is rather a sweet letter, even with the somewhat titillating image with which he concludes it:

[T]he other day a young lady went in at the end of the beach without anything at all and made quite a sensation. Her bulldog waited for her on the shore and looked extremely proper and dignified. But he must have found it trying. Eventually the lady emerged to dive and roll very cutely into a great white bath-sheet.[22]

There is only one other mention of the relationship with Beck in Thayer's correspondence. It occurs four years later, in 1925, when she, after conferring with her parents, told him that she was ending their relationship.

The final decree in the divorce was entered October 10, 1921,[23] by which time Thayer was in Vienna. His letters to his mother from this period are full of news about his friends, the artwork he is buying, and the theaters he attends, but there is no mention whatsoever of Freud, and when she raised the possibility of visiting him in Vienna or the two meeting up somewhere, he flatly refused her. Alyse Gregory was aware of Thayer's work with Freud, but when she asked in a letter how the analysis was proceeding, he rebuffed her. "News from Vienna you must not expect," he wrote. "I move tapping my way among not wholly unfamiliar but not for that reason the less awful shapes."[24]

Vienna, then a city of about 2 million, had been impoverished and destabilized following the Great War and the collapse of its monarchy. The Socialists had control of the city and were carrying out extensive reforms aimed at improving the lot of the workers, but unemployment was high and the economy fragmented. Many artists and entertainers had moved to Berlin, which was wresting from Vienna the title of cultural capital. With royalists and the Catholic Church allied against the Socialists, and with feuding among the leaders of the various political entities, the city was racked by conflict and periodically rocked by riots.[25]

In a letter of December 11, 1921, Thayer described his own experience amid this uproar. Earlier that day, his hotel had been invaded, but fortunately the rioters had not reached his rooms on the upper floors.

My own point of contact with the rioting occurred when my taxi was stopped before I had got to the Hotel that evening just after the invasion of the hotel. A man jumped on the front of the car and turned off the power and others opened the door and tried to pull me out intending to strip off my fur coat I was wearing. I might probably also have lost my pocket book and my gold watch and my dignity had I not done the only thing possible by jumping out right in the faces of the people at the door and startling them, which gave me time to leap a few yards further and to attain a group of militia-men who were keeping a few square feet of order in a sea of disorder. I was then sufficiently near the hotel so that I was able to get inside where order had by that time been established and where soldiers were keeping the doors. Of course earlier in the afternoon I had observed that a great many windows had been smashed and that all the shops were closed and that demonstrations were being held before the House of Parliament, but thought that things would pass off without any aggressive attack on houses or hotels, or on peaceable citizens like myself. Earlier that afternoon, a couple of hours before, my taxi driver had warned me that we could not go where I wanted to go and refused to drive me there telling me that about ten taxis had been demolished, but I persuaded him to take me a roundabout way to the address. On the way however we had to cross one of the main streets which we had thought free and what should we see but a parade with red banners coming down this avenue upon us as we neared it. We had to turn about so quickly that we almost turned over in the snow and the parade stopped and was about to pursue us or at least stone us when we got under way so rapidly as to make this pursuit futile. . . .

Of course the thing was rather picturesque with the enormous crowds of black clothed people moving, silently for the most part, everywhere in the snow covered city. . . .

But now I feel that everything looks more suspicious and hope for no further such unpleasantness during the winter in Vienna. Of course I consider the selfishness of the American Senate immediately responsible for the disturbance. Thousands of people are starving and hundreds of thousands are living on the verge of starvation and it is no wonder that there should be trouble.

He continued to seek out work for the *Dial*, and soon the magazine was running a "German Letter" and publishing translations of his favorite Germanic writers, including Arthur Schnitzler, Hermann Hesse, Hugo von Hofmannsthal, and Thomas Mann. Thayer's passion for German and Austrian culture was matched by the Francophilia of his partner, James Sibley Watson, and the two often argued about the relative merits of each.

Tom Eliot had begun writing the "London Letter" for the *Dial* in April, but 1921 was turning out to be a difficult year for both Eliots, as the stresses of their marriage and of Eliot's heavy schedule of work and writing (he was working on *The Waste Land* at this time) took its toll. In October, Vivien wrote to Thayer to tell him that St. John Hutchinson would take over the "London Letter" while Eliot was recovering from illness. She explained that Tom had suffered a serious breakdown and had to recuperate. At one point, she voiced the unhappiness she had felt since marrying Eliot and settling in England. "Toward the end of November I *want* to go—somewhere. I don't know yet, and it doesn't matter much, but I must escape from England or it will smother me. Have been trying to escape for five–six years!" She also grumbled that she hadn't finished her own breakdown yet, to which Thayer replied coolly, and perhaps cruelly, "Goethe once observed speaking of his love affairs that it was pleasant to see the moon rise before the sun set. But such is not I presume the case with nervous breakdowns, especially when they are both in the same family."[26]

From a letter to Alyse Gregory written in January 1922, we get a better idea of how things were going in Thayer's sessions with Freud.

You have expressed interest in my affair with the Great Master. As I mentioned in my last letter, there are excellent reasons why I should not want to venture myself at present into any complicated study of our relationship. But as yesterday I confessed to some of my stumbling blocks to the Professor himself, I now see no reason why I should not mention (in this most provokingly guarded fashion) one or two things. Firstly, I was reminded by the speed with which he made his diagnosis of my case of your criticism to me of his apparently almost too immediately certain diagnoses of certain cases instanced by him in his most recent book. You may recall that I had received the same impression from these passages in the book and agreed with your feeling of hesitation before analyses that were not anyhow to the layman obvious. Of course this inability on the part of the layman to O.K. the diagnosis of the specialist may be due merely to the layman's lack of acquaintance with the subject in question. Certainly, not only from conversations with Dr. Freud but also from my conversations with Dr. Clark, I have received more than once minor diagnoses which I did not at the time accept and which were afterward substantiated by further experience of my own. In the case of Dr. Clark my scepticism [*sic*] was not often aroused, for the simple reason that Dr. Clark did not often make any statements of sufficient interest to arouse even scepticism. With Dr. Freud the exact contrary is the case. He bristles with the most startling and penetrating comments upon apparently superficially meaningless details in dreams, free associations, and daily experience. Therefore a natural sceptic like myself is constantly being jolted. But here, as I have said, as in the case of Dr. Clark, later experience has often substantiated what at first struck me as wild guesses. But not always. And in the essential foundation-lines of Dr. Freud's diagnosis of my neurosis—a diagnosis made during the first weeks of my stay in Vienna—I am not in agreement with him. As I have already been here for three months, this is certainly discouraging. Neither of us budges. Of course I came here, as you know, with the best will in the world and really do not want to be my usually contentious and pigheaded self. Yet I cannot honestly accept the diagnosis. Perhaps I might mention that the diagnosis is distinctly more serious than that given by Dr. Clark and most unpleasant. Of course I realise that herein may lie that cause of my inability to accept the diagnosis. But I do think I am capable of looking at the case critically from the outside and even when I try to do so I cannot accept the diagnosis in question.

So I really do not know whether I shall be staying on in Vienna until the summer (which I shall do if Dr. Freud and I agree that I am receiving any help from the analysis) or whether either Dr. Freud or I may feel forced to break off things sooner, that is, any time.

. . . I really appreciate the advantage of intercourse with a man for whose intellect I continue to have the highest regard. It is therefore the more unfortunate that in regard to my own particular case I cannot yet really agree with him.

You will, I fear me, definitely without further information take Dr. Freud's side of this affair when you learn that I have now gone so far as to remember a long harangue on the part of our contemporary James Oppenheim in my rooms at the Benedick a couple of years ago. [Oppenheim was a poet and novelist who had founded the magazine the *Seven Arts*.] He then explained to me in Oppenheimesque the divergence between Jung and Freud and the brightness of Jung and the limitations of Freud. At the time and after further conversation upon the subject with Dr. Clark, I did not agree. . . . Now I hesitate, and I have been forced with a thousand apologies to mention the matter to Dr. Freud yesterday. He took my difficulty very pleasantly, but you will realize how delicate the situation now is and that this may be the beginning of the end. I have even mentioned to Professor Freud that Zurich [where Jung, Freud's rival, practiced] is on the way back to Paris. You see how low I am fallen. . . .

I'm sorry not to be able in writing to go into details of our differences. I confine myself to reporting then that so far as I can see I am exactly as I was when I came to Vienna. . . .

Please write and comfort me in my great troubles![27]

Freud's belief that paranoia arose in the mind as a defense against unwanted homosexual desire is widely known today, a fact that checks off one more item supporting the theory that Thayer's "great troubles" sprang from such suppression. This is certainly possible, but we should remember that Thayer was himself thoroughly aware of Freud's thinking on the issue. Soon after sailing for Europe, he had written to Gregory, "If I'm a homo wanting to be changed he refuses absolutely [to see me]."[28] Considering that Freud was evidently unwilling to treat neuroses arising from homosexuality and that Thayer would spend two years in analysis, during which time one would think the matter would come to light, one has to conclude that Thayer's psychological difficulties were more complex.

The year 1921 had begun with great promise. *The Dial* was successful in every way except financially and conferred great prestige on Thayer and Watson. Thayer's social life was busy, and he was, with the divorce of Elaine and the creation of a trust fund for Nancy, beginning to bring some order into his chaotic personal life. Mostly, though, 1921 was the year in which he finally sat at the feet of the "Great Master," where Thayer had hoped he would find the knowledge and wisdom that could set at rest his inner disorder. But just as the experience first at Harvard and then at Oxford had in the end disappointed, just as he would eventually be disillusioned even by his great hero of the intellect, Santayana, Freud himself was beginning to lose his lustre, and in his letter to Gregory we see Thayer doing something wholly unexpected: questioning not only the conclusions but also the "limitations" of this magician of the mind.

The only things that did not disappoint Thayer were literature and art. This may be why, despite the stress of publishing the *Dial*, and despite the fact that he and Watson were spending a small fortune on the magazine, and despite the fact that he often talked about getting a "divorce" from Watson and walking away from the magazine, he could never bring himself to do so until the final stages of his madness. And in the feverish buying of artwork in which Thayer indulged in this period it is possible that we are seeing a man desperately clutching to himself the beautiful things that brought him some moments of joy and mental quietude and which just might, he believed, shore him up against insanity.

13

ASSESSING THE MODERN

It is astonishing how stupid people are! How could anyone
think that The Dial wanted to be modern? Certainly no one
who was acquainted with the editor.

NICHOLAS JOOST

In January 1922, Ezra Pound was editing the final version of Eliot's poem *The Waste Land* and noted to the poet that he had "writ to Thayer asking what he can offer for this."[1] So began the negotiations over the publication of the poem in the *Dial*, a process that was almost sabotaged by miscommunication, misunderstandings, and one horrifically garbled telegram. More than anything, though, the fiasco that ended with the publication of the century's most famous poem was almost certainly a manifestation of the rivalry, resentment, and downright bad feeling that had grown between Eliot and Thayer.

Thayer had not been impressed by Eliot's productivity as the writer of "London Letter." Sickness, family difficulties, and a nervous breakdown had taken their toll on Eliot in 1921, and on a couple of occasions Vivien had had to write to Thayer apologizing for and explaining her husband's inability to respond to Thayer personally. This no doubt miffed Thayer, who was a stickler for propriety in such matters. Things came to a head in January 1922, when Gilbert Seldes, still editor of the *Dial* at this point, rejected a "London Letter" that had been written by St. John Hutchinson, a friend of Eliot's. Seldes described it to Thayer as "horrid and vulgar and tedious and totally impossible," and Thayer duly passed on this judgment to Eliot. Eliot replied urbanely that he thought it as good as any he had written, suggesting that the payment for the piece be deducted from his own future earnings from the *Dial*.[2] Eliot had written Hutchinson asking him to take on the assignment, and no doubt Hutchinson had picked up from that letter some of Eliot's obvious disdain for the work: "The idea is a sort of chat (which I do very badly) about the intellectual life and the life of the intellectuals in London at the moment—not criticism of new books etc. so much as to communicate to the lonely reader in Chicago or Los Angeles a pleasant comforting sense of being in the know about activities in London."[3] It had not exactly been an exhortation to excellence.

In the same letter to Thayer, Eliot offered *The Waste Land* for the *Dial*. "I shall shortly have ready a poem of about four hundred and fifty lines, in four parts, and would like to know whether the *Dial* wishes to print it (*not* to appear in any periodical on this side) and if so approximately what the *Dial* would offer. I should like to know quickly as I shall postpone all arrangements for publication until I hear. It could easily divide to go into four issues, if you like, but not more."[4]

Thayer had already been approached by Pound regarding the work, and now here was Eliot pushing the same poem at him, in the same letter in which he somewhat airily waved off Thayer's unhappiness with the "London Letter." This apparent attempt to railroad material into the magazine, coupled with the fact that *The Waste Land* had obviously been written at a time when Eliot was supposedly so stretched with personal difficulties that he had been unable to produce the "London Letter" or even respond personally to Thayer's letters, must have considerably aggravated Thayer.

Thayer managed to make a more or less civil response, though he could not resist showing himself less than sympathetic regarding the bout of influenza that supposedly had forced Eliot to write from his sickbed. "[I]t is good to know that you have taken up the old-fashioned custom of answering letters," he noted. "I hope I shall not have to await another case of influenza before receiving another letter."[5] He agreed to accept *The Waste Land*, sight unseen, for $150.

Soon after, however, Eliot learned that the *Dial* had at one time paid writer George Moore £100 (then about $440) for a short story, and this so enraged him that he fired off a telegram to Thayer demanding £50 for his poem.[6] But when the cable arrived in Vienna, it was impossibly garbled, reading "cannot accept . . . under !8!56 pounds = eliot +"[7]

"I presume there is some error upon the part of the telegraph service," Thayer wrote in response to this apparent demand for £856. "Were you to let me see the poem and to let me know why it is you feel that *The Dial* should make an exception in this case to its general rule, I should be happy to consider the matter further. But in the meantime I have had to notify *The Dial* that we are apparently not to receive the poem."[8] (To the Dial staff he had said, "If Eliot's long poem was anything like Pound's Cantos, perhaps we are unwillingly blessed.")[9]

It took all the considerable diplomatic skills of Watson, who took time off from a family European vacation and traveled to Vienna to discuss the matter with Thayer, to get the negotiations back on track. The upshot was that Eliot received the $150 Thayer had originally offered for the piece and was also promised the two-thousand-dollar Dial Award. The poem appeared in the November issue of the *Dial*, after its appearance in the October issue of Eliot's own magazine, *Criterion*.

The irony of all this, as the scholar Nicholas Joost pointed out in correspondence with Watson in 1966, is that Thayer never paid Moore £100 for anything. The "short story" Eliot referred to was probably Moore's continuing three-part "Imaginary Conversations," which appeared in three separate issues of the *Dial* in 1919, before Thayer even had control of the magazine. "It was most interesting to learn that it was Johnson's Dial that paid that famous, magnificent sum to George Moore," Watson wrote. "Of course, that was the beginning of the trouble with Eliot. He didn't distinguish between the Dial of Johnson and the Dial of Thayer."[10]

Though himself an Anglophile in his younger years, Thayer greatly disliked the excessive Englishness that Eliot adopted. "When one hears Mr Eliot talk," he wrote, "one shuts one's eyes the better to see him, in patent-leather boots with deer-skin . . . tops, a morning-coat, and a stick with an ivory knob representing the head of a King Charles Spaniel of pedigree. He speaks with a so spotless accent one might take him for the English Spotless Laureate of some green and English Spotless Town."[11]

He found *The Waste Land* "disappointing,"[12] but it is Eliot's "mincing, priggish, pedantic" prose,[13] not his poetry, that Thayer most frequently remarks on in his personal notes. Eliot's attitude in his criticism of others is that of "so extremely consciously the Daniel come to judgement," Thayer wrote. Thayer attacks the paternal superiority he sees in the poet's critical writings: "Although Mr Eliot often asserts, in castigating his contemporaries (like the father to the naughty son) 'It hurts me more than it does you, Charlie,' nevertheless one smells the sadist."[14]

Thayer once pointed out how "queer" he found it that Eliot, "who approves of metaphysical verse should be opposed to poetic expression in critical prose."[15] Here is a paragraph on Eliot's prose that also demonstrates Thayer's own highly metaphorical critical style:

Eliot's prose is back-handed, vigilantly defensive. Like M Moore's it is skeletonal (sp?) And like a skeleton, it walks stiffly. And like a skeleton walking, it is very *distingué*. It is like a Gothic cathedral walking, too. Only, the flying-buttresses seldom fly. And it is, of course, not French: it is English Perpendicular canted slightly backwards. In his case one feels it has faced too closely the continuous explosion of the American magazine. All is in order, but all is awry. Stylistically, as intellectually, Mr Eliot is always in order. But that order—that nobly retained architectural . . . formation— that order is permanently and basically wrenched. It and he are always more or less off center. His sentences are like perfectly formed tin soldiers of which the bases are so bent as to make the soldier always lean slightly backward. They face the enemy, and their *term,* like their *ton,* is *parfait . . .* But they are not as they might have been. "And bent the bough that might have grown full straight."[16]

When Thayer uses the term "modern," it is more often in reference to art, not literature. In the fine art of his day, he saw a living contemporary aesthetic expression that he found lacking in much of the literature of the time. Indeed, in both Eliot and Joyce, those twin titans of modernism, Thayer saw too much of a slavish reverence for and adherence to old ideas of order and orthodoxy.

Joyce's scholastic design of Ulysses (scholastic because so logically ordered and balanced, as well as leaning against, written against, the authority of Ulysses) is typical of the . . . scientific . . . way of life of contemporary movement. Eliot's finding of Hamlet a failure is a crying example of the same tendency. He too leans upon the ancient models of drama, he too exacts logic and balance everywhere. But in behalf of Shakespeare and in answer to all these men, we may affirm that no trained perfected *logical* circus-horse or cavalry-horse or race-horse ever could give his rider the thrill Mazeppa had. The ultimate emancipation (exhilaration) of the spirit occurs when the reins are fallen loose upon Pegasus' unbroken neck.[17]

Over the years, Thayer reluctantly and with something less than grace accepted the fact that his old rival Eliot was becoming more and more successful, but Eliot's was not a success he found admirable. He wrote, "Upon the narrow carpet which his conscious prejudices and his unconscious inhibitions grant him, Eliot can curl, flop, and tumble most learnedly, and to the king's taste."[18]

The lives of Thayer and Eliot seemed to run in parallel. Each had attended Milton Academy and Harvard, each had gone to Oxford for postgraduate work, and each would become the editor of a respected journal. It was in England that their friendship was at its seeming warmest, until, that is, they both pursued (or were pursued by) Vivien Haigh-Wood. The relationship seems to have soured from this point on. Granted, their correspondence remained largely civil (with the howlingly notable exception of the negotiations over the publication of *The Waste Land*), but in the more private arenas of letters to others and personal notes, neither had much complimentary to say about the other.

As for Thayer's opinion of Eliot, one must search hard indeed to find in his writing a fond word about his old schoolmate. Eliot's poetry is rarely referenced. He mentions that Eliot's "Rhapsody on a Windy Night" was probably suggested by a T. E. Hulme poem[19] and asks himself whether Prufrock's phrase "trousers rolled" means "trousers *turned up*." Indeed, his comments on the verse are all very minor, except perhaps for his insightful comparison of Eliot's metaphors with those of John Donne.

In his longest and most sympathetic entry on Eliot, Thayer references a Puritan minister and a battlefield of the Great War and compares Eliot's output to excrement.

> One can never imagine Mr Eliot exploding. And explosion more than anything else is what this constipated Mather requires. After the wet bombs of De la Mare, Davies, et cetera, one is glad of the Eliot dryness. But here in this elaborate interior mechanism something is definitely lacking, or rather, misplaced, out of gear. These bombs of Mr Eliot can upon the Aubusson describe the most elaborate of orbits. They can sit upon the left hand of (ascend into the air and sit upon the right hand of) the gas chandelier. They can maunder of paper-flowers and milk-glass moons. And sometimes there is a ragged succession of precise little explosions—almost. Of a defecation so elaborate, so contained, so magisterially baroque, so unerringly to the point (so pointed and precise). These fluted massives [missives?] are, after the sputterings of most criticasters, the inadequacy, the absurd brevity of whose intestines is evident, a real relief. (Applies still better to his verses.)[20]

And *that* is one of the more complimentary passages. Here is an entry showing a reluctant admiration of the rising poet:

> Fame is like a mantle; and one would wish that so young a man (as Eliot) should wait until this mantle lie more firmly upon his shoulders, before he should draw it so majestically about him. But if Mr. Eliot is ridiculous, it is in great part the ridicule of genius. Victor Hugo, a greater poet than Mr Eliot will ever be, was also, here and there (par çi par là) ridiculous.

While Eliot's poetry is only infrequently referred to in Thayer's notes, the prose comes in for a good deal of criticism. He writes of the "queer, pathetic fin-de-siècle prose of T. S. Eliot,"[21] comparing its progress to the "gait . . . of a frail man in a top hat leaning backward because the hat is heavy."

He shows a cynical admiration for Eliot's diplomatic skills in writing about other writers: "Mr Eliot treading the narrow path between disloyalty to his friends and disloyalty to the interests of art occasionally finds the going difficult. The two sides of this narrow path coalesce, may seem to cross each other—but Mr Eliot keeps on walking, intelligently, on the void."[22]

In 1925, when he came across a magazine advertisement for Eliot's *Collected Poems* that noted *The Waste Land* was out of print, he scribbled "Ha! Ha!" in the margin and sent it to his friend Alyse Gregory.[23]

•

Considering both Thayer's loathing of many of the technological advances of modernity and his disdain for much of the moder*nism* that was the artist's response to the forward thrust of the age, it is astonishing and ironic that he played such a large part in the establishment of modernism, and that his magazine in many ways charted the directions of art, literature, and criticism for the twentieth century. Thayer was unimpressed by the reverence toward industrialism and technology shown by some artists of the period; his own background was in the textile and manufacturing industries of the American Northeast, and he found nothing particularly intriguing or romantic in the factory. (That he disdained industry, which had provided him with his fortune, was a contradiction that did not bother him.)

He did though have an understanding of the movements then swirling around the artistic sphere. He understood that some artists, unable to ignore the rapid progress of technology and the thrust of the modern, were finding methods of embracing these forces in their work. Of Marianne Moore he wrote, "MM's use of quotations [is] like Picasso's of newspapers; and is influenced by infringement of mechanical upon our life: thus even by sea the noise of steamers etc. becomes part of aesthetic whole."[24] The use of collage as in the introduction of disparate elements, often unexplained, into a work of art was a not uncommon practice among the modernists. But there was also the danger, he felt, of allowing one's aesthetic to be overcome by an unthinking emphasis on integrating the artifacts and images of the modern world: "Modern artists' attempt to be angular is inferiority complex to accepted overimportance of machinery."[25]

Picasso was for Thayer the greatest artist of the era, and naturally he gave much thought to the subject of cubism. Thayer's view of Picasso's work in cubism was surprisingly similar to Pound's view of Eliot's creation of himself as an artist. Pound was both astonished and impressed at how Eliot had trained himself to become "modern." Eliot had in fact remade himself, and this, of course, was Pound's exhortation to the writers and artists of the time: "Make it new." Thayer saw Picasso's cubist work as a similarly heroic individual effort to achieve a new level of skill and understanding. "Picasso develops Cubism to wholly wean himself of wistfulness and adolescence: it is a gesture of stark manhood," he wrote. Thayer also divined that style, as much (or even more) than subject, added meaning to a painting. "Abstract art can be as personal as representational [art]," he said. "Picasso's cubes betray a rugged willfulness."[26] It was perhaps this insight into the ideation that went along with the creation of an artist's style that would cause Thayer to lash out so at Leo Stein for his remark a few years later that Picasso was "in no serious sense a thinker."

And yet Thayer saw cubism only as a means to an end, one that could be dispensed with once its purpose was achieved. It would always be pedagogically useful, he thought, proof that "arrangement of color and line in itself give aesthetic content," but he added that this was "scarcely the part of genius." He also may have believed that any style could be abused and cheapened by overuse, and in the popularization of cubism he saw how it might easily be coopted by commercialism and propaganda. He once suggested the method would be ideal to create subway frescoes.[27] One would love to have heard Thayer's opinion of Picasso's *Guernica*.

His other favorites in art included Matisse, who "just swims in fluid colour, as angels do in fluid light,"[28] and Gaston Lachaise, of whom he said: "What a gulf separates Lachaise from all other post-Aztec Am[erican] sculptors. He taught the American that peacocks have ears."[29] The reference is to the detail achieved on Lachaise's bronze sculpture of three peacocks. He was also most admiring of the work of his friend Charles Demuth, whom he described as "the only painter in America about whose work I very much care."[30] He disliked Goya, with his "canvas explosions" and "ornate farts,"[31] and Rockwell Kent, whose work "lack[ed] holly"[32] (to achieve the full Christmas-like effect of its sentimentality, no doubt). The great American painters, he felt, were only Charles Turner, Whistler, Marin, and Demuth.[33] Sargent was "no more a great painter than an efficient graphophone is 'a great singer.' Mere crass 'talentism.' *Rien de plus.* Unblushingly so."[34]

Thayer had a dim view of American culture in general. A mock epitaph he wrote for himself went:

Scofield Thayer 1889–19—
Though born in the States,
English[35]

In his early adulthood, he regarded England as the mother country and the United States as at best a colony and at worst a historical bad joke. This was not an unusual point of view among certain members of the cultured and the literati, who saw something admirable and even heroic in the existential expatriation of Henry James and others, who had chosen to return to the source. This view evolved somewhat in Thayer as he became disillusioned with England ("I find England + the English sluggish") and more enamored of the culture of Austria and Germany.[36] His antipathy to the United States, however, was unremitting.

The inferiority complex toward European culture that Ralph Waldo Emerson urged his compatriots to overcome in his 1837 lecture "The American Scholar" lingered still, and it infuriated some that men of talent such as Henry James, Ezra Pound, and T. S. Eliot should choose to live in self-exile from their native culture, since this was an implicit acceptance that America was indeed culturally second-rate. (Thayer wrote, "In Germany poets walk like prophets, in France like cocks, in England like gentlemen; in America they skulk.")[37] Against such a point of view some writers angrily agitated. Indeed, one literary nationalist subsect of American modernism, which included the poet William Carlos Williams and the fiction writer Robert McAlmon, was singularly dedicated to creating an American literature. (This no doubt fed into Thayer's mocking of McAlmon when the writer eventually married a wealthy heiress and moved to Europe.)

The idea of a literary and intellectual tradition was as important to Thayer as it was to Eliot, and Thayer viewed the American tradition as something of an embarrassment compared to that of Europe: "Germanics in Italy mixed with the latins and exploded in the Renaissance. In America they were too good to mix with indians and their explosion is only a noisy report with an unpleasant smell."[38] As an avid student and patient of Freud, the "Great Master," it is not surprising that Thayer's approach to understanding and explaining his dissatisfaction with America would include that of a Freudian: "Even the historical background of America is like that of a neurotic. Thus we can see and remember back only to the Pilgrims, or, at its dizzy best, Columbus. Behind we are aware there are red aboriginal tomahawk profiles in the thicket; but of understanding, of sympathy, there is none. This is like the break in a neurotic's history."[39]

Thayer had a good grasp of the modernist directions being taken by literature. His thoughtful and admiring essay on Joyce in the *Dial* of September 1918 had been the first American survey of all of Joyce's work from *Chamber Music* to *Ulysses*.[40] Thayer finds that the "little songs" of Joyce's early verse comprise "a remarkable perfect echo of the best in early seventeenth century prosody" and notes that *Dubliners*, with its "singular, spare, athletic phraseology," was Joyce's most perfect work. *Portrait of the Artist as a Young Man* had sections of immense power and facility, he says, but finds the last part of the book, which followed Stephen's thoughts in the school infirmary, "jotty and spasmodic," a style he compares to pointillism. Thayer refers to Pound's proclamation that Joyce excels beyond impressionist writers because of his selection of detail and then takes the thought further:

> Joyce has become impressionist in a much more subtle sense. He gives us, especially in "Ulysses," the streaming impressions, often only subconsciously cognate to one another, of our habitual life—that vague, tepid river of consciousness to which only our ephemeral moments of real will or appetite can give coherence. Joyce succeeds in this undertaking to a remarkable degree. The chief fault of this method is its jerkiness, peculiarly inapt to interpret the calm flow of our sensations merging so noiselessly one into another. Some of us feel it a pity that he who could write the strangely sinuous final pages of "The Dead" should now have adopted so different a medium. But there is a time for all things.

Here Thayer considers the weaknesses of Joyce's choice of style, particularly its inability to capture the smoothness of the thought stream. Thayer generally found the stream-of-consciousness approach to offering a verisimilitude of cogitation lacking largely because of its *un*stream-like qualities as it jumped from one thought to the next, as it must in orthodox prose in which one sentence follows another, whereas there is no evidence that the bolus of existence created by the constant cognitive give-and-take among impression, response, memory, thought, and emotion is chronological. In *Finnegans Wake*, of course, Joyce would strive to bring this experiment to its conclusion.

Thayer was quite familiar with the stream-of-consciousness style. He greatly admired the Austrian writer Arthur Schnitzler, who had in 1901 published the novella *Lieutenant Gustl*, an early experiment in interior monologue. Freud was also a fan of Schnitzler's, telling him, "You have learned through intuition—though actually as a result of sensitive introspection—everything that I have had to unearth by laborious work on other persons."[41] Thayer noted the importance of the Austrian writer to the modernist movement: "Schnitzler, as befits a scientist, has twice been a forerunner—of Freud and of Joyce."[42]

Just as Thayer was not at all impressed with those other products of high modernism, Eliot's *The Waste Land* and Pound's *Cantos*, he thought *Ulysses* an aesthetic failure. One of his main complaints was the constant reference to a narrow view of classical form he saw in some of the moderns.

Thayer had been an early supporter of Joyce, and in 1919 he had given the writer seven hundred dollars at the request of Padraic and Mary Colum.[43] Joyce had just lost his patron and was in his usual financial difficulties. It is true that two years later, after being approached by Lewis Galantière, Thayer declined to help Joyce further, but there was no spite in his refusal. "Of course I admire Joyce as much as you do," he responded from Vienna. "But I am not able to extend any financial help to him at present."

> The Dial has cost me personally to date over 100,000 dollars and indeed has been taking more than my income. I feel it so important for the welfare of American art and letters and therefore of American artist and writers that The Dial should continue its work that I am unwilling to withdraw from this venture. . . . I feel that it is up to others this time to help Mr. Joyce.[44]

Just as his published survey of Joyce's work up to *Ulysses* is full of admiration, so in his personal notes we see his delight in Joyce: "Of Joyce's style: so elastic a stride." But Thayer also thought that Joyce's head had been turned by the praise heaped upon him by his contemporaries, and that their urging of him into further experimentation had set him in the wrong direction.

> The case of Joyce is parallel to that of Tennyson. The latter was led by the unintelligent adulation of the great public to spread himself in methods not natural to him . . . who was only an intense, unhappy lyricist; so Joyce has been led by the unintelligent adulation of the smaller public to spread himself in methods unnatural to him, who is only an intense, tortured register of misery at once in his own heart and in his natal environment.

Thayer's final word on Joyce was that he had run the impressionistic novel into the ground. The result, ironically, was that Joyce's writing, which had been the jewel in the crown of modernism for those who revered the progressive, had stalled and soured. This, Thayer felt, was the tragedy of Joyce's genius. "Never before since the world began has a man of such talent written so dull a book. Never has a book been so lavishly fitted up with obscenities and been so dull as Ulysses."[45] Thayer showed more disappointment in what he felt was Joyce's misuse of his talent than he did in any other writer. "Something in Joyce curdled," he wrote.[46]

14

A MILLIONAIRE IN RED VIENNA

In 1922, there was much foment and instability in Vienna, which after the Great War had been left largely impoverished. Following the death in exile of the former emperor Charles, services were held in his memory throughout the city. Demonstrations and counterdemonstrations often followed these services, one of which Thayer witnessed.

> I was in my room at the time and from my little balcony saw the crowds marching up the Graben singing the old Austrian national anthems. They went before the Houses of Parliament and attempted to force an entry. The police of the present weak government seem rather afraid to interfere as vigorously as was necessary to disperse people. But the news that the workmen who form the backbone of the present government and are of course socialistic and violently opposed to these royalists, the news I say that these workmen were arming themselves in the factories of the suburb Floridsdorf to march upon Vienna and themselves disperse the royalists seems to have decided the Government to risk more vigorous action, and mounted police then succeeded in dispersing the crowd without bloodshed. Had this not been the case there would have been a pitched battle between the royalists and the workmen which would certainly have lost many lives and might have led to an upset of the Government.[1]

His sessions of psychoanalysis with Freud continued, and evidently he and the doctor had made peace after their disagreements. He wrote to Alyse Gregory: "Speaking of the doctor, I might mention that he and I, thanks to recent 'good' dreams and rather agreeable recent remarks of his own are to each other somewhat reconciled. We talked things over from the practical point of view yesterday and he now goes on record as feeling that we are making some advance and is hoping that in time we may get somewhere."[2] In the same letter, Thayer continued a thread of gossip about the curious relationship between Marianne Moore and her mother: "Yes, the mother of Marianne is a whopper and who would not give his hat to psycho-analyse Marianne?" Marianne Moore never married, and she lived with her mother until the latter's death in 1947.

The Dial, though popular and prestigious, continued to lose money at a steady rate. By 1922, the best that could be said was that the magazine might, in a few years and with the right fiscal management, reduce its annual deficit, which the year before had been about $100,000, to just $20,000. "With Dr. Watson paying half of this I should then feel able to keep up indefinitely," he wrote his mother. "But of course I hope—though not sanguinely—to run the paper eventually without any deficit at all."[3]

One of the major problems in distributing the magazine was its artwork. Samuel Craig, business manager, complained to Thayer that various booksellers refused to advertise in the *Dial* because its art was generally viewed as "degenerate."[4] Indeed, a well-known and powerful New York book publisher, Henry Holt, had been greatly offended by the magazine's frontispiece in the December 1921 issue. This picture, a photograph of the sculptor Gleb Derujinsky's *Leda*, is a realistic depiction of Leda's being ravished by the Swan. According to Watson, Holt looked at the picture, said, "Why, it's coitus," and withdrew his advertising.[5]

Craig wanted to remove all such risqué artwork from the magazine and sell it separately as a quarterly supplement to the *Dial*. Thayer did not agree to the removal of art from the magazine, but the idea of a putting together and selling a collection of reproductions of works of modern art did strike him as a good one, and he began working feverishly on what would be called *Living Art*, a collection of what he felt was the best art of his time. "I realise that those who have understanding for modern art are not numerous nor particularly monied," he wrote Watson. "Nevertheless I had thought we could ask fifteen or twenty dollars for such a folio and get that price from a few hundred people."[6] Much of his time over the following year would be spent in choosing pieces for this folio and overseeing its publication.

Thayer had by this time struck up a friendship with the novelist and playwright Arthur Schnitzler. The two had met the year before, when Thayer described him in a letter to his mother: "Schnitzler is in my opinion the most distinguished of contemporary prose writers and certainly the most important Austrian man of letters. Although a Jew, he appears quite German, having clear light blue eyes, a light skin, and a grizzly beard and hair. He is a small man with a large head. His house was the most orderly I have ever been in, in this respect reminding me of my own apartment in New York."[7] One notes Thayer's sensitivity toward, and the need he feels to comment on, the fact of Schnitzler's Jewishness. He had made a similar remark the year before in speaking of Freud: "I had in Paris the sweetest letter imaginable from him and forgive him for being a Jew."[8] Charges of anti-Semitism against modernist authors are not unheard of. Pound is, of course, the most infamous, but the truth is that disdain and even hatred of Jews can be found in many of the writers and thinkers of the period, and so it is not surprising to find it among those who edited and wrote for the *Dial* or were in some way connected with it. Kenneth Burke, an editor, described the magazine's music critic, Paul Rosenfeld, as "a greasy Jew" and wrote that Sherwood Anderson, whom he also disliked, was "a victim of Jew aesthetics."[9] Thomas Craven, the magazine's art critic, would after his tenure at the magazine refer to Alfred Stieglitz, whose work appeared in the *Dial*, as "a Hoboken Jew without knowledge of, or interest in, the historical American background."[10] Albert Barnes referred to Gilbert Seldes, another editor at the magazine, as a "weak mugged jew."[11] Even mild-mannered, Progressive Alyse Gregory complained about the Jewish presence around Patchin Place, which included "vicious gambling Jews roaring at each other exactly under my back window"[12] and the nearby row of law offices "occupied mostly by jews" who would employ detectives to follow girls in the street and seek to solicit them. "If the girls showed any signs of response, the detective would immediately put them under arrest," Gregory wrote. "He would then march them up to the office of one of these lawyers, who would promise to dispose of the case on the guarantee of a future payment. The girls, usually penniless, would sign anything to get their freedom and would be saddled with a debt, remorselessly exacted, that might take them years to pay off."[13]

Various maxims in Thayer's personal notes refer to Jews several times:

There are at least two varieties of Jew—those who tip too little and those who tip too much.

Jews have one advantage over all other peoples: they presumably do not suffer so much in the presence of Jews as do all other peoples.

The Jews were Nomads and remain so in absence of Natural Magic, humour, and other emotional impediments. They travel light. This is one reason why they often arrive first—and a reason resented by more heavily-laden, more attached peoples.

Al Jolson, this greasy mixing of Jew and nigger. We go by turns hot and cold. We comprehend the passion of Voodooism—and of the pogrom also.[14]

By undergoing psychoanalysis with a Jewish doctor whose ideas he revered, and by living in Vienna where many members of the large Jewish population were active in literature and the arts, Thayer was forced to reconsider this kind of unthinking, offhand anti-Semitism. He wrote to his mother:

Last night I was at Schnitzler's "Professor Bernhardi," a rather serious problem play in regard to the relationship between the Jew and the Christian in Vienna. As you know, the Jews in Vienna are even more in evidence than in other parts of the world. Schnitzler and Hofmannsthal, the two most distinguished living men of letters in Austria, are both Jews and Freud and Adlon, perhaps the two greatest living scientists in Austria, are also Jews.[15]

Another letter to his mother takes up the matter again.

Dr. Schnitzler sent me tickets for the opening of his play "Regien" on Tuesday evening. . . . This play, written a great many years ago, was put on here last winter and was then withdrawn because of the anger and indeed rioting of the Catholics, incensed over what they considered its indecency. The fact that Dr. Schnitzler is a Jew was perhaps the reason for their excitement over the play. Jews in Vienna are more influential than anywhere else in the world and indeed the intellectual life of Austria is chiefly Jewish. Perhaps for this very reason the Christian population is in part at least violently antisemitic.[16]

Thayer was spending a great deal of money in Vienna. He wrote long letters to his mother explaining his purchases of art and insisting that they were all sound investments. Interestingly, he never once mentioned to his mother his sessions with Freud, which were costing one hundred dollars a week. Since arriving in Vienna, he had twice written to Herman Riccius in Worcester, his personal business manager and family advisor, asking for letters of credit to buy more art. It may well have been that Thayer's family was beginning to worry about him, and perhaps that is why, in October, Florence boarded the *Aquitania* for Europe. Thayer wrote to her:

I just received your telegram saying that you were coming on the 'Aquitania' and indeed that you were sailing today. . . . I had received no definite information that you were coming abroad until a few days ago when I received simultaneously letters from yourself and Mr. Riccius and from Elaine all of them giving me this information as though it were something that I knew already. Either you are mistaken in thinking that you wrote me that you were coming or your letter miscarried.

I wonder are you intending to come to Vienna to see me or will there not be some time before our relatives sail with whom I understand you intend to return? Of course it is absolutely impossible for me to leave Vienna.[17]

He was also still trying desperately to persuade Alyse Gregory to work for him at the *Dial*. She had turned down Thayer's offer of being a secretary at the magazine, a post that would actually be that of a very powerful stand-in for Thayer. "It would please me to run The Dial in this corrupt eighteenth century fashion," he had written. In October, he offered her the editorship at seventy-five dollars a week (managing editor Gilbert Seldes and business manager Samuel Craig each received only fifty dollars weekly). "You would . . . have entire charge of what material is to go into the paper, that is to say you would go through all the manuscripts submitted and would yourself decide what to accept," he wrote, but then almost immediately contradicted himself by telling her what should and shouldn't be included: "I feel forced to refrain in future from publishing such matter as the silly cantos of Ezra Pound and as the very disappointing 'Waste Land' . . . and I should like to secure for The Dial the works of such recognised American authors as Edith Wharton."[18]

The letter also shows the beginnings of his suspicions toward those who worked for him. At this time, his main concern seems to have been his editor. "I find from Americans that I meet abroad that Mr. Seldes seems always to give the impression that he does not know whether I am ever returning to America and that anyway my connection with The Dial is of the faintest," he wrote. "Mr. Seldes has been taken up on this score a year ago and has most insistently assured his innocence. I am wholly dissatisfied with his attitude toward The Dial and toward myself, also with his incompetent or unpardonably careless editing of such important departments as the Notes on Contributors (which could be a good feature and are puerile) and of our own advertisements both in The Dial and in in other journals and in pamphlet form." The excoriation continues: Seldes "writes exactly as he did for the Harvard Monthly . . . what he writes almost always tires me and his theatrical criticism and his Comment I find comically influenced by my own contributions to those sections and not for the better." He refers to "catastrophic errors in management upon the part of Seldes and Watson" and goes on to say, "I am as usual not on speaking terms with Mr.

Watson and now in addition 'off' with Pound, Eliot and Cummings."[19] One senses here a growing feeling of helplessness in Thayer, a loss of control and a sense of isolation largely brought about by his pushing people away. Gregory was the only friend he ever felt he could trust completely, and he may have felt that putting her in charge at the *Dial* might help him regain some of the power he had lost by not being present in the New York offices. Thayer was a notorious micromanager. When he was in New York, a postmortem would follow every issue of the *Dial*, and every error both large and tiny would be traced back to its source. Trying to maintain such control from four thousand miles away must have been hugely frustrating for him.

At the end of the year, he received a letter from Gregory in which she once more rebuffed his offer of employment at the *Dial*. He accepted her decision graciously, but that is perhaps the only gracious moment in the entire letter, which is full of spite, anger, and sadness. He first notes with satisfaction that the *New Republic* is giving away copies of *The Waste Land* with subscriptions, which proves to him that he and Watson "were both lacking in discernment" in their decision to publish the poem. He goes on to grumble that the magazine is not available in Paris bookstores and that he intends to ask "the irritating Samuel Craig" to explain.

"Seldes writes me that Charles Demuth reports himself on his deathbed," he wrote. "He being the only painter in America about whose work I very much care it seems only natural that he should immediately die. Apparently it is really dangerous to be friends with me, as although not yet an old man at least half my friends are already under ground." The Demuth scare was a false alarm. The painter suffered ill health all his life, but he was not to die until 1935. And yes, Thayer had lost several close friends at an early age—Randolph Bourne, Alan Seeger, and Valentine Farrar—but so had many others, thanks to the Great War and the influenza epidemics of the time. Death had been a focus of Thayer's ever since he lost his father. He may even have been unconsciously attracted to those who experienced death in their younger years. Elaine lost both her parents at an early age, and in Louise Bryant, Thayer somehow stirred up emotions regarding the loss of her grandfather as a teenager.

Perpetually on the edge of sanity, and loving the sea as he did, it is not surprising that Thayer should use a maritime metaphor to describe the tenuous human grip on existence and express that, in mortality, there might be some relief from the torture of living: "We live on shoals in sea of death, breakers of death crash about me, calm beyond under the sun, with only the beating of the sea's slow heart."[20]

The letter of complaint went on:

I only wish that he [Watson] could under the influence of some subtle feminine hand be so worked upon as to decide to withdraw from The Dial leaving me to carry the full burden and run things as I damn please. Of course I thought from the first year that I could put the paper on a self-supporting basis within two years if I could have [an] absolutely free hand not so much to do as to forbid doing, that is to say to prevent the publication of such nonsense as in the December number the incestuous rot of Anderson, the silly pseudo verses of Williams, the ridiculous negro imitations of [Rudolf von] Huhn and the slip-slops of [George] Biddle. I also found the Marianne Moore contributions most disappointing. Her bit about that awful Freeman book was really for so intelligent a young woman pretty bad. You know I once thought of her in a certain connection. I guess in this case I thought to the right conclusion.

(One infers that the "certain connection" of which Thayer spoke was the editorship of the *Dial*.)

The December issue about which Thayer was so damning was in fact stellar. It opened with the first part of Thomas Mann's novella *Tristan*, translated into English for the first time by Thayer and Kenneth Burke. Mann himself provided the "German Letter" and T. S. Eliot the "London Letter." The number also included "The Poetry of Drouth," Edmund Wilson's seminal essay on *The Waste Land*, and book reviews by Bertrand Russell and Kenneth Burke. The magazine's art includes photographs of sculptures by Alfeo Faggi and the line drawings of Emanuel Fay.

But Thayer's mood was black. He disliked the direction literature and the *Dial* seemed to be taking. Death and disagreements had shrunk his cadre of true friends. His power at the magazine was waning. Everyone in Vienna, it seemed, had a hand out, eager for his dollars. By the end of the year, the high hopes with which he had recommitted himself to analysis the previous January were sinking. "The analysis goes on much as always," he wrote Gregory. "As did Henry Adams, so here one can in the abstract accept the tenets of evolution without perceiving much advance from the character of Julius Caesar to that of Ulysses S. Grant."[21]

15

TEUTON VERSUS FRANCOPHILE

In the summer of 1923, Thayer was in Paris, his time with Freud having come to an end. Thayer gives no reason for ending his sessions with the "Great Master," although a letter toward the end of his period in Vienna to Alyse Gregory suggests that he himself had set a time limit. "I do wish I might be with you in Europe for part of the summer," he wrote. "When I leave Vienna . . . I shall, after two years forced compression, be chock full of the Great Man. I should think that it might be amusing to you to get reactions when they are still full of spring. I shall, I fear be only dragging myself off to some un-Viennese-as-possible sandbar to get my breath after these two years which have consisted chiefly of disillusionings and grippes [sic]. 'I could a tale unfold!'"[1]

Psychoanalysis is supposed to be about self-discovery and insight, but in it Thayer found mostly the cold finger of disillusionment that had touched so many parts of his life. He records how shocked he was one day to suddenly see Elaine, whom he had all but worshipped, become an ordinary, even banal girl. His expectations at both Harvard and Oxford were knocked down by the quotidian realities of collegiate life. His reverence for Santayana soured. And now, having spent two years with Freud, the man who had supposedly unlocked the secrets of the mind, Thayer found himself full of stories about Freud and his ways but empty-handed as to understanding. We might also note that at this point Thayer's epithet for Freud has slipped down the scale from the "Great Magician" to the "Great Master" to the "Great Man."

Indeed, Thayer may have worsened, especially after an intimidating meeting at his Paris hotel with Barnes, who was furious that Thayer had rebuffed his suggestion that Thomas Craven be given the Dial Award. Cummings and at least one other acquaintance noticed in the summer of 1923 an agitation and unrest in Thayer during his stay in Paris that may well have been caused by the confrontation with Barnes. Cummings had visited a happy Thayer in Vienna earlier that year, and Thayer's letters of the time to Elaine (the two remained on good terms) had shown a rare lightness of spirit. But in Paris that summer, Cummings reported meeting a Thayer much different from either the one who had left America two years before or even the one he had seen in Vienna six months earlier, finding him increasingly paranoid.[2]

Marianne Moore also picked up some gossip about Thayer's behavior in Europe that summer from the novelist Glenway Wescott. She wrote, "He said Scofield Thayer is in wrong everywhere, refused an article by M[ina] Loy on G[ertrude] Stein, was offensively aggressive and insolent when calling on Gertrude Stein and that she 'showed him the door.' . . . [His] high airs and disgruntlement with the present state of affairs was colossal—entertaining . . . us very much."[3]

Thayer himself had been aware for some months of the effect he was having on others, but he put it down to his sardonic and cynical nature. In Vienna, he had earned some notoriety for unpleasantness. "I noticed that Dr. Schnitzler is very guarded with me," he confessed in a note to Alyse Gregory. "I have heard to my amazement that I have acquired the reputation of not always being generous in my remarks about my Viennese hosts. . . . [E]ven in the furthest corners of the earth simple upright people always catch on eventually to our embittered sort. And we have not Randolph's excuse. Unnatural."[4] The glancing reference to Randolph Bourne, whose poor health and disfigured features would have truly warranted bitterness, is a sweet one.

The year 1923 brought Thayer other discomforts. The strain of having run the *Dial* at a loss for more than two years was evidently beginning to tell, not only on Thayer but also on his partner, James Sibley Watson. The two had had a long-simmering disagreement about the ratio of French to German submissions in the *Dial*, with Watson championing the former (his first piece for the *Dial* after taking charge of the magazine was an appreciation of Rimbaud), while Thayer's preference was for German literature, with which he inundated the magazine during his stay in Vienna. "[W]ould it not be possible to publish German things less frequently—to send few things that must go in right away?" a frustrated Watson asked in a letter, pointing out that Thayer had already sent enough "to last 2 years."[5]

The good news at the *Dial* was that Alyse Gregory had finally agreed to become managing editor, taking the place of Seldes. Both Thayer and Watson had long sought the services of Gregory, but she, feeling that she wasn't up to the job, had repeatedly rebuffed their advances. One night soon after Thayer had returned from Europe, however, he and Watson made the pilgrimage to Gregory's apartment in Patchin Place, and after Thayer regaled the other two with a lively chat about the idiosyncrasies of the European writers he had met—Thayer seems to have regained some of his old lightness at this point—the men offered Gregory the editorship and she finally agreed. "The real purpose of the visit was to persuade me to change my mind about taking over the management of The Dial," she wrote. "I did not say I would not consent to so flattering an offer, which was equivalent to saying I would."[6]

Thayer and Watson were also at odds over Ezra Pound. Watson admired the work Pound did for the *Dial*, whereas Thayer roundly loathed both his verse and his prose. "I personally abhor Pound's cantos as I abhor his Paris Letters. My feeling toward Pound is shared by pretty much everybody of intelligence I know. You and Eliot remain notable exceptions. Cummings, to name one out of hundreds, considers Pound mad—'getting more Idaho day by day.'"[7] When Kenneth Burke forwarded to Thayer the most recent cantos of Pound, Thayer responded impatiently: "The Pound Cantos are quite impossible, as I should have thought it would have been obvious without sending them to me. As I had gathered from his recent contributions to the Dial and the Criterion the man is obviously (let us hope not permanently) intellectually gone to pieces."[8]

Apart from *The Cantos*, which he dismissed as "silly,"[9] what Thayer most detested about Ezra Pound was precisely what he is most praised for today—his ceaseless promotion of those he deemed important. Thayer greatly distrusted writers who were adept at public relations, a distrust that led to him faulting those who had the knack of calibrating and satisfying readers' tastes. "M. Twain the Amy Lowell of his generation," he wrote. "He, too, knew how to sell himself to his people."[10] He saw Pound as "the official barker outside the tent—or is it a pagoda?—of imagism et al."[11]

Thayer found profoundly irritating both Pound's need to appear more learned than anyone else and his assumption that the world would be a much better place if people would simply follow his, Pound's, curriculum. "Mr. Pound is all for getting on," Thayer wrote. "Goethe said that Byron when he began to reflect became a child—Mr. P. becomes a school-master and one unduly eager to rush us on to our ninth grade."[12]

Thayer had at first been quite taken with Pound after meeting him during his time in England. He discussed him at length with his friend Valentine Farrar, who died in the Great War. Farrar dismissed Pound's emphasis on "newness" and was suspicious of the suggestiveness of the verse. He wrote Thayer, "Pound seems to be hugging to himself some artificial little mystery of no significance, and teasing people to guess at it."[13] Thayer thought highly of Farrar, and Farrar's dismissal of Pound may have been the beginning of Thayer's disillusionment with the poet, which grew into a positive dislike.

Pound was one of the writers about whom Thayer and Watson always disagreed, and this may have arisen from their respective preferences for German and French literature; Pound was more steeped in the French and Romance traditions and so was more congenial to Watson's taste. Thayer saw irony in Pound's eagerness to dress himself in the culture of the French, since this betrayed the kind of vulgar Americanism from which Pound was trying to flee. "The intense Americanism of E.P. is obvious not only in his grovelling before all things made in Paris; but even more saliently in his worship of the new as such. These men are not interested in beauty, they are connoisseurs in novelty, and . . . as in other notion shops we find some diverting contrivances. Pound is an inventive Yankee, and it is good to have such people tinkering around."[14] We see from this that Thayer came to distrust what he saw as Pound's emphasis on what was merely new (he was suspicious of startling effects, even in poets he admired such as Cummings), but we cannot deny that his distaste for Pound may have been colored both by his annoyance with Pound's aggressive promotional style ("That agitated agitator")[15] and simple snobbery: he sneered at the fact that Pound's father was named Homer and that he was born in Idaho.[16]

After the "Paris Letter" of February 1923, Pound would not appear again in the pages of the *Dial* for five years, until after Thayer had severed his connections with the magazine. Watson would have the last word, though, giving Pound the Dial Award in 1928.

Freud was yet another bone of contention for Thayer and Watson. Thayer had persuaded Freud to submit to the *Dial* an article discussing a seventeenth-century church account of a man selling his soul to the devil. Thayer considered this a "scoop" and was eager to see it in the *Dial*,[17] but Watson and Burke put off translating the piece, making one excuse after another, until Burke finally cabled Thayer saying that it had been rejected. "Watson has just turned down an extremely good article from Freud which I had got after a year and a half's labour," Thayer grumbled to Alyse Gregory. "You can realize how I feel. But I am awaiting some explanation from him. I hope he has a good one. Our relationship is most strained and I may have to return to America immediately, either to keep The Dial afloat or to sink it plumply."[18] He complained also to Burke, saying that he didn't understand why Freud should be rejected for controversy when the magazine had printed Sherwood Anderson's "Many Marriages," which dealt with the themes of sex, rape, and incest. He also pointed out an error in one of Burke's draft translations from German. "I want the Thomas Mann's story title translated Death in Venice, not The Death in Venice," Thayer wrote. "I had not thought it possible that there should be any disagreement as to how this should be translated. Der Tod is understood by every reader to be Death personified."[19]

Thayer traveled a good deal in 1923, going from Vienna to Paris to buy paintings, returning to Vienna, traveling to London for further purchases, and then in August returning finally to the United Sates and to his beloved Edgartown. Much of his time in Europe during this year was dedicated to producing the *Living Art* folio, a labor-intensive endeavor that required him to select and buy the works he needed for reproduction, to send the works on to America before the summer (when he feared a newly implemented law would tax works of art at American rather than European prices), to produce and distribute the folio, and to arrange for an exhibition and reviewing of the collection and the folio in New York City. Thayer quickly found he had taken on too much. "I regret having undertaken the folio as I regret having undertaken The Dial," he wrote his mother. "As The Dial gave me no time to write independently in America, so the folio has given me no time to write independently in Europe."[20]

It was also during the summer of 1923 in Paris that he attended the champagne dinner party on a barge on the River Seine thrown by the wealthy expatriate couple Gerald and Sara Murphy to celebrate the opening of Igor Stravinsky's ballet *Les noces*. Thayer himself describes the "very charming" occasion. "With lanterns and music the picture was pleasing," he wrote. "A great many interesting people were there, some of whom I enjoyed meeting—Picasso; the greatest of living composers, Stravinski; the young French poet Jean Cocteau; Tristan Tzara, the founder of Dadaism; the writer, Cendrars; the Americans, Damrosch, the painter Dougherty, and the Princess de Polignac née Singer Sewing Machine."[21]

Naturally, Thayer placed first in this list of attendees the one he felt was most important: Picasso. He had come to Paris for the express purpose of meeting the great man, and the morning after the gala on the Seine he visited Picasso in his studio. "I found him even more charming than upon the previous evening," he wrote his mother.

> As I presume you know, I admire him more than any other living artist. He had many wonderful things in his studio, but none of them, unfortunately, buyable. At his special representative's [studio] . . . I bought two drawings for the same figure I offered for the same two drawings a year ago, but which offer was not accepted as the German agent had to get a percentage in addition to Rosenberg. I paid $250 for the two. I wanted to buy a large and important canvas and would have been ready to pay ten times that much for such an oil painting. Unfortunately, Rosenberg has only second rate Picassos at present, having sold the last important one to the Museum of Fine Arts in Prague a week before my arrival; a picture my friends tell me I would have appreciated and which it is too bad I missed being able to get.[22]

Like many wealthy collectors, Thayer was taking advantage of the sinking French franc. "I am buying the pictures by the highest priced and the best painters in France for about one quarter of what I would have paid . . . before the war," he wrote.[23]

By mid-August, Thayer was back in Edgartown. He wished to God he'd never come back to the States, he wrote Alyse Gregory, adding that Edgartown was "utterly depressing." He had begun wearing false teeth and was suffering from a gum abscess. "And I have tremendous dreams which command me back to Vienna. I really consider going."[24]

We cannot be sure, however, that the idea of more sessions with Freud was what was attracting him back to Vienna. Thayer had spent some of his free time in Vienna attending dance recitals with his friend the artist Adolf Dehn, whom Thayer had hired to help assemble the Living Art folio. In 1922, Dehn had met and fallen in love with Mura Ziperovitch, an eighteen-year-old dancer with the Ellen Tels troupe (the two would eventually marry), and it may have been through this connection that Thayer met other young Viennese dancers. Thayer struck up a relationship with one of these, the then fifteen-year-old Marietta de Grisogno. She was, one notes, the same age Elaine Orr had been when he first met her. In Marietta's early letters to Thayer, the girl sounds extremely fond of the older man, though at first it is difficult to conclude whether she is being flirtatious or simply trying to sound grown up. In one letter, in German, she expressed concern that a picture of himself that he said he would send her had been lost in the mail. She enclosed a photograph of herself and a friend, saying she wished he were there so that they could play tennis and go hiking. She enclosed an edelweiss she had picked for him on a hike, and she asked if he was angry with her. She yearned for him, she wrote, and burned with desire for a letter. She signed herself "your eternally honest little friend who loves you very very much."[25]

In another letter, she thanked him for sending her money and said she was "unutterably" happy since she could "pursue my career with no worries.[26] She was taking personal dance lessons from Ellen Tels, she wrote, and she begged for a letter from him. Marietta's mother also wrote Thayer around this time, thanking him for the gift of money to Marietta and apologizing for the way her daughter was "bothering" him.

As time went by, Marietta's letters became more forward. At the end of the year, she sent Thayer Christmas greetings and again complained that he didn't write enough. She'd like to write him how much she loves him, she said, but it "wouldn't be proper for a girl of 16." She ended her letter with a New Year's toast for her beloved patron: "!!! Hoch Mister Scofield !!!" (literally, in German, "up with Mr. Scofield").[27] Thayer, who had perhaps entertained the thought of enjoying the girl sexually, allowed himself a moment of vulgarity and scribbled in the margin, "Something for Freud!"[28]

16

BARNES IN ERUPTION

I am never tranquil without a fight at hand.

ALBERT C. BARNES

Many aesthetic battles were fought in the pages of the *Dial* in the 1920s, especially in the first half of that decade, when the magazine became arguably the most influential cultural journal of its time. One of the most bitter and damaging of these conflicts was between Thomas Jewell Craven, the magazine's art critic, and Laurence Buermeyer, philosopher and tutor of the industrial chemist and art collector Albert C. Barnes. The controversy, which eventually flared into physicality (although not between Craven and Buermeyer), demonstrates the passion that was brought to these matters at the time, and the clashes of the various aesthetic philosophies that struggled for the upper hand in the early days of modernism. And even though Craven and Buermeyer each may have firmly believed in his own position, they were in fact fighting a kind of proxy war for their respective employers, Barnes and Thayer. The end result was a victory of sorts for Barnes. The consequences for Thayer, who was growing more mentally unstable during this period, were dire. Barnes would eventually become the bête noir of Thayer's paranoid vision of the world. "It appeared that Dr. Barnes was at war with *The Dial*," wrote the art critic Henry McBride. "Threatening death and destruction to the magazine and ready to use any means to accomplish his ends, and as a matter of fact, it is to the strain of this conflict . . . that I have always attributed the nervous collapse of Scofield Thayer which followed shortly after and brought on in its turn the death of *The Dial*."[1]

Barnes and Thayer had some things in common—they were both rich men who loved art, especially the more contemporary work coming out of Europe, and both feverishly amassed great collections of art. The two were also drawn to the growing field of psychology, and both greatly admired the philosophical writings of George Santayana and Bertrand Russell. But there the similarities ended. Thayer had inherited his fortune, while Barnes was a self-made power-house of a man from Philadelphia whose fortune came from the product he helped create and aggressively promote, Argyrol, a silver-based compound used to treat infections. Thayer was raised as an American aristocrat, while the iras-cible and pugnacious Barnes came from a working-class background. Thayer disliked physicality; Barnes was a former boxer who was not above responding to disagreements with brutality, threats, and blackmail.

Barnes's first and only piece of art criticism in the *Dial* was an appreciation of Renoir published in the February 1920 issue. In that article, he argued for a "psychology of aesthetics" through which the great artist could enrich human experience

> by recalling memories and feelings originally associated with perceptions sometimes so nearly forgotten as to have left only the cumulative residue, the "hushed reverberations" which we know as "forms"; and these "forms" necessarily constitute the totals and essence of experience, education and culture. For that reason, art is practical, never exotic, in that it deals with ideas that have served some purpose in human life.

The quotation demonstrates Barnes's approach to art, a neo-Platonic romanti-cism couched in the pragmatic-sounding language of scientific thought. Barnes received a check for the article, which he returned to the magazine to be used "to better advantage."[2]

Thomas Jewell Craven was one of the regular art critics at the *Dial*. Barnes generally admired Craven's writings but told him that he needed "contact-experience with good paintings."[3] When Craven responded that he was unable to afford study in Europe, Barnes invited him to Merion to view his large and growing collection. Craven visited Barnes several times in Pennsylvania, and their relationship evidently deepened. In March 1923, Barnes was still pushing Craven to complete his education by visiting Europe. "There is something in Paris quite different and very much more real, honest, genuine, than the so-phistications and bunk that reach us here through the ignorant ventriloquist [John] Quinn, the fat-headed literary street-walking of Clive Bell and the supe-riorities of that arch-Adlerian Ezra Pound," he wrote. "We've had it so long and it has been so accepted without analysis that it permeates the whole spirit of modernism and stifles the positive creative talent we have plentifully in America."[4] He also began campaigning to have Craven given the annual Dial Award, which was both prestigious (the award had previously gone to Sherwood Anderson and T. S. Eliot) and, with a cash gift of two thousand dollars, extremely generous.

Barnes's intentions in putting Craven forward for the award aren't easy to fathom. He may, of course, have been selflessly trying to advance the career of a talented young man, but the history of Barnes as a shrewd and ruthless strategic thinker suggests otherwise. Barnes was also at the time trying to persuade Craven to write a book on art that would be funded by the Barnes Foundation, which he had established in 1922 to "promote the advancement of education and the appreciation of the fine arts." Naturally, Craven's being awarded the Dial prize would not only give the project both cachet and publicity but also further Barnes's own beliefs regarding art. Whatever Barnes's motivation, Craven was thrilled at the idea of receiving the prize. "Needless to say, your proposition excited me considerably," Craven wrote. "I have, in one or two moments of extreme optimism, visualized the Dial prize; but have quickly dismissed the idea: my relations with the magazine have been most amicable—I have never had a single piece of work rejected and have been able to get work whenever I wanted it, but I have always fancied that I am not 'modern' enough to qualify for the annual award."[5] Craven's last remark is of interest. Craven saw in much contemporary art what to him was a dismaying emphasis of materials over meaning, of technique over substance.

Barnes's support for Craven was not without caveat. As mentioned, he thought Craven needed firsthand experience with the art of Europe and its creators and critics, and Craven's dismissive remarks on both Renoir and impressionism no doubt irritated him. Further, he regarded Craven as lacking in knowledge of psychology, which Barnes believed to be an important tool for the critic. However, he also viewed Craven as the best art critic writing in America, and he knew that the *Dial* had unusually strong influence with the critics and tastemakers of the time. Barnes would have to get his ideas out via the *Dial* at least for the near future. He would eventually found his own magazine, he said, adding darkly that he would then deal with Thayer. "I'll attend to him when the Foundation gets its journal going," he wrote.[6]

Barnes's modus operandi for tackling those who stood in his way was generally the frontal attack. He even explained his tactics in a letter to Thayer at a time (one of the few) when the two were on reasonably good terms. He spoke of a contemporary art exhibit he had mounted in Philadelphia and which had been criticized by the press as being offensive and degenerate.

> I selected the most important of the papers for retaliation and broadcasted a letter, which I signed, asking the public to judge the paintings on their merits, not on the ignorant abuse of a yellow journal. Three days later, the newspaper made a second abusive attack in an editorial. The next day I mailed a second letter asking the public if Philadelphia would stand for the inhospitality of vituperation of their spiritual guests by a newspaper with a known record as a protector of criminal vice. The newspaper made no reply so, a few days later, I mailed a third letter . . . [saying that] artists recognized everywhere else as honest and capable were viciously maligned by a Philadelphia newspaper whose personnel were made up of sexual perverts, clandestine fornicators and illegal traffickers in booze. I sent the letter to clubs, judges, prohibition officers, vice-crusaders, high police officials, district attorney's office etc. I expected to be arrested but not a step was taken by the newspaper. For weeks the city had one of the worst and most talked about scandals in its history with the curious anomaly that not even a hint of it appeared in any of the newspapers. But the exhibition was crowded every day and artists whose names had never been known here—Picasso, Matisse, Modigliani, Soutine etc.—were talked about by people of all ranks. I felt pretty good because we not only put over the show to the public but I think we paved the way for a more circumspect treatment of future modern shows by the newspaper.[7]

This letter really is a startling confession as to the lengths to which Barnes was willing to go in what he believed was the service of art. One notes first his patience, the fact that he did not attack the newspaper and its staff until the second blow had been struck at his beloved exhibit, and then the escalating and unrelenting ferocity of his attacks as he senses that the other side is not prepared or willing to defend itself.

Barnes was so eager to have Craven receive the Dial Award that he offered to pay the two thousand dollars himself if Craven were chosen. Thayer and Watson mulled over this very tempting idea; they agreed with Barnes that Craven deserved recognition, and it was no doubt attractive to think of Barnes footing this particular bill since the magazine was losing money heavily. But they balked at allowing Barnes or anyone else to choose the recipient of the award. Watson also considered the option of giving Craven a special award from an "anonymous giver for the best 'artistic criticism' by an American" and other "honour-saving subterfuges,"[8] but in the end he and Watson decided to reject Barnes's proposal and his money. This would turn out to be a mistake; Barnes wasn't accustomed to being rebuffed.

Barnes and Thayer were both in Paris in the summer of 1923. Thayer had made the journey from Vienna to work with Gilbert Seldes on the *Living Art* folio, and Barnes was in Paris visiting his dealers and artists' studios. What exactly happened between the two men on July 3 in Thayer's room at the Claridge Hotel is not fully known. We do know that voices were raised and insults flung, and that Barnes finally stormed out. It seems that Barnes had wanted to tell Thayer face to face what he felt was wrong with the art criticism in the *Dial* and that Thayer had given Barnes short shrift and spoken down to him. In any event, Barnes was infuriated and wrote Thayer, warning him not to consider the interview a victory "if you wish to keep your professional skin" and threatening to publish "before competent judges of the basic principles involved." He concluded, "I'll be in Paris long enough for you to try to finish what you started."[9]

Barnes then wrote to Craven, saying, "Thayer is a lolly-pop—soft, gummy, unreal and absurdly pretentious. I hope Thayer answers my letter because I've got something to say to him that I can't very well spit out unless he gives me a pretext."[10]

Barnes was hoping that his letter to Thayer was provocative enough to cause Thayer to speak incautiously, so allowing Barnes to escalate the matter even further. But Thayer's response of July 5 was curt and evasive: "Dear Mr. Barnes, Your letter of July 2nd, the occasion of which and the intention of which I do not understand, was duly received."[11] This was not quite enough to give Barnes the "pretext" he needed to "spit out" what he had to say. But that would come soon enough.

Craven was not writing regularly for the *Dial* at this point. Henry McBride, for whom Barnes and Craven had scant respect, was the regular writer of the "Modern Art" segment. However, Craven had produced for the journal an ambitious two-part article entitled "The Progress of Painting" that comprised a somewhat hurried history of art along with a careful measuring of the modern schools, including impressionism, expressionism, cubism, and futurism. At the heart of his argument was that "form" was the sine qua non of art and that modernism was not so much a revolution as a readjustment, an attempt to return to art the form that the impressionists had all but destroyed. Only Cézanne, he argued, saw the wrong path art had taken and brought it back on track when he "awakened the modern mind to the significance of the past, to a conception of real form, solid, thick, material, and plastic."[12] The article's swipes at impressionism must have been galling to Barnes.

Curiously, and despite the events in the Paris hotel, upon returning to the United States, Barnes and Thayer resumed a more or less civil correspondence. In August, Barnes wrote that he had at hand two paintings of Thayer's (a Picasso and a Pascin) to whose "formalities of importation" to the United States he had agreed to attend.[13] That same month, he offered Thayer photographs of the works in his collection for publication in the *Dial*, and he later received from Thayer a handwritten note of thanks.

At around the same time, Barnes's protégé Craven was beginning to go rogue, pointing out in a letter to Barnes that he had agreed to write a book on art for the foundation only on the condition that he write free from any influence. Barnes finally withdrew his offer to publish the book and complained about Craven in a letter to Thayer, at the end of which he became almost conciliatory: "I've been writing you a devil of a lot of late but it's probably because that in spite of the present apparent different view-points, I really believe that our ideals are pretty close in fundamentals."[14] The lovefest would not last.

Despairing of using Craven to get his ideas into the *Dial*, Barnes turned to his old friend and tutor Laurence Buermeyer, who was by this time employed by the Barnes Foundation. Buermeyer wrote a response to Craven's "Progress of Painting" article entitled "Some Popular Fallacies in Aesthetics" and submitted it to the *Dial*. Thayer wrote back to Barnes, saying that the article "together with Craven's reply," would appear in the February 1924 issue.[15] No deal, said Barnes; Thayer must first submit to Buermeyer a copy of what Craven was planning to say or return Buermeyer's manuscript. Thayer wrote to Buermeyer refusing to do so, and this was all Barnes needed to "spit out" what he had threatened after the interview with Thayer in the Paris hotel. He wrote back to Thayer:

> I have just read your letter of November 29th to Buermeyer and I don't like the two-barreled intimation that he is not telling the truth. I got him into the trouble and I'll get him out—so be careful what you say to him, for in the present situation he is I. If you again intimate that he is a liar or otherwise not clean, I am very likely to get stirred up sufficiently to tell you why (and quote from Havelock Ellis's Psychology of Sex) I think you're a pervert—and illustrate the story with photographs. Then throw in for good measure the current rumors why you're a grass-widower, put in good readable shape the known Vienna events, a copy of the letter I wrote you in Paris, how I embarrassed your valet, the positive legal proof

that you're such a boob in your own field of journalism that you buy para-
phrases from the Bible, and reprints from standard authors and then sell
such counterfeits to the public as original contributions. After that, I'll
likely go to New York to rough-house you.[16]

What kind of a "pervert" Barnes means, we don't know. We do know that
Thayer had something of a reputation as a homosexual—Hemingway famously
called him "Scofield Buggaring Thayer." However, it should be remembered that
Hemingway was as fond of calling men he didn't like homosexual as he was
of referring to women who offended him as frigid old virgins. There is some
evidence in Thayer's papers of his being bisexual, but the vast majority of his
writings on sex supports the conclusion that he was mostly heterosexual. The
"grass-widower" comment no doubt refers to the fact that Thayer had separated from his wife, Elaine, soon after they returned from their honeymoon in
California. The "known Vienna events" possibly refer to some kind of embarrassment suffered by Thayer during his time in that city, or it may simply be
a case of Barnes tossing various charges at Thayer in the hope that some will
stick. Then again, undergoing psychoanalysis carried a stigma in some quarters,
and Barnes may be referring to Thayer's sessions with Freud. The case for there
having been a Viennese scandal is buttressed by Thayer himself the following
year in a letter to Watson from Martha's Vineyard: "Hildegarde . . . last night
informed a quartet who were at the moment camping about me: 'He likes 'em
young,' . . . [f]rom which we perceive the perfection of the radiographic communication just now installed between the ancient capital of the Hapsburgs and
this quaint village of the Reverend Mayhews."[17]

The standoff between the two men continued until Thayer finally blinked and
agreed to publish Craven's reply to Buermeyer in a later issue of the magazine.

If at this point Thayer breathed a sigh of relief that the matter was finally over,
one could not have blamed him. But the relief would be short-lived. In March
1924, the *Dial* published Craven's response to Buermeyer's article. There were
many things about it that no doubt infuriated Barnes, not the least that this was
a magnificent and well-received issue of the journal. It included the first English
translation of Thomas Mann's *Death in Venice*; reproductions of pictures by
John Marin, Maurice de Vlaminck, and Jack Yeats; book reviews by Bertrand
Russell and Edmund Wilson; a philosophical dialogue by George Santayana;
an essay on comedy by Herbert Read; and a line drawing of Charlie Chaplin by
Cummings. Such company would have given anything more gravitas merely
by association. Barnes's ire may also have been stoked by Craven's article being

inflammatorily entitled "Psychology and Common Sense," or by the dismissive tone of its opening sentence: "The mild, academic carping of Mr Laurence Buermeyer is not the first cry of distress provoked by my writings."[18]

Craven rejected the charges of exclusivity, defended his careful weighing of the merits of the moderns, and reasserted his belief that an art critic should not have to "accept every eccentricity parading under the banners of the new movement." He categorized Buermeyer as "an excellent general psychologist" but one who "takes his modernism without reserve." He restated his view that form was the soul of art as opposed to such things as color, tone, and "a decorative line." He returned to the matter of Renoir, granting that Renoir was undoubtedly important as an artist but chiding him for his effect on younger generations of artists who aped his superficial methods and led art away from its true path. He once more rejected the impressionists with "their glamourous formula, sunlight and stupidity" and ended by describing himself on the side of the artists. Buermeyer, he said, "approaches art in the conventional attitude of the dealer and the curator."[19]

Barnes once more erupted, and again it was Thayer who received the full force of his fury. "I believe that in publishing an article such as Mr. Craven's you are merely coming back at me—as far as your vicarious courage will let you—for my letter of December 3rd expressing my willingness to tell you why I think you are a pervert, that rumor makes you a cuckold, that your yellow streak is indelible, that you are a welsher," he wrote. He retracted his former apology.[20] Thayer stopped responding to Barnes at this point and had managing editor Alyse Gregory and his secretary write in response, but this served only to anger Barnes the more. He addressed his letter charging Thayer with sexual perversion to the magazine staff in general and dared Thayer to sue him.

Barnes kept up the pressure, writing a second time to the staff of the *Dial* and even making a veiled threat of death. "Your habit of neglecting or ignoring conditions and refusing reasonable and legal demands is likely to precipitate—oh, almost anything!—at critical moments," he wrote. "A mere prince—said to have been a fruit—sent to heaven in 1914, increased our income taxes and put the French in the Ruhr."[21] One assumes Barnes is referring here to the assassination of Archduke Ferdinand and to the Great War.

Finally, Alyse Gregory wrote to Barnes that the *Dial* would publish a further reply by Buermeyer "as a communication."[22] Barnes asked whether this would be the last word on the matter, and Gregory replied that it would.

Buermeyer's "communication" (there was some face-saving for the *Dial* in that the piece was printed as a letter rather than an article) appeared in the April 1924 issue. Buermeyer reasserted that Craven's art criticism was greatly derivative of Fry's and charged Craven with distorting his, Buermeyer's, arguments. The matter of "form" and its definition, which was at the heart of the original argument, here receives only a single paragraph, and in it Buermeyer points out that Craven's definition is so similar to Fry's that both deserve to be targets of the same criticism.

Barnes was content with this and said so in a letter to Thayer full of his usual rationalization and triumphalism. "I am satisfied with that publication as your public statement for having participated in dirty fighting," he wrote. "I am satisfied with the technique operative in performing the public duty forecasted in the letter of December 3rd, 1923, wherein I wrote to your editor:—'You give Buermeyer a square deal or you will answer to me in the way I elect.'" He concluded, "I hope that in future we can live in the same world without either of us transgressing the rule generally accepted as sound for decent living."[23]

This seems to have been the last communication between the two men. However, each remained much on the other's mind. When, in the summer of 1924, Thayer had a run-in with Leo Stein, brother of Gertrude and an art collector and critic in his own right, over reporting in the magazine what had been a private conversation, Barnes immediately wrote Stein to offer his help. Barnes offered his most threatening letter to Thayer for Stein's use, continuing eagerly:

> Another method would be for you to demand an apology or you will attend to him physically with a horsewhip. I'll stand by and prevent outside interference. Another method (I have done this with good results) is to invade his office, break a window or smash a chair and thus get yourself in the hands of the police. Sympathetic friends provide bail and arrange for newspaper reporters at the hearing. After that, publicity is only a question of skill.[24]

During the course of their correspondence, Barnes related to Leo Stein a couple of damaging anecdotes about Thayer.

> Last summer, I saw Thayer buy a painting by Picasso showing Picasso himself having his cock sucked by a woman. Aside from the fact that it is a good likeness of Picasso, the picture is only pornographic, not art. Thayer has a collection of dirty pictures devoid of art value. He has a vicarious orgasm when he shows them, by dramatic candlelight, to the elect of his circle. I leave it to any psychologist, regardless of school, whether that

constitutes exhibitionism and whether his attack on you is or is not, basically, sadistic, a pretty uniform factor in the syndrome.

One day last summer, Paul, Jack and I were looking at a Matisse which I had bought, when Picasso came in. He started to knock the Matisse and I told him that Thayer who likes his (Picasso's) work had admired the same Matisse the day before. Picasso replied:—"Thayer—I would like to piss on him." It seems that the sad fate of poor Thayer has ever been to be the victim of unrequited affection, like the eternal cuckold.[25]

Stein eventually declined Barnes's assistance, preferring to simply let the matter drop, and saying as much in a letter to Thayer. Thayer wrote Gregory: "You will be glad to hear that Stein has written me from Florence . . . 'amiably,' calling me 'absurd,' etcetera, etcetera, etcetera, but, thank God, saying he is through. I had feared he might become an incubus. Let us hope Doctor Barnes will not hear the voice of Duty commanding him to assume the rôle of Ersatz-Incubus."[26]

Of course, the tormenting incubus of Barnes had already taken up residence in Thayer's mind and would be part of the hallucinatory menagerie of terrors that would eventually bring Thayer to insanity.

17

FEUDS GALORE

M.D. somewhat the quality of a small, white palfrey.

SCOFIELD THAYER

Marietta de Grosogno's letters continued into the new year of 1924. In February, she thanked Thayer for the "unfortunately short letter" she had received from him and talked about the books she was reading: *Memoirs of an Idealist* by Malwida von Meysenberg and *Memoirs of a Socialist Woman* by Lily Braun. She said she was ashamed to admit they were the "first serious books" she had ever read. She was learning to type and did her dance exercises one to two hours per day. The girl was still very eager to see Thayer again, and she said she was "almost frightened" by his saying that he hoped to see her in a few years in America, because that suggested he didn't plan to return to Vienna soon. Does he not *want* to, she asked, or is he not *able* to? The time they spent together was "like a beautiful, bright, pure dream," she said, one that gave her no peace. His letters to her were too short, she repeated; nor did she find in them what she was seeking. She closed with, "Is it so hard to write a few friendly words to a little Viennese girl who's thirsting for them?"[1]

This "little Viennese girl" was evidently struck by Thayer and was eager to be part of his world, perhaps with dreams of a more intimate friendship. The two would stay in touch for several years, though we don't know if they met again or whether there was any kind of physical relationship between them. She was obviously important to Thayer in some way. He had always been attracted to young girls—the woman who became his wife was only fifteen when they met, and his correspondence and personal notes contain many references to pubescent girls.

Toward the end of his public life, Thayer certainly did show an interest in girls that most people at the time would have regarded as inappropriately young. Later that year, when a group of young campers pitched their tents close to his Martha's Vineyard home, they were warned by Hildegarde Watson about Thayer's proclivities. "He likes 'em young," she said.[2] (This was evidently a reference to an incident that took place in Vienna, perhaps the one to which Barnes referred in his threatening letter to Thayer.) From his personal notes, we know that Thayer was not attracted to mature women. He once wrote: "All women over thirty should wear mourning. For their youth. There should be a law."[3] Physical weakness was exciting to him: "I like girls with arms as thin as sulphur matches; arms that can be broken between forefinger and thumb."[4]

Thayer finally wrote back to Marietta in August. It was a longish, chatty letter that focused on his travels and his ailments and discomforts (he had stomach troubles at the time, and the noise level in New York was becoming more than he could bear). He spoke of their being together again the following year: "It is possible I may get to see you in Vienna in the spring; on the other hand I may be detained by business in France and Germany until the autumn, when at the latest I hope ardently to be with you again. I should hope to remain in Vienna through the following winter."[5]

Otherwise, as far as Thayer was concerned, Marietta seemed very much out of sight, out of mind. And indeed, there was a great deal else going on in his life. Alyse Gregory took on the role of managing editor from Gilbert Seldes in February 1924, a passing of the editorial mantle that was noted by Ernest Hemingway: "Seldes, his sphincter muscle no doubt having lost its attractive tautness, has left The Dial," he wrote Pound. "An aged virgin has taken his place."[6] Hemingway's poems and short stories were famously rejected by the magazine.

Thayer, eager to show art lovers the work being done by contemporary artists, arranged an exhibition of his paintings at various galleries, including the Worcester Art Museum, and was greatly irritated when the museum asked him to withdraw two works to which it was felt that the more conservative museumgoers might object. Also in 1924, the *Living Art* folio finally came out, and the *Sunday Times* carried what was generally a very favorable review. Thayer must have disliked the half-apologetic opening of the article, however: "The public is like the Frenchman who was glad he disliked spinach, because if he liked it he'd eat it, and he hated it. The public delights in hating modern art, otherwise it would have to look at it. To make the public look at it is the aim of its friends."[7] Still, the author of the review saw the folio largely as a success, despite her opinion that some of the color reproductions missed the mark and that the realism of photography had an "afflicting property" on the sculptures.

Thayer, of course, ferreted out the two errors in the review:

> My dear Miss Cary, I am sure you will be anxious to correct in your columns a slight mistake in your kind words upon the Dial folio in the Sunday Times. You call attention to what you find to be a misspelling of the English word "morn." Why . . . should a proofreader have balked at the spelling of so simple a word as "morn"? The word in question—Morin—is correctly spelt. The [M]orin is a river in France. Would you further be so very good as to correct the error in the spelling of my name? No doubt this is merely the oversight of the proofreader.[8] [His first name had been given in the article as "Schofield," a common enough mistake, and one that never failed to nettle him.]

The "Comment" in the March issue of the *Dial* carried Thayer's response to the errors and to what he saw as wrong-headedness in the review. He concluded: "THE DIAL is taking up a modest collection for the benefit of The New York Times. It is our desire to enable this ambitious contemporary to purchase an atlas of France."[9]

Indeed, 1924 was a year of feuds for Thayer and the *Dial*. The two biggest, of course, were, first, the proxy war fought by the magazine's art critic, Thomas Craven, against Albert C. Barnes's stand-in, Lawrence Buermeyer, regarding artistic aesthetics; and, second, his argument with his hometown newspaper over Johansen's remarks about the *Dial* being an "intellectual sewer." The combative Thayer also had several other set-tos that year. One was with J. Middleton Murry, editor of the *Adelphi*, a British magazine. Murry had published in the *Yale Review* of January a criticism of Cummings. Murry was of the mind that Cummings was a literary fraud whose style masked the banality of his verses. He was particularly incensed by Cummings's use of the small *i* for the first person singular pronoun, which he explained by speaking as he thought Cummings would: "i use i because i do not wish to insist upon my personality. In this poem i am not I. i am merely a sentience."[10]

Thayer dismissed this strategy as the "journalistic dodge" of forcing an adversary to take an obviously untenable position. He explained that Cummings, in creating his own style, had "commandeered and impressed into his poetic service typography itself." He went on:

He [Cummings] employs punctuation, capitalization, and spacing (both between words and between lines) with more freedom than have other poets. He regards them merely as means to the expression of his aesthetic fact. He ignores the limitations of accepted literary usage developed largely for the purpose of lucid, logical reasoning, a purpose which, rightly or wrongly, he does not acknowledge as pertinent to art. He therefore employs capitals, ignoring English usage, only for emphasis. As in all other languages than English, so in the idiom of Mr. E. E. Cummings, the first person singular does not, in itself, require a capital.[11]

Murry, according to Thayer, was a "genus critic, species billiard-ball, [who] caroms about between his rectangular limitations very smoothly."[12] More importantly, Thayer's remarks are one of the first attempts, if not the first, to describe the idioprosody that Cummings was at the time creating.

The other spat was with the art critic Leo Stein. In the April 1924 issue of the *New Republic*, Stein had written of Picasso: "His intellectual baggage is of the slightest, and the total output of intellect in his work is negligible. Picasso is thoroughly intelligent in the ordinary human way, and is ingenious to the last turn, but he is in no serious sense a thinker."[13]

Thayer may have been reminded of, and was perhaps emulating in his response, Ezra Pound's annoyance after being mentioned in the *Dial* of November 1919 as "too clever to be a poet." Pound had responded in an open letter to the *New Age*: "Sir,—The identification of poetic genius with stupidity in the cutting . . . which you have so kindly sent me, will surprise no one who considers the source of the statement or the place where it appears."[14] (Watson also wrote the *New Age* to explain that the remark was ironical. Pound was somewhat mollified.) Whatever his motive, Thayer leapt with glee onto Stein's remark. "We are all sorry to observe the announcement of Leo Stein's insanity in the current issue of the New Republic," he wrote to his friend Demuth.[15] In his June "Comment" in the *Dial*, he recalled Stein telling him an anecdote about Renoir using a book of essays by an art critic to prop up the model stand in his studio, and concluded from this that the artist was "in no serious sense a thinker." He went on to suggest that Stein might have a successful career in America producing advertising copy.

An irked Stein responded by letter, saying he had never told such a story and that he didn't even remember having met Thayer. Thayer published this letter, along with his own reply, in the August issue of the *Dial*, giving details of the two men meeting at the Yale Club in New York City. He also, in his most irritatingly gassy prose style, repeated his dismay at Stein's dismissal of Picasso's intellect, when Thayer regarded him as "the chief ornament of our time."[16] He concluded by reading into Stein's penciled-in additions to his typewritten letter some kind of psychological "blocking." He had his lawyer check the letter for libel before publishing it.

The feud extended into the October issue, when Thayer printed a second letter from Stein in which Stein noted that he and Picasso had been close friends for ten years, which gave him, he felt, the right to discuss the painter's intellect. Stein also dismissed Thayer's "heavily-creaking irony" and his ful-some prose ("What a lot of words you use to say so very little!"). He concluded by saying that whether his statement would be the last word in the matter "rests, obviously, with you."[17]

Thayer of course had a rejoinder, at seven-and-a-half pages the longest "Comment" ever published in the *Dial* and more than twice as long as the letter that provoked it. Thayer was obviously greatly enjoying the give-and-take of the aesthetic kerfuffles he was bringing to the magazine's "Comment" section and no doubt thought that controversy wouldn't hurt the journal's circulation. His main point was that an artist's ignoring the writing of critics was no measure of his or her intellect and that painting was in and of itself an intellectual pursuit. He defended his praise of Picasso and charged Stein not only with missing the significance of the artist but also with using his position and intellect to mini-mize Picasso's importance and diminish his recognition.

The predatory Barnes had been watching this episode unfold with great in-terest. He wrote to Stein, expressing his outrage at Thayer's having published what was obviously meant to be personal correspondence from Stein and ea-gerly offering to help Stein in any way he could.[18]

Barnes helpfully sent a copy of this letter to Thayer and to the staff at the *Dial*. "Barnes is again in eruption, if possible even more virulently than before," Thayer glumly wrote Cummings from Edgartown. "He is putting the whole Barnes Foundation at the disposal of his friend 'Leo,' and they are going to 'get' me. Being a signally honorable man, Barnes honored me with a copy of his letter to 'Leo.' I am seeing a lawyer, but presume I can or should do nothing anyhow at present."[19]

This fresh "eruption" of the volcanic Barnes agitated Thayer greatly, stirring up both his incipient paranoia and various health complaints. That summer he had the well water tested at his home in Edgartown and was convinced that he had contracted typhoid.[20] He complained of "singing" and "shooting pains" in his ears.[21] Later in the year, Thayer's secretary Eleanor Parker, who was staying with him in Edgartown, wrote this mysterious note to Alyse Gregory:

Mr. Thayer wishes me to tell you that he thinks he has now discovered what has been the matter with him, and has therefore started upon a self-administered cure. As a result he feels so weak that he remains lying down most of the time and is not dictating letters, although he can read your letter and Dial communications of every kind when he sits up for an hour or two during the evening.[22]

It was around this time that Thayer spoke to Watson of an "ailment in my own person which I have been pursuing with such singular unsuccess from Worcester to Vienna for upwards of twenty years and from which I have been suffering and maimed since my fourth year."[23] To which of his many physical difficulties Thayer refers here we don't know. He was treated at various times for colitis, indigestion, back problems, foot problems, vision difficulties, and pain and hypersensitivity in the ears. Since he was a Freudian, the ailment and the maiming of which he speaks may well have been psychological, though the weakness brought about by his "self-administered cure" suggests the physical.

In 1924, Thayer had also, on Freud's advice, persuaded Cummings of the rightness of Cummings and Elaine Orr getting married,[24] and he set about persuading Orr of the same.[25] His efforts were successful, and the two were married by Cummings's father in the family's Cambridge home in March. Nancy, then four years old, was left with her nurse in New York, and the couple spent the night at the Fairmont Copley Plaza Hotel in Boston. The marriage was apparently consummated but only once that night. Cummings wrote, "I can't get erection a 2nd time/lack of pash-ness."[26] The fact that the true parentage of Nancy had been hidden from Thayer's family for so long must have weighed heavily on Elaine's mind, because just two days after the wedding ceremony she wrote to Florence Thayer, "It hurts me to tell you now that Nancy is not your grandchild."[27] Cummings also tried to explain the unusual three-part relationship to his family, writing to his mother, "Incidentally, you may be sure that, so far as Thayer is concerned, there was never the slightest deceit involved, & that we three (Elaine, Thayer, & myself) are now & have always been the best of friends."[28] In April, Thayer agreed wholeheartedly to have Cummings adopt Nancy and paid for the adoption process. Why the couple's being married mattered to Thayer, considering his strongly antimarriage views, is a puzzle, and one can only surmise that he saw this as a regularizing of Nancy's parentage that might avoid future complications. This was possibly also the reason that Elaine herself agreed to the marriage because just three months after the ceremony she told Cummings she had met somebody else and wanted a divorce.

Cummings was dashed. He bought a gun from Watson, considered killing himself, Elaine, and Elaine's new love, Frank MacDermot, and wrote obsessively about the marriage and its failure.

Staff changes at the *Dial* included the hiring of Alyse Gregory as managing editor in place of Seldes. Gregory and Thayer had been close friends since they had been introduced to each other by Randolph Bourne. They later discovered that they had met as children at the home of Gregory's uncle, who had been a Harvard classmate of Thayer's father.[29] Gregory was five years older than Thayer, attractive despite her somewhat plain style of dress. Both Thayer and Watson were attracted to her. She was a woman of sharp intellect, passionately interested in the literature of the time, but with little self-confidence. She was probably Thayer's closest friend—he is atypically unguarded and vulnerable in his letters to her—and she shared his bouts of social nervousness and psychic uncertainty. "Today I called on Miss Gregory," Malcolm Cowley wrote to Kenneth Burke soon after she took over editorship of the *Dial*. "She has the air of always being embarrassed, or was it assumed for the occasion?"[30]

In her memoir, *The Day Is Gone*, Gregory fondly recalled this period:

> The offices of *The Dial* magazine and *The Dial* Publishing Company occupied the whole of a large, old-fashioned, three-story house in a downtown residential section of the city, once fashionable, but now left to retiring old ladies, peering from behind dusty lace curtains onto the street below no longer populous as in their youth. The word *office* is hardly, however, a suitable one to describe the spacious square, homely rooms, with their casual collection of shabby furniture—selected, apparently, as little for display as for efficiency. They had something of old New York about them, its serenity and its leisured dignity.[31]

The top floor of the building, she recalled, was a dining room where the magazine staff and contributors met to dine and mingle with visiting authors and artists. Thayer's Japanese servant, Oni, cooked and served. "Dr. Watson was apt to be absent on these occasions, and Scofield would preside at the head of the table, communicating by his air of frozen civility a feeling of constraint. When I remonstrated with him once, saying that I feared he had been bored, 'Not bored, in torture,' was his reply."[32]

The contrasting sides of Thayer mentioned here by Gregory—in her apartment a chatty raconteur, at the Dial dinners an aloof and unnerving host—shows the mercurial complexity of the man over whom Gregory pondered so much.

Gregory was "intensely anxious" to do well at the magazine and was equally determined to treat contributors with respect and courtesy. As a writer, she had herself received many rejection slips, and her empathetic personality made her acutely aware of the damage a harsh rebuff could inflict.

Of her time at the magazine, Gregory recalled in particular Thayer's attention to detail, how he once waited for a cable from Germany concerning a single comma, and how a small, last-minute change to a piece by W. B. Yeats caused Thayer to destroy an entire run that was ready to go to the newsstands and print the issue anew.[33]

The most painful part of the month for any editor of the *Dial* was the postmortem held after the publication of each issue, when Thayer came to the meeting with a meticulous list of errors, each of which would be "remorselessly tracked" to its instigator. "These were painful occasions, redeemed by the presence of Dr. Watson, whose quick and indulgent understanding offered balm to all," Gregory wrote.[34]

Alyse Gregory by this time was in a romantic relationship with Llewelyn Powys, a member of the famous literary Powys family. Powys suffered from tuberculosis, and Gregory was in a constant state of anxiety about his health. Her letters are full of talk regarding Powys's temperature, his strength, his appetite, and his weight. At this time, fresh air was considered a necessity in the treatment of the disease, and Powys and Gregory often slept outside in all but the coldest months of the year. In the spring of 1924, Watson was planning a trip west to hunt in the Rocky Mountains, and he invited Powys along. Gregory feared the exertion of such a trip on Powys's frame, but Powys himself, a great lover of nature who had, despite his disability, a truly adventurous spirit, jumped at the chance.

Watson, a taciturn and modest man, has left very little of himself in the records of the period. Much of what we know of him comes through Thayer, who was perpetually amused by Watson's reluctance to reveal his emotions. Once, when told by Gregory that Watson was "very enthusiastic" over some drawings, Thayer remarked drily, "I wonder did he dance the sailor's hornpipe."[35] It's interesting, therefore, to read what Powys had to say about Watson:

> He was enormously rich, yet liked to appear poor. He was extremely wise, yet preferred to be thought foolish. With a small black bag, held in the long sensitive fingers of an artist, he was to be encountered on a perpetual peregrination through the side-streets of Greenwich Village. He made one think of the silent, evasive eels one hears about, eels that find their way to the ocean from remote ponds, sliding their sinuous bodies through

night-dusky, dew-drenched pastures. He possessed a subtle, cynical mind, which he did all in his power to conceal. He was an extremely able doctor, who never practiced, and an extremely clever writer, who never wrote.[36]

Powys's impressions of Thayer and Watson together give us a sense of how truly odd this couple was.

It would have required a Henry James to tabulate and record each interesting tarot card of this astounding association. And yet these two millionaires, in the face of the crass stupidity of the Philistine world, in the face of the sneering hostility of a score of pseudo-literary cliques, had managed to produce in America a journal which, without any doubt, is the most distinguished of its kind to appear in the English language since the publication of the *Yellow Book*. But how quaint it was to see these two working together for the aesthetic enlightenment of the Western world! It was like seeing a proud, self-willed, bull-calf bison, fed on nothing but golden oats, yoked to the plough with a dainty, fetlocked, dapple-grey unicorn, who would, an' he could, step delicately over the traces and scamper on the edge of the prairie, where, under the protective colouring of a grove of pale wattle trees, he might be lost to the view of the world.[37]

Powys is perspicacious regarding the tastes of both men. Thayer was certainly more the classicist in his preferences, comfortable in the past and suspicious of modernism's eagerness to celebrate and apotheosize the contemporary world, which for Thayer was often harrowing and ugly, while Watson was truly enamored of the advances, both artistic and technological, of the period. He would in a few years try his hand at moving pictures, producing two movies destined to become favorites of those who study early avant-garde cinema, *Lot in Sodom* and the first-ever production of Poe's *The Fall of the House of Usher*. Both would feature his wife, Hildegarde.

By September, Alyse Gregory and Llewelyn Powys had moved to rural Montoma, New York, for the sake of Powys's health, and Gregory edited the *Dial* from there, going into the city when needed. That same month the couple married, despite Gregory's progressive attitude toward and reservations about the institution. She wrote, "I remember riding back through heavy rains that filled the rivers to overflowing as they came pounding tumultuously down the mountain-side and roared by under the thin wooden planks of the bridges across which we passed, and feeling strangely sad."[38] She explained to Thayer, "[I]t is only Llewelyn's delicate health that could *ever* drive me to it," and "I hope you won't despise and reject me and look at me with distant disdain, because of course no one will understand my *real* feeling better than yourself."[39] In her journal, she wrote, "It is what Llewelyn wanted, but some cloud lies upon my spirit as if I had betrayed something in myself."[40]

In the summer, Thayer was treated for colitis and some kind of vision problem at a New York sanitarium and was forbidden to read or write.[41] He recuperated in Edgartown, where he had hot poultices applied to his stomach. To avoid using his eyes, Thayer had his mother read him the short stories submitted to the *Dial* that Gregory passed on to him. Florence Thayer was shocked by some of the more risqué submissions, and Thayer asked Gregory to start noting for him which stories where suitable for his mother to read. He added that he had struggled through "Passion" by Djuna Barnes "because of the title and because of Djuna Barnes," only to find that the story was quite harmless. "I find I might just as well have let my mother read that to me also, as the story is, morally at least, not shocking. Except in so far as bad spelling and bad typing are always shocking."[42]

Thayer's private life continued to be a busy one. A teasing and coquettish letter from an admirer regarding an evening the two spent together suggests that Thayer's interest in younger women was as strong as ever. The letter reads, in part:

Sunday at Sundown

I'm wishing you're as happy as I.—
My dear Mr. Thayer,

I'm asking that you extend me your kind permission to explain the matter of some recent communications purporting to come from me . . . Pause . . . Granted? Thanks! I shall continue.

I truthfully aver, Mr. Thayer, that since that evening when we two met (we weren't alone—Goethe was with us, or, at least he was with me) I have made no attempt to communicate with you, telephonically, or other wise.

You think me presumptuous. I do not at all blame you. I am. I am young—vigorously, vivaciously, young—passionately young. Youth, however, demands expression; expression conveys a meaning. Is that meaning, though, always read aright?—But—

At this dangerous (but delectably sweet) age of effervescent youth there must be exercised a certain amount of reserve (stop laughing so loudly!) to keep this effervescence in check.

The letter goes on in this manner for some time, talking of Thayer's "passion for flesh" and complimenting him for holding back his physical appetites during their time together.

You may not know it but I do, that, if you were not the man of clean morals; if you were not the man who respected chastity in a woman—no matter who that woman—you might very easily have overpowered me by your physical force. This might have happened if you really thought as you said you did, that a kiss was merely, and should be merely a momentary satisfaction of a sexual desire. But subconsciously, you know it should not be. Subconsciously you felt that a kiss is a divine expression of two hearts, two souls that have come to one clean understanding. . . .

There is one thing I do resent. You said, "I don't believe it," when I declared that I had never permitted any man to touch my lips. It hurt me, Mr. Thayer, because it is true; because I had experienced an abundance of reserve to counteract my passionate desires, and had succeeded; and because you laughed at this success that I am highly proud of.

Do you want to smell the tea rose? I hope you'll consider its fragrance more entertaining than hair tonic. I know you will. I'm smiling now—and happy. Good-bye, Mr. Thayer,

[P.S.] Don't forget to smell the petals before you throw the whole "business" into the fire. They're really sweet.[43]

From this letter we get an inkling of Thayer's modus operandi in flirting with young girls, which seemed to include talk of poets and poetry, the joking acknowledgment of the age disparity that gave each something the other desired—his sophistication, her youthful beauty—the turning of the conversation to the subject of intimacy, and the sounding of the youngster as to the extent of her experience.

Even the normally proper Alyse Gregory joked about Thayer's appetite for young flesh, mentioning that the Montoma postmaster had a daughter who was "sprightly" but "a little too old for your purposes."[44]

Marietta's letters, in both German and English, continued to come. In one, dated December, the girl thanked him for a check he had sent and told him she had learned to apply her own makeup. "Soon spring will arrive and with it my dear Mr. Scofield," she wrote.[45]

18

ANNUS BELLI

The January 1925 issue of the *Dial* announced that Marianne Moore had been given the Dial Award. Moore had also joined the staff of the magazine, acting as an editorial stand-in for Gregory, who was still mostly working out of her home in Montoma, where Powys's tuberculosis was responding well to the mountain air of the Catskills.

The magazine continued to be both prestigious and unprofitable. In January 1925, Thayer wrote to Gregory: "Do you realize that in the January 1925 number we have fewer pages of paid advertising than ever before since we took over The Dial? This even though we now have (at least so a Miss Gregory, late of New York, informed me) a modicum of prestige and several times the number of subscribers we had when we took over The Dial?"[1]

In that same letter, written from a hotel in Bermuda, where he said Eleanor Parker, an office assistant at the *Dial*, had joined him "surreptitiously," Thayer also discussed an essay by William Carlos Williams, possibly one Williams wrote in praise of Marianne Moore; it argued against the mystical in poetry and praised the solid, organic nature of modern work such as Moore's. The essay was, in many ways, a refinement of the old imagist ideas: "With Miss Moore a word is a word when it is separated out by science, treated with acid to remove the smudges, washed, dried, and placed right side up on a clean surface."[2] Thayer hated the essay's emphasis on the new and the modern. "[L]ooking over The Dial," Thayer wrote Gregory, "the most remarkable thing about it is the fact that, although I am the Editor of it, no one who knew me would guess this fact. This is of course attributable to many things, but chiefly to Watson's constant and subterranean pull to the left. I myself detest all Modern Art."[3] One assumes that the Williams essay had been requested to be run with the announcement of Moore receiving the Dial Award, but, if so, Thayer and Watson disagreed over the quality of the piece.

It is true that Thayer defended the work of the modernists in the *Dial*, but one doesn't need to look far, even in his apologia, for the telling line. Thayer wrote to a San Jose News editorial writer who said he didn't understand *The Waste Land*: "I also find many blind passages in The Waste Land, indeed even in the Observations of Miss Moore. But after all it is the privilege of even the best poets to be their best only intermittently. And perhaps better to be unintelligible than to be May Queen."[4] Here Thayer is not arguing that unintelligibility is a good thing, but rather that it is a fault, the result of poets not being at "their best." Thayer distrusted this resistance to yielding a meaning to the reader, which was becoming a hallmark of much modernist verse. Watson must have eventually won the battle over Williams's essay, for the piece appeared in the May issue. Tangentially, Williams also claimed that around this time Thayer proposed to Moore, who declined the offer.[5]

Thayer was unable to get to Vienna in the spring as he had suggested he might to Marietta, but his friend Adolf Dehn wrote him letters about the amorous adventures he was enjoying there. One spoke of a "glorious" night out: "I danced like a madman, and found 2 beautiful sisters who are going to let me see them," he wrote. "No, no, I fear they're not to your taste but cheer up. I do think I know of a naïve little thing of 17, or thereabouts, who is, so you have something to look forward to."[6]

"It is the same Vienna, scarcely a change," he wrote in another letter sent in June. "It is a poorer Vienna however, the coffee houses are empty, the cabarets + theatres too, the prices are distinctly higher. The [illegible] + the Socialists still beat each other on the university steps, flowers are sold on the Freiwag by the hardfaced, black nailed mother, although no hard-breasted daughter is there to help, the Feló School is full of sweaty adolescence."[7]

Marietta's letters continued to arrive faithfully. She wrote that she dreamed of Thayer standing in the middle of her blooming garden, about to pluck all the blooms from the trees. She looked down at him from a window, saw what he was going to do, and cried. She dreamed of him often, she wrote. Was he coming to Vienna? She was crazy to see him. She had been accompanying a young cello virtuoso on the piano.[8] In another letter, she offered to come to the United States and nurse him through his many illnesses ("with Mama, of course") and added, in English, "Oh I love you soooooo."[9] On Valentine's Day, Thayer cabled Marietta a dozen red roses.[10]

He also wrote to Marietta that he would not be able to visit her in spring as he had wanted since Alyse Gregory had announced that she and Powys were going to marry and move to England. This meant more work for him at the magazine until he could find a replacement, and any possibility of his visiting Europe would have to be put off until the fall. He also asked her not to fall in love with the cellist. He received in reply one of Marietta's longest letters to him, all in English.

Oh, this Miss Gregory, how I despise her. . . . But in the autumn come *surely* Mr. Scofield. I am so impatient to see you, that when I was reading your [letter] I began to weep. Yes really to weep. But your last, long letter consoled me a little and with the last four words I was *very* satisfied. [The letter is lost, so we can only surmise what those four words were.] Six long months I must wait until the autumn, but when you write me often and always so fine letters, the time will [go] by much shorter for me. Mura Zyperowitsch [who would later marry Adolf Dehn] is now two weeks in Vienna and she is again dancing with us. But she is not so good as before and has much unlearnt. She has now shorts hairs and looks very lovely, but I don't like her so much. I have a good reason for that. I will explain you also why.—

I was so laughing when I read: "Don't fall in love with the cello virtuoso!" Oh, don't fear that. I love only one man and he is living very far from Austria. We must take a ship and drive over the ocean when we will come to his native country. I cannot describe how much I love him. I would give up my life for him. The most of time I must think at him, when I play piano, when I am dancing, when I go in the street alway. I must think at him. And he? Oh he has certainly not the slightest notion from my great pains. But enough you must not hear such sad things. . . .

Love as ever to you my dearly Mr. Scofield

Your grateful Marietta

Gregory, good Progressive radical that she was, was against marriage as an institution but had deferred in the matter to Powys. It also was he who desired the move to England, and Gregory ceded to him in this matter as well even though her post at the *Dial* was prestigious and well-paying. "It's disgraceful of me to have persuaded Alyse to give up The Dial but I WANT TO COME HOME," Powys wrote to a family member.[11] Later, when Powys took up a long relationship with another woman, Gregory would be similarly accepting of his open infidelity. Gregory was always a true lover and a loyal friend.

In late spring 1925, Thayer seemed full of joi de vivre, an eagerness to engage with and enjoy life that carried no hint of the anguish that would beset him later in the year. In May, inviting an old classmate to the Vineyard, he bragged that he could offer for his guest's pleasure wine, whisky, Chartreuse, Benedictine, apricot brandy, *The Oxford Book of English Verse*, a rhyming dictionary, and "Girls to be avoided or encountered at your discretion."[12] Also in May, Thayer received a letter from a young woman named Doris Beck in which she apparently ended a relationship that had begun as long as four years before, when her letters to Thayer first appear.

> I have thought things over a great deal and discussed them with my parents and agree with them that seeing "friendship" between us is impossible due to my predilection for getting dramatic and due to *your* circumstances that nothing else is possible, have come to the conclusion it is best ended—
>
> I want to be happy and find pleasure in *various* things but knowing you prevents that so I ask you sincerely not to write or try to see me *ever* again.
>
> This is very difficult for me to do but I am determined so ask you not answer this—and mean all I have said and do not want half-ways.
>
> Doris Beck
> Thanks for the two books which I am reading—.[13]

The letter is both illuminating and puzzling. It tells us that Thayer obviously had some kind of relationship with the girl. (Note that the parents are evidently aware of this relationship, as was Marietta's mother. Thayer seems to have gone out of his way to ensure that his dealings with young females had the blessing of their parents, even though the parents may not have been aware of all that may have been going on.) But the reasons for her decision are hard to discern. She ends the relationship because mere "friendship" between the two is impossible due in part to Thayer's "circumstances." This is perhaps a reference to the fact that at this time he was planning to go to Europe for a long period, perhaps for good. He was also at this time divorced, so if Doris Beck is alluding to marriage, there was certainly no barrier to this, apart, of course, from Thayer's loathing of the institution. Then again, we do not know what Thayer had told Beck of his "circumstances." One would not put past him the ability to tell a lie that might forestall the possibility of ever again entering into a marriage.

Meanwhile, the faithful Dehn continued to send Thayer reports about Marietta and to ask about his other romantic adventures. "Your Marietta was not at the school when I was there," he wrote.

I shall go there again to see her + write a note especially. Mura says she is truly charming; that she has grown much + that she is poorly dressed. . . .

Would you let me know how the twin-romances ended—or are they ended? Be sure to greet Miss Parker warmly. Is all well between you?[14]

Thayer responded:

I trust you did eventually see the little girl of whom you alarmingly write that "she has grown much." I require more exact data. . . .

As to what you entitle euphemistically "The Twin Romances," and as to *your* Miss Parker, I shall let you come here to learn details. Suffice it to say that something you once suggested in regard to Swanny turned out justified, that Tingle-toe may now by superlatively entitled as the Lite Princess of Tangoland, and that Miss Parker is now in an asylum (or sanatarium if you will) at Bloomingdale, New York. The latter fact has not occurred with[out] leaving its mark upon me. I have spent most of this month in New York with lawyers and have spent all my money, too.[15]

Dehn made one more effort to find Marietta in Vienna. "I went to the [dancing] school again before leaving as I had promised but the little Marietta was not there and I was told she would not come again for her season was over. I got her address as clearly as I could . . . and went there to pay an official call + greet her from you. The Hausbesorgers [custodians] at both numbers insisted no-one of that name or description lived in their houses, so I lost out. I'm sorry for I was curious." Dehn's letter then turned to other romantic conquests, including one by the name of Böcka. "She is very lovely and gay," he wrote. "For the first time I played with her.—Too bad you aren't here—I'm sure she'd please you. . . . She told Mura she is alone here with another girl + although she was chic she is very poor + poses I believe. So there!"[16]

One notes in Dehn's letters references to the poverty of the girls he sees in Vienna. There was great austerity resulting from postwar economic devastation, and dancing school students were often the daughters of families straining for upward social mobility.

Thayer's relationships with women continued to be, as he put it, "messy." After returning from Bermuda with Thayer, Eleanor Parker had suffered a breakdown and been hospitalized, as he mentioned to Dehn. A letter from Parker's mother to Thayer asking him to make a financial contribution to the hospital stay hints at what seems to have been a complex relationship. "It is very expensive, eighty dollars a week, and as I feel her breakdown was caused by her overwork for you I shall trust to your help to meet the bills," she wrote.

She need know nothing about that if you feel it might militate against her recovery. Your suspicions as to what she might say to hurt your reputation, shows me how much she had to bear and I agree with others that the wonder is that she did not break down sooner. I am much better informed on the subject than I was when I saw you and I have corroborated all the statements she has made.

When she called you Tuesday it was to remind you that you owed her for two "bets" she had. When I told her she should call off bets of that kind she said you already had won more than she had and this would make her even.[17]

Thayer was indeed a hard taskmaster, and there are records of others in his employ who left because of his demands and rigorous standards. The first paragraph also carries a whiff of a threat regarding aspects of Thayer's behavior that might affect his "reputation." The fact that Mrs. Parker had gone out of her way to "corroborate" her daughter's statements suggests that such knowledge gave her useful leverage over Thayer.

Thayer responded by throwing money at the situation—throwing it judiciously, however—and admitting nothing. "I enclose a check for $100 to cover the two bets which Eleanor remembers that I owe her," he wrote. "As all bets made between us, so far as I can now recall, were made for $50 each, $100 is presumably the owing. I had thought that all bets between us had already been liquidated and indeed that Eleanor had come out even or ahead of the game. But I am glad now to be able to rectify the error."[18] These "bets" are indeed curious. Thayer evidently had a taste for the occasional wager, once betting Amy Lowell one hundred dollars that E. E. Cummings would become part of the canon of American verse. The bets with Eleanor Parker, however, seem of a darker nature. The amount stated, fifty dollars, would have been more than her weekly salary. It seems not only inappropriate but also almost pathologically cruel for a man of Thayer's wealth to indulge in bets with an employee (even if the two were in an intimate relationship) who could not afford to lose. In the same letter, Thayer reminded Mrs. Parker that "Dr. Wood" had said Thayer should not share in the expense of her treatment. He also asked that she and her family reserve judgment regarding what had transpired. "I myself retain the hope that Eleanor, again herself, will see this affair in a different light from that in which she and apparently you all now see it," he wrote.[19]

In May, Alyse Gregory left the magazine and America for good to live with Powys in England. She left Thayer a note:

Friday 4 p.m. I felt so sad that I could not go to work after you left. I could only sit and try to keep the tears from my eyes so that no one would discover my distress. But when Mrs Granville brought in vacation money which I neither earned nor deserved I did not know where to go. Suddenly everyone about me seemed unreal and I could think only of old memories of your kindness, of long and happy talks, of something I feel in common with you that I feel with no one else. I do love you, dear Scofield with a lasting affection and always shall in spite of my touchiness and quickness of temper. I do appreciate your goodness, your distinction. I wish that I might in some way have lightened your burden. In leaving America I leave you. I have been happier and more at peace at The Dial than ever before. I can't thank you. I can only pray for your peace and happiness.[20]

It was at this time, June 1925, that Marianne Moore took over full editorship of the magazine. Ellen Thayer, a cousin of Scofield's, had also joined the staff. Ellen had been at Bryn Mawr with Marianne Moore, where she had received a Valentine verse from her:

Lady, lady is it true
That you love me as I love you
No of course it isn't true
But say it is, my lady, do

Moore walked into what was very much a baptism by fire. Conrad Aiken had written a review of Amy Lowell that was particularly harsh, so much so that he had second thoughts about it and cabled Moore asking that the review be tempered before publication.[21] Moore immediately cabled Thayer at Martha's Vineyard saying it would be possible to substitute a short story for the offending section,[22] but evidently Thayer decided that the piece should run, and Moore was forced to lie to Aiken, saying that the magazine had already been printed.[23]

Some, such as Edmund Wilson, cheered the change of editorship. He wrote: "This [the hiring of Moore] is at least an improvement over the old regime at *The Dial*, when, so far as I could see, the contributions were never read, the editors were never in the office, and the magazine knocked itself together every month without human intervention except on the part of the proofreaders and stenographers. Marianne Moore is really awfully nice and very intelligent; but I am afraid that her co-editor Watson will prevent her from making the magazine any different from what it was before."[24]

Wilson's opinion of how the magazine was put together is gainsaid by the flood of correspondence regarding the magazine that ran between Thayer and Gregory during the period of which he speaks so critically. The staff was indeed working extremely hard at the magazine, though the lack of a "presence" at the Greenwich Village offices due to Gregory's working from Montoma was no doubt irritating to writers. As to the quality of the magazine's content during the period of which Wilson speaks, one might point out that in a six-month period the magazine published fiction by Virginia Woolf, Jules Romains, and Maxim Gorky; articles by Oswald Spengler, George Santayana, and Bertrand Russell; verse by Marianne Moore, Carl Sandburg, and Wallace Stevens; and reprinted the art of Pablo Picasso, Georges Seurat, Edvard Munch, William Gropper, and Adolf Dehn. Not a bad inventory for a journal that "knocked itself together."

Moore also found herself at the center of an office intrigue involving the hospitalized Eleanor Parker and Dorothy De Pollier, another secretarial employee of the magazine. Both women were aspiring writers and had evidently submitted work to the magazine under pseudonyms. Thayer disapproved of this and had Moore go through wastebaskets in search of proof. De Pollier broke down into tears when questioned by Moore and resigned the following day.[25]

Thayer was haunted by a growing paranoia. He told Gregory that he believed his mail was being opened and read.[26] He was convinced that Barnes was again "active" and "in eruption," as Thayer phrased it, and was in fact the dark force behind the "fantastic and sinister happenings"[27] that were occurring. The Barnes Foundation had been dedicated with great fanfare in March. In June, Thayer received from Barnes a letter so "threatening and obscene" that he asked Watson to bring a gun to Martha's Vineyard for his protection. Watson complied.[28] "I spend most of my time in New York with lawyers and detectives," Thayer wrote Alyse Gregory from Martha's Vineyard. "The rest of the time I spend here with my colitis returned acutely, and an enormous correspondence with lawyers, etc. It is of course B[arnes], who is now so much worse than ever before you cannot imagine it. Neither can I mention it on paper."[29] The same letter continues: "I only hope I do not have to ask you to return to this country to bear witness to my good character in a court room . . . I would to God I had gone abroad instead of going to Edgartown. One lawyer even advises my going now. But my other lawyers oppose it, and I have decided it is the part of wisdom to face the music here, anyhow for the present."

We already know that something had taken place in Vienna in 1923 that Thayer thought Watson and his wife might frown on (Barnes had also made reference to "the known Vienna events"[30] in one of his threatening letters to Thayer). Now Thayer was speaking of an incident in the United States requiring the hiring of lawyers (the detectives seem to have been hired in reference to his suspicions about Barnes). What was the music he said he must face?

Gregory herself had become more worried than usual about Thayer. She sensed that his obsession with his own body and mind was not merely the egotism of a rich, powerful, and attractive young man but rather a symptom of a mental inability to process the feelings of others—or perhaps a determination not to do so. "S. T. is like a cold sharp sword blade playing all about one in the air descending now + then," she wrote.

> Does he lack a certain penetrative imagination? Does he attach the effect to its cause + at the same time transcend it with an aesthetic insight which negates any human feeling or does he merely lack enough imagination to connect? Does he get an added pleasure by understanding the suffering . . . or does he negate the suffering altogether? The reason he likes Marianne Moore is for her intellectual veracity which is exactly what tires me. . . . Her philosophical speculations lack any broad foundations.[31]

Thayer became more and more skittish. "I am nervous in this exposed house," he wrote Watson from Edgartown in June, "but I hesitate to invest in a dog, which, it appears is more likely to bite my girl friends than to bite Dr. B."[32]

News continued to reach Thayer from Vienna, from where his friend Adolf Dehn reported his ongoing amorous adventures: "I ran into Böska at the Dome on the night of the 4th of July so a friend of his little friend went with us to a little dance hall + we had a mad evening till 2:30.—Really she's a fine person + a body which maddens. She asked about you."[33] Marietta also wrote. She and her mother (a father is never mentioned in her letters) had left Vienna and were living in an idyllic little village in the country. She said that her yearning for Thayer was getting stronger and stronger. She had not been dancing in order to renew her strength so that he would be satisfied with her in the fall.[34]

Thayer finally left New York for Europe at the end of July on the *Aquitania*. He told his friends that he was leaving so as to focus on writing.[35] Marianne Moore tried to persuade him to remain in the United States, but after a two-hour lunch she concluded that her effort was in vain, saying, "I am afraid you are, Mr. Thayer, a spiritual expatriate."[36]

19

FREUDLESS IN VIENNA

If Thayer hoped that returning to his beloved Vienna to write would help his state of mind, he was sadly mistaken. Whatever the external problems were from which he may have been running away—Barnes's threatening letters, the demands of Eleanor Parker's family, or a mysterious incident in Edgartown that he mentions in a letter only after arriving in Europe—they were at least fleeable. Not so the paranoia that was, more and more, insinuating itself into his mental processes. At some level, he realized his own helplessness and the need for a steady, even-minded, friendly presence to help him through the forest of fears that his life was becoming. He realized this need even before sailing for Europe, when he evidently asked his old friend Stewart Mitchell to join him. Mitchell did not reject the offer outright, but he would not make the trip. He sent flowers to Thayer's cabin, perhaps as a consolation for not being able to make the visit. Thayer would not let go of the possibility that Mitchell would join him. He cabled back, "FLOWERS LOVELY PLEASE DO NOT DISAPPOINT ME."[1] Thayer cabled his old friend Cummings, saying he would forward the funds for his passage, but Cummings had not yet recovered from the blow of having lost Elaine Orr and was still trying to see her. One of her telegrams to Cummings from the period reads, "SORRY FEEL MEETING WOULD BE USELESS AND PAINFUL TO BOTH OF US."[2] Cummings's *XLI poems*, published that year, was dedicated to Elaine. Thayer also tried to persuade his partner Watson to come to Europe, dangling the carrot that he, Thayer, might be willing to buy the *Dial* outright.[3]

The same letter to Watson eventually moves on to the subject of Thayer's psychic isolation, which had intensified to the point that he feared losing his sanity if he did not see his friends. His paranoia had also ballooned almost out of control, and he complained that his attempts to buy paintings were being thwarted by unknown persons of great wealth.

> The situation about me in Europe (wherever I go) is such that I need (if I am to retain my sanity: *I mean this literally*) as many of my friends about me as I can muster. I was therefore much disappointed that Stewart [Mitchell] could not come; also that Estlin [Cummings] (to whom I cabled last week) had to remain in America. I am exposed almost *hourly* to every indignity and mental torture to which it is possible for human being to be susceptible. The doings in America were child's play compared to these here. Money is obviously being spent like water. Although I myself have drawn two thousand dollars on my letter of credit since landing, I am always overbid. . . . It is obvious that several thousands dollars have already been spent against me in Germany (where I have been one week).[4]

We have no idea what indignities and mental tortures Thayer was suffering, but in his words we hear once again the cry for the company of trusted friends. This reaching out to others for help would become more and more desperate as his mental illness worsened. The irony, of course, was that his paranoia would not allow him to trust others.

The letter goes on:

> Please not to believe that I am already insane. And please to forgive one who is much put upon if you read between the lines of this letter something which should not perhaps have been given place for between lines of mine. And if you ever felt sympathy for O. Wilde when he stood in the railway station handcuffed and under guard en route (as he would have said!) to Reading Gaol, and there received in his face the spittle of a bystander, please now do extend your sympathy to me.

The allusion to Wilde is of interest. Thayer had made another Wildean reference in a letter written toward the end of his psychoanalysis by Freud, saying that he was to "return after two years imprisonment more criminal or, if you will, more insane than before."[5] The scholar Walter Sutton suggests that here Thayer is comparing himself to Wilde insofar as Wilde was sentenced to two years' hard labor, and Thayer was in Vienna being analyzed by Freud for the same period. The fact that Thayer saw himself remaining as "criminal" or as "insane" as ever despite Freud's efforts also carries a soft echo of Wilde's resigned post-prison remark, "A patriot put in prison for loving his country loves his country, and a poet in prison for loving boys loves boys."[6] Thayer closed the letter with a series of paranoid requests. "Please seal with wax any letters you write me. And address me at London. And if you cable, don't cable anything you don't want broadcast all over Germany as soon as or before I get it myself."[7]

The pathological mistrust apparent in these instructions is found in most of his writings around this period. He had begun closely examining the letters he received, convinced they were forgeries—even those from Alyse Gregory, despite the fact that Gregory's handwriting was strikingly idiosyncratic. He believed that his pursuer or pursuers had brought not only him "to the verge of insanity" but were also the reason that his friend von Erdberg had suffered a series of heart attacks.[8] He wrote Gregory, explaining his flight from America and speaking of the horrors he was forced to face in Europe:

> I stopped three weeks in N.Y. seeing Pierce Clark [his American psychiatrist] often. I even started analysis with him. But the last was too much for me. And for a reason I can't give you here I couldn't return to Edgartown. So I arranged to be with Erdberg at Hiddensee [an island in the Baltic Sea]. But from the time I boarded the Aquitania (already in a dangerous nervous condition) I have been subjected to every conceivable mental torture (I had always thought the phrase "mental torture" rather silly before!). A horrible scene in Berlin. Further horror in Hiddensee. . . . Then we sought refuge under the roof of Dr. Fritz Klatt, a friend of von Erdberg. . . . I have had a nerve-specialist up from Vienna. He has to leave to-day. I expect Dehn day after tomorrow. I trust him.
>
> I should flee to you, but I know I should be followed. And any movement on my part now puts me in the most horrible excitement. (Half the people about me think me already insane. The nerve-specialist wants me to go in a "sanatorium.") Also I should not dare to be in an isolated house.
>
> I have hesitated weeks before writing this letter. But I think if you were going through what I am going through now I should want you to let me know of it. . . .
>
> P.S. I have in the little difficulties of my life cried "Wolf" so often that now that the animal or rather the whole pack is actually at my heels, I cannot perhaps expect full credence.[9]

Gregory had invited Thayer to stay with her and her husband, Llewelyn Powys, in their tiny cottage at White Nose, a clifftop home in Dorset. He declined, on the grounds that any travel would excite him too much.

The awareness of his own mental illness is perhaps the most tragic and painful part of Thayer's condition. But he was also able to separate his self-confessed paranoia from the belief that he was indeed being followed, watched, and acted against.

> [A]ny travel in my present condition aggravates my excitability. Also it gives opportunity to the curs which continue at my heels to stage all manner of nuisances which, were I quite myself, would be only silly, but which now work all too immediately upon my all too active Persecution Complex. Here the Klatts look after me quite touchingly and Adolf Dehn bluffly encourages with allusions to dainty things I am to inherit in Vienna . . . I have . . . decided—God willing—to remain here trying to quiet down.[10]

It must have soon become obvious to Gregory, reading this letter, that its intent was to persuade her to go to Thayer. Thayer told her that he had begged Freud to take him on once more as a patient but that the great man was too busy. He planned to take a house on the Hohe Warte, an exclusive area of Vienna where there were "no motors, no dust, no smoke, no noise, no Danube mists." He continued his letter, writing rhapsodically of the aesthetic utopia they—he, Gregory, and Powys—might all enjoy together.

> But I want—and O so much—to have you and Llewelyn share the sun, the castellated expanse of the Kahlenberg across the valley, a garden of bergamots (from Oxford Book of Eng Verse), home of literary composition of the most measured variety, Viennese éclairs, the opera of Mozart, the theatre of Rheinhardt, and the ballet school of Elen Tels, gently and philosophically with me. Really, you know, I think you would be then above even rheumatism! The air is good on the Halse Warte, and if need be we shall heat the house till our éclair turns into chocolate puddles.

Thayer was never more pitiable than when he was fearful of loneliness. He was used to getting his way simply because he had enough money to make his offers all but impossible to turn down, especially among the generally impecunious artists and writers who constituted a great number of his friends and acquaintances. But Gregory was never easily persuaded to do what did not arise from her own desires and ambitions, and Thayer knew that if she was going to be persuaded to make the journey to Vienna, he would have to make a good pitch. He turned to emotional blackmail:

> Lest you still hesitate, let me add that if you turn my love and my hospitality down, I don't believe I shall try to stick it Freudless in Vienna. In that case I think I shall return to New York (after a month's Viennese

jocundity) and to the arms and bosom of L. PIERCE CLARK. I mean this seriously. I don't feel at present—in my morbid condition and impossible circumstances—like trying to stand on my own feet.

Thayer's request makes any potential declination on Gregory's part a rejection of his "love and hospitality." He also knew that Gregory was aware of the fact that Clark had been able to do nothing for him and that Freud had become what he believed was his only chance for a cure.

The letter went on to maintain its emotional pressure, but with new tactics: painting a life free of domestic chores and the need to support oneself that most writers would jump at and the promise that Powys's health would be taken into consideration:

> You would of course have no trouble of any sort with me in the house, so far as I can help it. Yet if you don't like me, you can put me out; and if you don't like my housekeeping, you can correct it and me. And you shall have a proper quiet place to write. And a revolving aërated summer-house— with painted German cupids upon it—shall, if you and Llewelyn so desire, be set up for sleeping purposes among the bergamot.

The letter, this heightened romantic idyll, ends with the harsh and bathetic reality of money:

> I take the liberty of enclosing a check to cover travelling expenses, taxi-cabs in Vienna, etc.
>
> O please don't send me back the check! Please write I am to have your *sanity* and *your indignation* across the tea-table from me only four weeks hence in the City of the Emperors![11]

One supposes that Thayer could not see how insulting it was to enclose what must have been a substantial check in a letter to a close friend. It shows not only how little he valued money in his confused mental state but also how little he understood about how others, especially someone who was both poor and proud, might regard it. Thayer was generally used to people holding out their hands for his money—there are many unpaid IOUs among his papers—and saw it not as a moral force but as a useful remover of inconveniences. He was more aware than most of what money could not do.

Gregory returned the check, and his next letter to her was a brief one. The manner, by turns cajoling and imperious, of the previous letter is replaced by, if not humility, then at least a resignation: "The sad residuum of a discarded hope received." In the postscript Thayer notes that he has started writing verse.

[D]eserted by friends and health, I have adopted a new motto, "A Poem a Day Keeps the Doctor Away."

Love![12]

Thayer had indeed at last begun to write, and was producing poems that were being published in the *Dial*. Indeed, it is at around this point that his work for the magazine moves from being wholly prose to largely poetry. His verse, with only a few exceptions, was unapologetically formalist.

Thayer also kept up the pressure on Freud to take him on again as a patient, but Freud pushed back. He wrote that he was ill and had reduced his sessions with patients. At the age of seventy, he said, he didn't want to take on more sessions.[13] But he relented somewhat in another letter, telling Thayer to call him when he arrived in Vienna.[14] Thayer suggested that Freud put off one of his current patients to take him on. Freud said he could not do that, but that there was a distant possibility that one patient would leave Vienna at Christmas, and, if so, he would take Thayer on.[15] Freud eventually agreed to have a session with Thayer, but he refused to take any money for the work.[16]

His determination to see Gregory remained, even as his thinking grew more and more erratic. He asked Gregory if he could stay with her and Powys, but as soon as she agreed to this he decided he could not travel.[17] He then asked her to become his secretary, which he described as a sinecure that offered a good salary for halftime work with no typing and no stenography.[18] As ever, she declined. "You withdraw my last hope of earthly peace," he wrote back.[19]

Thayer's behavior was beginning to trouble his colleagues at the magazine. His complaints about various staff members, his accusations of their working against him, his insistence that they be fired: all these things served to disrupt work at the *Dial*. At the end of November, Watson wrote an unusually unguarded letter to Marianne Moore about the situation. The letter mentions Herman Riccius, a lawyer from Thayer's hometown in Massachusetts who had done business with Thayer's father and who acted in the family's legal and financial interests. It also mentions Kenneth Burke, who had been working as an editor and translator at the *Dial*.

Mr. Riccius argued that for us to be or to seem to be compliant would be helpful in whatever attempt at treatment is going on. However, as I pointed out to him, to agree to all these whims would be absurd, since they cannot be expected to last forever and not be supplanted by different ones, equally urgent. And if they are really "fixed," the situation is hopeless anyhow, and new ones will presumably be added. It seems to me the condition cannot persist long in its present stage. Either something will happen, calling for a general readjustment; or else he will develop sufficient insight to stop this nonsense. The only German doctor who has seen him recently is said to be hopeful and to regard this winter as a time for his friends *not* to interfere.

If S.T. were in this country one might be able to give him a moral shakedown such as you have once or twice attempted. To do so by letter to any purpose seems impossible, I tried it and he sent me a funny postcard. It is absurd, however, to lie to a man (i.e. say you believe him when you don't) in order that he may continue to have faith in you. . . .

I did inform Burke (who has a right to know everything) of the latest developments. He is leaving, as I understand it, really because the situation is too unpleasant for him to care to stay on. He is not leaving as a therapeutic measure and does not believe his going will be of any service to the patient. He shares your opinion that S.T. has not sufficient contact with the world—too many valets, etc.[20]

20

RETURN OF THE PRODIGAL

By January 1926, Thayer's paranoia had turned its suspicious eye onto the staff at the *Dial*, whom he accused of slighting him and of plotting behind his back. What Marianne Moore called Thayer's "[i]rrational discontent with staff" at the *Dial* escalated to the point that he demanded that almost everyone except for Moore and his cousin Ellen Thayer, who had joined the staff, be fired.[1] Moore, Watson, and Ellen Thayer found themselves in the awkward position of trying to mollify Thayer while avoiding the wholesale removal of those who put the magazine together every month. His cousin Ellen wrote Thayer: "Marianne and I are eager to help you whenever we can. But we are at a loss to understand how the reorganization of the staff that you request can be anything but harmful to your real interests."[2] Ellen Thayer also wrote to Freud, saying that Thayer's mother, under the influence of the protective and loyal Riccius, wanted Watson and Moore to concur with Thayer's wishes to dismiss staff since she believed that this might in some way save his mind.[3] It didn't help that a precedent had been created when Thayer had caused the letting go of Kenneth Burke the previous November, perhaps still smarting over Burke's part in rejecting the Freud article Thayer had acquired a few years earlier.

In an attempt to calm Thayer's turbulent mind, Moore and Watson had allowed to be published in the December 1925 issue a letter he wrote to "The Editors of The Dial" from Prerow, Germany, complaining about his opinions being mischaracterized in an October 1925 "Comment." This "Comment" was, in fact, a wholly innocent essay (probably written by Kenneth Burke) that used as its opening a remark made by Thayer comparing the German writer Herman Keyserling with H. G. Wells. Thayer's response was four pages of sarcastic vituperation attacking the essay writer, the editors, and the magazine itself. Stewart Mitchell wrote to Watson and accused him of cruelty and negligence in allowing it to be published.[4] Remorseful, Watson wrote to Moore, saying that she should feel free to tell him when she thought Thayer's writings were excessive. Moore responded that publishing the letter was, in fact, the lesser of two evils: "[A]t the time, we were struggling manfully to prevent his turning from the office, nearly the whole staff and thus to prevent a broadcasting of everything that was destructive to him. He was like a child who was striking at parents, friends and servants and it was to his interest I am sure that we should have received the brunt of his displeasure. And he would not have endured to be thwarted in every direction."[5]

Thayer's overall mental deterioration was not a steady decline. He would, even for some years into the future, go from an obsessive and ingrained paranoia to lucidity and charm, and then back again. At this particular time, however, he was very much in the grip of his mental illness. He had asked Gregory yet again to come to him. She had innocently asked him about the Vienna environs, which he saw as a hint that she might visit him, and he reported himself being "heartened 1/10 of 1%" by the thought.[6] "I am not well. I am up to my ears in trouble—the same trouble, the Parker trouble," he wrote. (We don't know if the "trouble" to which Thayer refers is a continuation of the fallout with Parker's family about his relationship with her or if he was fearful of suffering a breakdown similar to hers.) "Even Freud was a couple of days ago by my plight moved to *tears*," he wrote.[7]

Less than a week later, he decided that he had to have Gregory with him in Vienna, and he sent her a long cable saying that his situation was "suddenly so appalling" that she simply had to come to him.

> I cannot leave Vienna and find myself without one friend to whom I can turn in my trouble[.] I ask you Alyse in the name of friendship to believe this is the most . . . serious telegram of my life and to come immediately without stopping to pack and to use aeroplane if you can then gain one hour every hour may make your coming too late please understand and believe me when I say . . . if you do not come you will regret it as long as you live please telegraph me urgent after you are en route in the name of Nelson Taylor I ask you not to wait one hour before starting.
>
> Scofield Thayer[8]

Of all Thayer's frantic, panicked telegrams and letters, this is one of the most dire. Not surprisingly, Gregory and Powys concluded from the urgency of the language that the situation was extremely serious and so made the trek to Vienna. They arrived on or before January 28, when Gregory wrote her mother to say she was in Vienna with Powys at Thayer's invitation and that he was sick with "an attack of the grippe" (Gregory was ever discreet).[9] Thayer mentioned the visit in a postcard to his mother, describing airily how he and his two visitors "motored up the Danube to Dürnstein where Richard I was held prisoner."[10] (Thayer had dedicated one of his juvenile histories to Richard the Lionheart and another to Napoleon, both great men who were imprisoned. These allusions, along with his persistent thoughts about Oscar Wilde's imprisonment, may have bolstered the notion that his two years on Freud's couch were an imprisonment. One might also point out as a matter of interest if not illumination that the frontispiece of Freud's 1920 A General Introduction to Psychoanalysis, a book Thayer undoubtedly would have owned, showed Moritz von Schwind's picture The Dream of the Prisoner.)

It was decided among the three that Thayer would accompany Gregory and Powys back to England and stay with them at the White Nose, their small home in Dorset. The move is mentioned in a curious letter from Thayer's mother to him. In the letter, which is full of otherwise unexceptional hometown Worcester gossip, she addresses him as "Leo," no doubt at his insistence, and the letter was not sent to him directly but was forwarded from his private banking company in London.[11]

At the last minute, perhaps when he was on the railway platform at Prerow with Gregory and Powys, waiting for the train, Thayer decided not to go. Gregory does not record the incident, but there is from Thayer this letter, evidently written immediately after his flight from his rescuers. (In the letter, Thayer refers to the cottage as the White Nore, as Gregory and Powys had thought it named; it was another Dorset dweller, Thomas Hardy, who told them otherwise.)[12]

Forgive me, Alyse!
My most dear and sweet and generous Alyse,

   I am not, anyhow to-day, coming with you to The White Nore.

   You have helped me a great deal by coming on as you did; and so has Llewelyn, as indeed I anticipated he would. Again I must apologise for that wire to you. You will recall I confessed to you in the taxi, the morning of your arrival, that the tugging in of "Nel" [perhaps the Nelson Taylor pseudonym] was only a means to be justified by its end. I must now confess to you the whole telegram was of a like nature. Some day I hope, perhaps at the White Nore, to tell you all about it. In the meantime perhaps our gentle and honest Dorset friend may make up his mind to illuminate.

He has been to me illuminating. . . . No, I did not and do not need observe the also gentle and innocent and *intact* Mr. Gilbert Seldes.

Anyhow don't read this letter as other than childlike fun. Don't miss that train! And do know I am in excellent health, among harmless friends, and anxious only to persuade them as expeditiously as possible to give up trying to fool one who, as we say in Vienna, was not born yesterday.[13]

Back in New York, Riccius had traveled down from Massachusetts to discuss the situation with Moore and Ellen Thayer. Moore was somewhat buoyed by Freud's reply to Ellen Thayer's letter. "I was greatly cheered by Doctor Freud's evident sanction of our retaining employees at *The Dial*," she wrote Watson. "Perhaps you know of his answer to Ellen's letter of inquiry? In which he said that it would be awkward for her to disregard Scofield's wishes but that it would be unjust to dismiss innocent persons and since there are two directors of *The Dial* might it not be possible for the other director to frustrate her cousin's wishes? He asked particularly that the fact of his reply should be kept secret."[14]

And yet Thayer continued to seek out people who could stay with him in Vienna. He even contacted Kenneth Burke about acting as his secretary, but Burke begged off on the grounds that he had plenty of work, his shorthand had degenerated, and he didn't want to live permanently in Europe.[15] Burke, who had left the magazine because of the abusive treatment he received from Thayer, is to be admired for a civil and polite response.

Meanwhile, Thayer's cables to Gregory became more and more bizarre. One reads: "This afternoon I dreamt actually of Oni [his former manservant in New York] and this evening we eat asparagus is dreaming like speaking and what has this to do with God[?]" It was signed, "Tolstoi." Others simply recite lists of flowers: "Dandelion Bachelors Button lilac Scofield" and "Dandelion Bachelorbutton Egerius Puritanus." Then came this: "I feel as though I had been tricked Samuel."[16] Samuel Taylor was the pseudonym he had used during the Chicago experiment.

At some point during this period, Thayer left Vienna and went to Germany, where he sent Gregory a postcard that read:

> Hedda!
>> On one count you win.
>> On one count you lost
>>> So there you are!
>>>> A.[17]

In late February 1926, Watson received a cable from Thayer saying he would resign from the editorship in June. Watson, who was probably jumping at the chance of unlinking the magazine from Thayer's whims and fantasies, cabled back, "Arrangement satisfactory." He wrote to Moore, "His intentions have been shifting rapidly since he left Vienna, and although such a brief answer may make him think momentarily that we do not care whether he resigns, he will probably be off on a new tack almost at once."[18]

Thayer seemed to have taken on with glee the role of gremlin to the *Dial*, and he further disconcerted Moore with his resignation announcement, in which he said he was "happy" to announce that he was stepping down. Watson asked Moore to try to persuade Thayer to remove the adjective.[19] Moore made a brave attempt, reminding Thayer of their long history and suggesting that he might one day wish to return to the position of editor. "When you are ready to take back the Editorship, it will be I who am 'happy' and justified in being so," she wrote. "But as I am sure I said in my recent letter, I feel that you ought graciously to withhold any such statement as that you are happy in resigning. Propriety and elegance have been characteristic of you and if you are not sorry in resigning, you at least ought not to say so."[20] The effort was in vain, and the eventual announcement in the June issue informed readers not only that Thayer was leaving but also that he was happy to do so.

Thayer's peregrinations around Europe continued, taking him through Germany, Switzerland, and Italy. During a stay in Venice, he received a letter from Louise Bryant, who mentioned a mysterious "story" about her that was making the rounds. Thayer responded:

Dear Louise . . .

You write very sweetly indeed and I am happy to know that the sweetness is all very real. It is also—particularly just at this time—most reassuring to have in hand your written statement of innocence as regards the "story" in question. One would not have any friends in any way associated with a thing like that. Least of all a member of your "frail" sex.

But really—to be even more serous—I am glad you write yourself my friend, I accept everything you say or do as from a friend, and am myself your friend.[21]

He also wrote from Venice to his uncle. The letter described the sudden increase in Thayer's production of lyric verse, which he explained was caused by "the expression of nervous strain on emotional tensions."[22]

Around this time Alyse Gregory wrote to her mother regarding Thayer's breakdown. Interestingly, Gregory puts the blame on the shoulders of Eleanor Parker. "Scofield was affected by his secretary who developed manic-depressive insanity," she wrote. "I *beg* you not mention to *anyone* about Scofield. He still writes brilliantly and has only recently written some beautiful poetry." Her letter also mentions Freud's advice in the matter and some of the paranoid ideas that haunted Thayer: "Freud said it was important that no one should pretend to believe S——because if he found one person to believe him it would fix his obsession all the more deeply. I can give you no conception of his extraordinary fantasies. He thought his apartment was filled with dictaphones and electrical wiring, and of course he suspected everyone who approached him."[23]

Much of the "beautiful poetry" Thayer was writing, despite his mental illness, was published in the *Dial*. Along with Alyse Gregory, Marianne Moore was one of the biggest champions of Thayer's poetry. Of course, one could assume that in publishing the boss's work, Moore and Gregory were simply showing their pragmatic awareness of which side their bread was buttered on. And yet we know that Moore did reject works by Thayer,[24] and in her 1926 essay "'New' Poetry since 1912," published after Thayer's withdrawal from the magazine, she is more than kind to Thayer's poetic talents. She writes of his work:

> Categorically "formal," as are George Dillon and Archibald MacLeish, Scofield Thayer is a new Victorian—reflective, bi-visioned, and rather willfully unconventional. We have a mixture, apparently, of reading and of asserted detachment from reading, emotion being expressed through literal use of detail:
>
> > I agitate the gracile crescent
> > Which calls itself a fern:
>
> and through what seems a specific reviving of incident. Tension affords strength, as is felt in certain verbally opposed natural junctures of the unexpected—"a gentle keenness," "gradual flames," "concision of a flame gone stone"—the mechanics being that of resistance.[25]

Moore, meanwhile, who would be officially named editor in July 1926, continued to put her somewhat prim stamp on the magazine. Moore had recently angered Hart Crane by cutting more than half of his poem "The Wine Menagerie" and changing the title to "Again." Crane went along with the changes for the sake of the twenty-dollar payment.[26] Kenneth Burke said that Moore had taken all the wine out of the menagerie.[27] According to William Carlos Williams, Moore "detested" Crane's work and called it "fake-knowledge."[28] Moore also insisted on not running three photographs showing nude sculptures by Aristide Maillol.[29]

Then there was the case of James Joyce, of whose work only one poem ("A Memory of the Players in a Mirror at Midnight") ever appeared in the *Dial*. In the summer of 1926, Sylvia Beach of Shakespeare and Company offered Moore a section of Joyce's *Work in Progress,* which was to become *Finnegans Wake*. "I should be very glad if The Dial would care to have it," Beach wrote. "Your review occupies the highest place among reviews and is the most appropriate one to bring out Mr Joyce's work." Perhaps knowing of Moore's reputation, she added, "P.S. There is nothing that the censor could object to in Mr Joyce's piece."[30] Moore cabled Beach that she could offer two cents a word but needed to see the piece first.[31] At the end of July, Beach sent a list of corrections Joyce wanted to make. Moore accepted the piece, saying that it would be published "in rather small portions."[32] In September, Beach sent two more lists of corrections from Joyce, saying, "this is final, he says."[33]

Moore was under the impression that Joyce's work was titled *abc,*[34] and Beach, who said she was "very glad" the magazine was taking the work, corrected her: "It has no title yet and he says anything will do. The fragments that were published by the 'Criterion,' 'Le Navire d'Argent' etc., were called 'From Work in Progress,' 'Extract from Work in Progress' so you may give it some such name."[35]

The publication of this work of Joyce's for the first time in the United States would have been a real coup for the *Dial*, returning to the magazine some of the avant-garde credentials that had been eroded either by what was perceived as its growing conventionality or by readers' familiarity with the journal, or both.

But something went wrong, and on September 17, Moore suddenly cabled Beach, "UNPERMISSIBLE TO PUBLISH JOYCE VERBATIM LETTER FOLLOWS."[36] The letter, written the same day, read: "We find that it would not be possible to publish the Joyce manuscript verbatim. We should be obliged if we are to publish it, to omit pages and parts of pages, reducing it by one-third—perhaps a half. We are very sorry that this discovery was not made before I had written to you. Do you feel that you must withdraw the manuscript? Or should you be disposed to have us indicate omissions subject to your withdrawal?"[37]

A subsequent letter, saying that the *Dial* could publish only twelve pages of the manuscript, made an attempt to explain the sudden about-turn. "Realizing that it has been your thought, as you know it was ours, to publish the manuscript intact, the request for so small a portion seems presumptuous and should you decline to grant it, we of course cannot but acquiesce," Moore wrote. "The coming of the manuscript in a vacation season has necessitated its having been sent from place to place and we are deeply troubled to have given the impression of inattention, whereas we could not have been more alert to responsibility than we were, or more anxious to have our decisions reached with promptness. The letter which I wrote to you accepting the manuscript was not held as I had asked that it should be until a final conference [was] held."[38] Beach replied with a curt cable: "JOYCE REQUESTS RETURN TYPESCRIPT WITH CORRECTIONS."[39]

What happened? Moore's excuse that the manuscript was "sent from place to place" rings hollow, considering that Thayer was now out of the picture as far as editing went, leaving only herself and Watson to read the work and make the decision. And Watson, we know, was more than comfortable with artistic experimentation. Moore's explanation that her original acceptance letter should have been but was not held "until a final conference" is frankly lame.[40] The truth was that she didn't like the piece, thinking it obscure, obscene, and not up to standard. As things turned out, *Work in Progress* would appear starting the next year in *Transition*, further causing the *Dial* in its later years to be perceived as orthodox and timid.

Thayer spent most of this year in Europe and at some point was joined by his mother (and perhaps by Herman Riccius), who came to retrieve him. Thayer had never mentioned Freud nor psychoanalysis to his mother in his many letters to her during his time in Vienna, but she must have known from Watson and from Ellen Thayer, as well as from her son's own paranoid letters, that something was seriously wrong. In the second half of this year, Thayer's correspondence lessens considerably, though there are several postcards to the ever-faithful Gregory. He wrote her from Lausanne, "This is the most depressing place I have ever been in."[41]

The company of his mother would not have been appreciated. In Thayer's notes, nobody is mentioned as frequently and with such loathing as is Florence Thayer. "One imagines my mother's heart as having electric-lighted plate-glass windows in it," he wrote. "Not excessively intimate."[42] Another note emphasized this lack of familial closeness: "My mother I love merely as I would love a parrot. There is no contact whatsoever with her as a personality; as this is agreeably with all other members of the family."[43] (Not all, perhaps. Thayer and his cousin Ellen were fond of each other.)

Being as sensitive to noise as he was, it is not surprising to find a good number of references in Thayer's writing to his mother's voice. He found particularly grating the timbre of her voice when raised, when it became "like a fish-horn, coarse" and made him realize, he said, that her hackle had been "permanently ruffed up," had been given "a Marcelle wave." It was, he said, "a voice mixed with gravel."[44]

In another note, he compares his mother's voice to his favorite trope, food-stuff. "The smell, taste and feel of liquid custard has always given me the suggestion of my mother's voice when tenderly emotionalized," he wrote. "Ordinarily her voice is, however, perceptibly less smooth,—rather like liquid custard in which the sugar is perceptible."[45] Her other physical features were found to be similarly unpleasant. Her teeth were "appropriate to bite a horse's neck."[46]

There is surprisingly little description of Florence Thayer's physical self. Her eyes are once described as having the color and quality of turquoise earrings Thayer had bought at the Grand Canyon,[47] and, in what is the closest we find Thayer coming to a softness of feeling for his mother, he talks of her face, in "occasional smiles," as expressing a "pristine sweetness." But he immediately makes reference to her "battered eyebrow," which gives her countenance, by and large, "a mangled (mountain) gentian quality."[48] Such floral metaphors aside, most of the time Thayer's comparisons for his mother are more domestic: "My mother like the smell of hot lamb."[49]

Thayer's major criticism of his mother seems to have been aimed at her egotism. Her ego, he said, was "permanently raw—like a raw throat."[50] This self-centeredness resulted in her always seeing herself as being wronged: "My mother *permanently convulsed* with self-pity: she has 'grown that way': there is no budging her."[51]

Thayer regarded his mother's interactions with the world around her as those of a snob.

My mother's furnishings, table-service, manner of eating, etc. are all determined neither by convenience (pleasure and comfort) nor by sensual or intellectual beauty. They are all determined strictly in accordance with the social scale: they are ordained or banned purely inasmuch as they stand high or low on the scale of contemporary usage among the Upper Class. She does not eat, lie down or regard a picture for pleasure or for comfort: she does all these things only in so far as the doing of them gives by suggestion to herself the sensation of being of that Upper Class, or indicates to others that she is of the class. Her whole life is thus based on competitive instinct and the social scale. Influence of the pleasure-pain principle has to be sought with a magnifying glass. Also the influence of sympathy.[52]

Thayer's remarks are interesting on several fronts. Thayer's argument is not merely with snobbery as such; he himself was a thoroughgoing snob (his mother's taste in silverware, he wrote, was "always for the bulbous,"[53] and he deemed it "[r]emarkable my mother did not have whipped-cream on her baked beans!").[54] Rather, Thayer is attacking his mother's inability to interact with the world on an aesthetic level. In her he found that the natural response of attraction to pleasure and aversion to pain had been subsumed to mere social correctness. She did not look for, and perhaps did not need, the pleasure or the comfort that art could bring and which was Thayer's raison d'être. Again, one thinks of his furious response to her comment on Lachaise's bust of Thayer. Indeed, in this intensely dysfunctional pair we find the same aesthete's hatred of and disdain for the bourgeoisie as was common in much of the avant-garde work of the period.

And if this complex relationship with his mother suited Thayer to Freudian analysis, how much more so when we see in his personal notes the conflation of Florence Thayer with Elaine Orr, his former wife: "My mother expressed her immortal affection for me almost always in the major key, even when whining and lachrymose. Elaine, on the contrary, spoke and wept invariably in the minor key."[55] And this: "By my mother I was seared, by Elaine singed."[56]

When the sad, homeward-bound pair arrived in Paris, toward the end of what may have been his last trip to his beloved Europe, Thayer received a note at his hotel from a Lillian Dat, who said she was seeking freelance work. "I saw by the Paris Herald that you were here," she wrote brightly. "You may remember that I worked as your secretary a few years ago and that I left because I found you too hard a taskmaster."[57] Thayer did not reply.

Another sign of Thayer's mental disorientation was noticed by Cummings, who wrote in a letter to Elaine of an incident at his apartment in Patchin Place that involved a man coming to complain that someone named Thayer had seduced his teenage son.[58] Thayer was, if nothing, tactful in his sexual adventures, and if the story is true it demonstrates an uncharacteristic lack of caution.

Having begun the year with Freud in Europe, he finished it by returning to America with his mother.

21

THE DEATH OF THE *DIAL*

Thayer was the engine that drove the *Dial*. It is certainly true that Watson played a more important role than he is often given credit for (Walter Sutton's excellent *Pound, Thayer, Watson, and "The Dial"* does much to correct the record on this matter), but once Thayer was out of the picture, it was to be only a matter of time before the magazine succumbed.

Still, by any measure, the *Dial* continued to be important. The January 1927 issue named Moore as full editor and listed Thayer merely as "Adviser." It also announced that William Carlos Williams, long appreciated by Watson, was to receive the Dial Award. The beginning of Williams's epic poem *Paterson* was published the next month, along with an appreciation by Kenneth Burke. In 1927, the *Dial* showcased essays by T. S. Eliot, Malcolm Cowley, Havelock Ellis, George Saintsbury, Bertrand Russell, Paul Valéry, and George Santayana; fiction by D. H. Lawrence, Thomas Mann, E. E. Cummings, and Maxim Gorky; and verse from Hart Crane (Moore did not tinker with "To Brooklyn Bridge" as she had with "The Wine Menagerie"), William Carlos Williams, Mark Van Doren, W. B. Yeats ("Among School Children"), and Scofield Thayer. From this point on, Thayer's contributions to the magazine were all poetry. The artists reproduced include Adolf Dehn, William Gropper, Matisse, Munch, Picasso, and Jack B. Yeats.

However, as the decade aged, the once-exciting ideas of modernism were undoubtedly beginning to show signs of age. In January 1927, the *New Republic* took a shot at the *Dial*, complaining that although the magazine was to be admired for publishing younger, lesser-known writers in its early issues, its current pages only continued to present these now somewhat overexposed favorites rather than the newer generation of writers. The choice of Williams for the Dial Award seems to have at least partly sparked the comment: "[W]ith all due respect to Doctor Williams, one is not sure that the prize-winning material of the Dial is not already beginning to run thin."[1] Gilbert Seldes was quick to respond, firing off a letter to the *New Republic* in defense of the magazine he had edited and for which he continued to write. It was not until the September issue, however, nine gestatory months after the initial criticism, that the *Dial* (probably through Watson) responded, rather weakly, in its "Comment" section, pettifogging the definition of what makes a writer "interesting" and arguing that the *Dial* published writing rather than writers. The *New Republic* fired back once more, and the *Dial* remained silent. As a literary feud, it was sadly (or perhaps mercifully) brief. What was significant, and the painful truth upon which the *New Republic* had placed its finger, was that the *Dial*, after being mocked and rebuffed in its early days, had come to be embraced so thoroughly by the cultured classes and had taught so well the appreciation of progressive art, literature, and criticism that, through familiarity, it had lost much of its edge and its luster.

Truth to tell, the *Dial* itself was beginning to note an irritating sameness and slovenliness in the work even of those who had once been its golden-haired boys. In the October 1927 issue, Conrad Aiken took D. H. Lawrence to task in a review of *Mornings in Mexico* for prose that lacked rhythm and was "tiresomely explicit."[2] Marianne Moore was evidently in agreement. "I'm glad you didn't think my review of Lawrence too drastic," Aiken wrote her. "I do think he needs to hear this sort of thing said—he has become too careless altogether."[3] In December of the same year, the art reviewer Henry McBride grumbled that the French section of an international art show was dated: "[W]hen the best the French can do is assemble three or four each of works by Monet, Le Sidaner, Maurice Denis, Ménard, [Ker-Xavier] Roussell, and Utrillo, even the presence of three or four rather repressed Matisses cannot go far towards conveying an air of contemporaneousness. One gets the idea, on the contrary, that one is in an old-fashioned, conservative art shop where nothing has been sold lately. Slightly stuffy!"[4] All in all, according to Moore, what had at first been a "spontaneously delightful" endeavor had deteriorated into "mere faithfulness to responsibility."[5]

A gossipy exchange between Williams and Ezra Pound in the summer of 1928 demonstrates how marginal the reputation of the magazine had become. At this point, both men had been recipients of the generosity of the magazine's owners through the Dial Award, but neither demonstrated anything close to a fondness for the magazine. Williams mentioned a rumor that the *Dial* was perhaps to be bought by the esotericist George Gurdjieff. Pound responded, "In some ways it wd. be highly fitting, though inconvenient, just as that orgum has show [*sic*] disposition to be useful." (The usefulness of which Pound speaks is no doubt the fact that he had received the handsome two-thousand-dollar Dial Award the previous January.)[6]

"Thayer seems to have all but nothing to do with the management of The Dial at the present time," Williams wrote back to Pound.

> If The Dial is sold and bought I am sure that it would mean the retirement of our Mary [Marianne Moore]. She will not sell out I know but would probably go back to the library—on starvation wages. Marianne gets little credit for her fight in New York but stands aces high with me for what she is doing, not—though—for what she is able to accomplish, unfortunately. The Dial is a dead letter among the publisher crowd. It almost means that if you are "one of The Dial crowd" you are automatically excluded from perlite society as far as influence in N.Y. goes. Shit! And yet I myself feel so disgusted with The Dial for its half hearted ways that I am almost ready to agree with anyone concerning its worthlessness.[7]

Several things are worth considering here. First, Thayer had been away from the magazine for more than a year at this point and had no more contact with its editors (perhaps less—we don't know much about his mental condition at this time) than any other writer submitting material. The only letter sent to him from the magazine's offices during this period was a somewhat patronizing note from Ellen Thayer hoping he found the city "restorative" after Thayer had paid one of his now-rare visits to Manhattan.[8] And Moore also mentions Thayer in a penciled note to Watson asking for permission to move a deadline, but this may well have been nothing more than Moore's imperturbable politeness.[9]

In short, Moore had been in charge long enough and was given enough independence by Watson to put her stamp on the magazine, arguably more so than any other editor before her. So it is nonsense for Williams to argue that she could accomplish more if she were afforded more freedom. Also, Williams defends Moore's efforts to change the policy of the magazine, but doesn't say how she was trying to do this. It would not have been a difficult thing for her to do. Watson respected her greatly and had anyway always been happy to step into the shadows to allow others to shine.

By early 1929, the end was in sight. Thayer's mother and Herman Riccius, both less sanguine than Thayer had been at the cost of supporting literature and art through the money-losing magazine, suggested to Watson that the issue for May that year be the final one.[10] Watson was willing to keep the magazine alive if it were felt that Thayer would benefit from its existence or if it could provide Thayer "refuge when he emerges from solitude,"[11] but Moore evidently was of the mind that there was little point without Thayer. "[I]f Scofield must be absent we'd better stop & suffer no selfish regrets in that matter," she wrote.[12]

After the publication of the final issue, Marianne Moore wrote to Thayer. She had been, along with perhaps Cummings, one of the few favorites of both Thayer and Watson. Her position at the magazine afforded her both income and time to write, and receiving the Dial Award helped make her name. It is unfair to say, as did Henry McBride, that the award "practically made" her career. Moore's talent and her method of creation, so congenial to the modernist outlook, would have always pushed her to the forefront of the literature of her time, despite her natural modesty. But the platform the magazine provided her was undoubtedly an important element in her success, and her letter to Thayer noted this.

> You and Doctor Watson for years and years have been devising ways to benefit others, and I looking on, have admired and approved; how often have I been taken aback and astonished by being myself brought into the circle and made a chief recipient. Work for *The Dial* has been rewarding from my first timorous day in the office; and certain parts of that work have been the most rewarding of any I have ever had a part in. Can you the better understand why I now feel that it is you and Doctor Watson who should be receiving from everyone associated with *The Dial*, expression of grateful remembrance?[13]

By the time the *Dial* died, in the final year of the decade, Cummings, Eliot, and Moore had all been anthologized[14] and the Museum of Modern Art was established. Modernism had moved into the mainstream.

22

THAYER IN ECLIPSE

As Thayer slipped into deeper and deeper eclipse, traveling between Bermuda, Boston, Florida, and his beloved Martha's Vineyard with nurses and servants, scholars of the modernist movement were beginning to comprehend the enormously important role that had been played by the "little" magazine in distributing and influencing the art and literature of the twentieth century. It is appropriate, perhaps, that the first survey of magazines and their role in influencing and distributing literature was undertaken by Ezra Pound in his 1930 article "Small Magazines,"[1] which somewhat idealistically traced the migration of literature to noncommercial outlets. Pound himself plays male lead in this entertaining rehearsal of the history of the small magazine, which is also appropriate, considering the labors he expended filling their pages with what he believed was the best writing of the time. Frederick Hoffman and his coauthors Charles Allen and Carolyn F. Ulrich were among the first to mine this scholarly vein and in 1946 published their seminal *The Little Magazine: A History and a Bibliography*. Hoffman and his colleagues were struck by the importance of the *Dial* in so many spheres, publishing as it did writers and artists both experimental and traditional who would come to define this aesthetic era in the country's history and whose influence showed little signs of abating. And while Pound's article had dismissed the *Dial* as being useful mainly in putting money in the pockets of impoverished writers, Hoffman and his colleagues saw the *Dial* as the best of its kind. "The Dial was one of the most important of the American experimental reviews," they wrote. "It represented more material than any other magazine, and to a greater number of readers; therefore, its leavening influence was far greater than that of its nearest competitor."[2] The quantity and quality of its contents, as well as the longevity of the magazine that was guaranteed by the deep pockets of its owners, ensured that its mark on the rest of the century in which it thrived would be profound. Wrote Hoffman, "America learned from *The Dial* critics more about the artistic process and more about the value of art as experience than it had learned during our entire previous history."[3] Hoffman also mentioned that Thayer had suffered a breakdown and disappeared from the literary scene. "Thayer has become a half-legendary memory around New York," he wrote.[4]

In 1949, Donald Gallup of the Yale American Literature Collection wrote Watson, noting the institution's interest in the *Dial*, and consequently the magazine's files were found in storage in Worcester. Gallup persuaded Thayer's guardian, Walter A. Edwards of the Providence, Rhode Island, law firm Edwards & Angell to transfer the papers to Yale. This was duly done, the papers arriving at Yale in 1950. Thayer's personal correspondence was to remain at the Worcester Storage Company.

Thayer's mother had placed most of her son's art collection on loan at the Worcester Art Museum, and in the early 1950s plans were laid for an exhibition of what had become known as the Dial Collection. Nicholas Joost, then a professor of English at Assumption College, was asked to write on the collection, and Thayer's guardian agreed that the correspondence and materials remaining in the storage warehouse that touched on the operations of the *Dial* be placed at the museum, where Joost could study them. Thayer's personal correspondence was to be separated and returned to the warehouse.[5] This was accomplished, after a fashion, in 1955. We don't know what criteria were used by Edwards and Joost in distinguishing between business and personal correspondence, and, of course, since Thayer was so profoundly involved in the magazine, many letters were a mixture of the personal and business. Edwards and Herman Riccius insisted that Joost, in return for being allowed access to the material, make no mention of Thayer's illness or indeed of any personal matters, a demand with which Joost was happy to comply. The restrictions under which Joost had to work are described in a letter he wrote to Alyse Gregory in 1965, evidently in response to Gregory voicing concern about her and others' privacy following the publication of Joost's *Scofield Thayer and "The Dial."* "Mr. Edwards went over every word of my manuscript—twice. He was excruciatingly careful to see to it that not a breath of libellous matter or potentially embarrassing matter got into print. . . . Your privacy is utter. I have been concerned with the Dial papers only as materials for research, and to tell the unvarnished truth, I've forgotten almost everything that I didn't put in the book."[6]

The Worcester Art Museum exhibition, which included lectures and a reading by Cummings, took place in the summer of 1959. One of the attendees was Yale's Gallup, who learned during his visit that much of the Thayer correspondence at the Worcester Art Museum was closely related to the *Dial* materials at Yale, and later that year Gallup approached Edwards about depositing the correspondence at Yale. Edwards declined, saying that he needed first to examine it but that he didn't immediately have the time. It would take eleven years, a change of guardianship, and Joost's wrapping up his research before the papers would finally arrive in Gallup's office at Yale in December 1971. Perhaps because of an oversight, four boxes of material related to Thayer and the *Dial* remained at the Worcester museum.

Some reviewers were not kind to Joost's book. There were few print references to Thayer after his removal from public life, and many scholars of the modernist period were eager to discover what had happened to him. Joost offered little personal information beyond Thayer's work for the *Dial*. He tried to brazen his way through this criticism, saying, "Scofield Thayer is not a figure of mystery,"[7] but the truth was that Joost's writing on Thayer did nothing to support such a denial. His work carefully avoided discussion of anything remotely personal in Thayer's life, reducing his struggle against insanity to a vague "illness," even though Watson had told the authors of *The Little Magazine* in 1943 that Thayer had suffered a "nervous and physical breakdown in 1925 and has never completely recovered."[8] Joost was also forbidden, by Herman Riccius, to mention the feud with Barnes,[9] despite the fact that it had been mentioned in print by Henry McBride.[10]

Ivan Sandrof, book reviewer for the *Worcester Telegram,* was well aware of these lacunae in Joost's work and took him to task for it. "Thayer, still living, is said to be an invalid, hopelessly ill, in an island institution, his affairs in the hands of an attorney," wrote Sandrof. "The full story will come to light, as it must, for Scofield Thayer played far too influential a role in American culture. Those who conceal the information, if they are aware of it, do nothing to advance truth, culture, or the right of the people to know."[11]

Reviewing Joost's book in the *New York Times Book Review* of January 31, 1965, *Partisan Review* editor Richard Poirier also noted the veil that had been drawn over the figure of Thayer. "Scofield Thayer's own insistence on the highly personal aspects of the enterprise makes all the more unfortunate that, while Mr. Joost's editorial history of the Dial profits from circumspection, his account of Thayer as a person is greatly impoverished by caution and uninquisitiveness," he wrote.

Obviously not an ordinary man, and still . . . a mysterious one, Scofield Thayer is nowhere submitted to the pressure of inquiry that would sufficiently reveal his highly personal relations to The Dial, its contributors and associates. . . . Mr. Joost could have written an even better book had he been more exploratory in the other direction, thereby revealing some of the less evident human and emotional energies crucially at work in determining the history of The Dial. As it is, the book doesn't fully answer the promise of its title.[12]

Joost must have been greatly frustrated by this. Writing the book as he was ordered to, carefully stepping around the topics of Thayer's personal relationships and his mental illness, must have been a truly difficult feat. And, whatever the book's demerits as a biography, Joost was able to put on the record a vast amount of information about the magazine and the period that otherwise might have been lost. Joost defended his work in a letter to the editor by saying it was not intended as "biographical gossip" and that Thayer's biography had "yet to be commissioned and written." He ended, "Finally, I can assure Mr. Poirier quite authoritatively that had I supplied the information he desired, I should not have been permitted to write the book."[13] To this Poirier in turn responded, "I suspected as much, but I hadn't wanted to say so."[14]

Joost further defended his project in a letter to Gregory. "I am amused at the reviewers who think that I've been ordered to hold back all sorts of 'secrets,'" he wrote.

I refer even to the excellent and sympathetic *TLS* review, with its mention of Pound and Eliot. Well, I used just about everything on hand, and Mr. Eliot himself told me that all his papers dating from the early 1920s had disappeared. There just aren't any "secrets," dread or otherwise, that amount to much. Of Mr. Thayer's own life, what really needed to be said beyond what I said except to explain in a sentence or two that he lived in Vienna to be near Freud and that the analysis didn't take? Unfortunately that small piece of information wasn't allowed and people have taken except[ion] to the with[h]eld facts. They are going to be disappointed some day.[15]

Joost persuaded one of Thayer's doctors to pass on to Thayer a copy of the book. "He was, I understand, 'more than interested' and kept it and read it after the doctor left," Joost wrote Gregory. "Next visit, he asked to meet with E. E. Cummings and T. S. Eliot and seemed much saddened to learn that they both are dead."[16]

Joost eventually managed to meet Thayer in person. It was the fall of 1968, and Thayer was on his way to Florida for the winter. Joost described Thayer and the meeting this way: "He's still erect, handsome, in excellent health; he has a cold, elegant presence that I find very daunting. He's a great man, and what a tragedy for himself and American culture that he hasn't been able to endure 'public' life."[17] The interview, such as it was, lasted only "a few minutes."[18] Joost reported no conversation taking place and, along with using the word "interview" in its primary meaning of two people seeing each other without necessarily speaking, couched his language in such a way as to suggest that Thayer was in fine fettle and that his withdrawal from public life had almost been a career choice. When Ellen Thayer heard of the meeting and how Joost had characterized it, she was skeptical of the portrait of Thayer drawn by Joost. "It would be really horrible if after all these years of suffering Scofield should get entire possession of himself," she wrote to a family member. "Mr. Joost must have seen and talked with Lazarus risen from the dead."[19]

Thayer was legally determined to be insane in 1937, and, following Massachusetts law, an annual reckoning of his income and expenses was maintained at the probate court in Worcester. A physician's certificate from Arthur H. Ruggles, M.D., superintendent of Butler Hospital in Providence, Rhode Island, placed in the probate file January 4, 1937, stated that Thayer suffered from "chronic and incurable mental disease which render[s] him incapable of taking care of himself or attending to any business matters" and that "he is not now capable or likely to become capable of taking care of himself."[20]

Thayer continued to write in both French and German but was often incoherent.[21] Evidently, none of these writings has been discovered. Margaret (Duggan) Coughlin of Maine was hired to cook for Thayer one summer in the 1970s when she was a freshman at Georgetown University. She later trained to become a licensed social worker. She saw him as an "elderly, unmedicated man" who dressed "in white flowy clean linen robes every day like a night dress."[22] Despite his mental illness, Thayer had retained his famous attention to detail. Cooking for him, Coughlin said, "was like cooking for 15." His Pepperidge Farm sandwich bread had to be cut at an angle, the crusts cut off, then put back in place. He would eat the sandwiches and leave the crusts. The broccoli tops had to be cut off, then cooked and put back with the stems and fanned out on the plate. He'd eat only the tops. His table setting covered half of a large oval table, and everything had to be in an exact spot. He wrote ceaselessly in his bedroom, which he rarely left except to eat meals. On occasion he would scream and slam his bed up and down.[23]

Because Thayer never dated his personal notes, we cannot be sure which of them, if any, came from the period after his removal from public life. But there is one that speaks of the psychiatric hospital in Belmont, Massachusetts, where he spent time. "The yellow brick bldg at McLean shows the direction to be at once heartless + incompetent," he wrote. "No one of heart wants red-brick. Any competent psychologist knows that sanatorial environment sh'd be not rebarbatively cold, but yellow brick so is."[24]

We also find in Thayer's notebooks a section of entries in which he mentions institutions at which he was hospitalized following his breakdown—Memorial Hospital in Worcester, Massachusetts; MacLean Hospital in Belmont, Massachusetts; and Butler Hospital in Providence, Rhode Island. He also mentions in these sections what he calls the "Clark affair," referring to the scandal his former analyst Dr. Pierce L. Clark found himself in after he was charged by a pastor with "alienating the affections" of the pastor's wife, who was one of the doctor's patients.[25] This also took place following Thayer's breakdown.

Some of these notebook entries are gnomic: "The Clark affair, like the Palace of the Sleeping Beauty at Beacon and McLeans, came to life at Butler."[26] Others seem to speak of his perhaps forced hospitalization at the hands of his family as his friends turned a blind eye: "I did not require charity: I required justice. I got what hypocritically pretended to be charity + was not even justice," and "The glib disloyalty of Cummings, Watson + Elaine Orr." There is also this: "At Mem. Hosp I was like a beautiful angel beating his wings in a . . . void in vain."[27] This is an echo of Matthew Arnold on Shelley, and there is an even more resonant plangency in the full quotation: "The man Shelley, in very truth, is not entirely sane, and Shelley's poetry is not entirely sane either. The Shelley of actual life is a vision of beauty and radiance, indeed, but availing nothing, effecting nothing. And in poetry, no less than in life, he is 'a beautiful *and ineffectual* angel, beating in the void his luminous wings in vain.'"[28]

Thayer died on July 9, 1982, in Long Hill Cottage, Planting Field Way, Edgartown. He was ninety-two and had outlived family, friends, caregivers, and guardians. There was no notice of his death in the *New York Times* or in the state capital newspaper, the *Boston Globe*. His hometown newspaper, the *Evening Gazette* of Worcester, Massachusetts, ran an eleven-inch obituary that had been prepared years earlier by his lawyers. There was no photograph. It made no mention of where Thayer had been the previous fifty-odd years or what he had been doing, saying only that he had retired in the 1920s and then traveled widely.

23

POSTMORTEM

In 1931, Florence Thayer began placing Thayer's artworks at the Worcester Art Museum, which would eventually house the greater part of his extensive collection. Naturally, the small and relatively young museum, which had opened in 1898, was delighted to receive such a trove of modern works, and many Worcester art lovers hoped that the collection would in time be donated to the museum. The feeling was evidently shared by some at the museum; an anonymous note in the museum's archives from September 30, 1931, records that the works were received on "permanent loan . . . to come to WAM eventually, probably."[1] Indeed, Thayer's collection remained at the museum so long (more than fifty years) that some staff members took for granted that the works were destined to remain at the Worcester museum. The collection, which included paintings, drawings, and sculptures by Pablo Picasso, Paul Cezanne, Henri Matisse, Pierre Bonnard, Marc Chagall, Gustav Klimt, Paul Signac, Gaston Lachaise, and Charles Demuth, was in many ways the heart of the gallery.

When he drew up and signed his will in June 1925, Thayer had just run in the *Dial* an excoriation of his hometown following the Worcester newspaper's publishing of a quotation calling his magazine an "intellectual sewer" (see chapter 1). Further, the one exhibition of his collection held at the Worcester Art Museum in 1924 had required the no doubt irritating removal of two paintings, a Picasso and a Braque, that might have offended the more conservative Worcesterites. So it was perhaps less than surprising that, when Thayer's will was opened, it was found that he chose not to bequeath his art collection to his hometown's art museum. The bulk of his collection, valued in the early 1980s at $14 million, went to the Metropolitan Museum of Art in

New York City, and twenty-two drawings by Aubrey Beardsley went to the Fogg Art Museum in Cambridge. Both gifts carried the condition that they were "for permanent exhibition."[2]

The city's perceived slights to his collection, in and of themselves, may not have been the only reasons for Thayer's spurning Worcester. The truth is that he had never had a particularly high opinion of his hometown or of its museum. He described Worcester as having "the cultural outlook of an Alpine village."[3] He wrote of the "squalor of Main St., Worcester,"[4] said that the city was "woundingly ugly,"[5] and compared it to a Swiss city he found just as dull: "Worcester is merely the under side of Basle. The only difference is, one is in heaven, the other Hell."[6] Indeed, to Thayer, Worcester displayed the same graceless greed and servility to the social order he despised in his own Worcester relatives: "Mothers of eligibles everywhere *glissent* about the millionaire; at Worcester *l'en vous colle*" (meaning that Worcester mothers of marriageable girls don't just mill around the millionaire, they are in his face.)[7] Of course, Thayer regarded his own snobbery as perfectly natural, and in one of his notations he compared members of his loathed hometown with Joyce and Cummings, writers whom he admired and yet whose relatively humble roots he could never pass over. "The battle-cry of the *canaille*: 'Suck my arse!' (Cf. Worc irish + Joyce + E.E.C.)"[8] As for the art museum itself, he regarded it as "more a jewel-box than a building,—and for mere platinum at that."[9] For Thayer, platinum did not have the prestige we impute to it today; he regarded this still relatively new metal as an ultimate symbol of contemporary falsity.

Thayer left the "residue and remainder" of his property, about $7 million, in equal shares to Alyse Gregory, Marianne Moore, Robert von Erdberg, and Robert Thomas Nichols. Gregory and Moore were his two women editors of the *Dial*. Erdberg worked at the Ministry of Cultural Affairs in Berlin and was a great friend of Thayer's, especially during his time in Austria. Nichols was another good friend, "the first to love me for my soul," wrote Thayer.[10] Nichols was a playwright, author of *Guilty Souls*, a drama that was reviewed in the anonymous "Briefer Mention" section of the November 1922 issue of the *Dial*. (His friendship with Thayer evidently did not translate into benign reviews of his work. The critique read, "The author of this play gives the effect of attempting to carry a greater weight than his shoulders will support.")[11] The four people mentioned in the will were dead at this point, and eventually five relatives (all cousins once removed) would come forward to claim the inheritance.[12]

With regard to the art, however, there was the question of what Thayer's will meant by "permanent exhibition." The phrase would seem self-explanatory, but as

the probating of the estate unfolded, it transpired that the Metropolitan was unwilling to state in writing how the works would be exhibited there. Consequently,
a hearing was held to determine the probate court's interpretation of the phrase.

The hearing was seen by many as the Worcester Art Museum's last shot at
keeping the collection that had been so important to the museum, not only for
its inherent worth, but also in the fact that the museum had been "collecting
around" the Dial Collection in acquiring new works.[13] Its loss would be, if not
a figurative tearing out of the gallery's heart, a painful and serious amputation.

Lawyer Charles B. Swartwood, representing the heirs, took the literalist point
of view and argued that "permanent exhibition" meant just what it said—that
the works should be continuously displayed in unrestricted public galleries.
John O. Mirick, appearing for the Metropolitan, argued that because the pieces
could deteriorate if continuously hung, "on permanent display" should mean
only that the works were available for viewing when requested. William Robinson, the Fogg Museum's acting curator of drawings, agreed with Mirick, saying, "The light exposure would cause harm. It would cause the paper to turn
color and the original esthetic quality would be forever lost." Swartwood asked
whether Robinson would hang a picture continuously if he were required to.
"[I]t would be like condemning it to death," he said. Smartwood tried a different
tack, calling to the stand Bartlett H. Hayes Jr., retired director of the Addison
Gallery in Andover, who said that he had several times "regretfully declined
gifts to the museum" because there were conditions attached that he felt the
institution could not satisfy.[14]

Both Mirick and Charles F. Dodson, representing the Metropolitan and the
Fogg respectively, argued that permanent display would cause deterioration
of the works because of exposure to light and extremes of temperature and
humidity, and it was this view that prevailed. In his decision, Judge Francis W.
Conlin ruled that the works in the Thayer collection need not be continuously
displayed on museum walls as long as they are accessible to the public upon
request. Conlin said Thayer "wanted the public to enjoy his works of art and
would not want them to be hung on the walls of the museum constantly and
continuously which would cause irreparable damage and destruction to the art
works he wished to have appreciated by many future generations." Pointing out
that the effects of light on works of art on paper were not well understood when
the will was drawn up, Conlin wrote that Thayer would not have preferred exhibition over preservation. "He loved his paintings," he wrote. "It was not his
intention to destroy his works of art."[15] The collection was to go to the Met.

Conlin's decision was arguably in the best interests of the art, but one has to wonder at Thayer's meaning in this note from his personal writings: "Art is like a woman. It does not wish to be put in a museum and studied: it longs to be taken home and loved, even though that love imply its own suffering. Museums like Minotaurs devour the fairest of mankind."[16] It is not a great stretch to consider that the "suffering" mentioned here might be that of an environment less controlled than that of a museum, a suffering that is made up for by the human love of art.

Thayer also made the point that a work of art that is not viewed may as well not exist: "Beauty is not in the eye of the beholder. Neither is it in the work of art—these are but the flint and tinder, which, being brought together, give the spark called beauty. As there is no sound when a tree falls if there be not present an ear, so there is not beauty unless some soul observe the object."[17]

The removal of Thayer's art from Worcester was by no means the end of the matter, and Thayer's will was to yield at least a couple more surprises. Among the items in Thayer's estate were three trunks, numbered C100, D77, and F33, that were stored at the Worcester Storage Company. A 1937 entry made in the state-required probate accounting of Thayer's effects said that the trunks contained "household furniture and articles of household or personal use."[18] When the trunks were opened they were found to hold correspondence, prints, and what the executors listed as an "erotic portfolio" including a Picasso that had not seen the light of day for a half century. This was the infamous *Erotic Scene*, also known as *La douleur*, which shows a boyish Picasso being fellated by a woman with long black hair. Picasso denied being the artist when he was presented with a photograph of the painting in the 1960s, but research has shown that the work is indeed his.[19] Another five years would pass after Thayer's death before the trunks were once again examined, this time as the files of the *Dial*, then at the Beinecke Rare Book and Manuscript Library at Yale, were being prepared for an auction that was eventually and fortunately averted. The trunks yielded more than ninety letters from Ezra Pound to Thayer, almost all of them written in the first fifteen months of the *Dial* being owned by Thayer and Watson. Walter Sutton called these "the 'new' or Worcester letters"[20] and used them as a basis for his book *Pound, Thayer, Watson, and "The Dial,"* which told for the first time the story of how these three men, sharing some tastes, utterly diverse in others, together forged the literary character of the *Dial*.

Today, little remains in Worcester connected to the life of Scofield Thayer. The homes he grew up in have been razed, the art he so lovingly collected is long gone, and the old families like his own whose fortunes were connected with industry and commerce are now mostly names on gravestones. Thayer's own remains were cremated and buried in Rural Cemetery at the Thayer family plot, right next to those of the mother and father he never seemed able to love or to forget. His own gravestone bears the same Greek cross he noted on his father's headstone. One wonders, considering his antipathy to America, his disdain for Worcester, and the revulsion he felt for his memories of growing up there, why he would choose this small, inward-looking city as a final resting place. He was careful enough in his will about his possessions and their disposition after his death, so why not his remains? Perhaps his feelings toward the city were much like those for his father, and under all the blustering dislike there was a trickle of fondness. It could also be that, as a formalist, he felt there was something proper in ending where one had begun. Or maybe he simply didn't care about the fate of his ashes, believing that the body was merely a vehicle to carry his essence through a lifetime, and once it had given up all it could, it could be dispensed with. He believed in the soul as something greater than mere mind, mere intellect, and the idea of a soul may have been important to Thayer because the other expressions of his self, his body and his mind, were damaged things that were unhelpful to the expression of the soul: "Soul struggles in material life as man under surface of water."[21]

GOD, STARS, AND SEA

THAYER'S POETIC LEGACY

We have just thirty-eight of Thayer's poems, twelve having appeared in the *Harvard Monthly*, one in the *Harvard Advocate*, twenty-four in the *Dial*, and one, "To One Who Was Betrayed," unpublished.[1] The literature on Thayer's verse is scant. As noted earlier, his writings were praised by Cummings and both Marianne Moore and Alyse Gregory, but the fact that all were recipients of Thayer's largesse through gifts and employment somewhat lessens the credibility of their support. Hoffman, Allen, and Ulrich, who effusively praised Thayer's work as editor of the *Dial*, mentioned only that he had also produced "some estimable verse."[2] Nicholas Joost, a redoubtable defender of Thayer in every other way, did little to defend Thayer's verse, only saying noncommittally that "The literary remains of Scofield Thayer rest in the pages of his *Dial*."[3] Such dismissal of Thayer's work is perhaps unduly hasty. His was certainly a poetry that carried few of the signatures of the modernist movements—he almost always preferred form to free verse, sentiment (in the sense of an expressed thought or emotion) to unexplained image, and the development of an idea as opposed to a disrupted or nonlinear narrative. But such poets were not unusual through the modernist era, with Frost, Yeats, Thomas, and others following a similar tack. And while it is undeniable that Thayer is best known for his unsigned "Comments" in the *Dial* and less so for the verse he published there in the later years of the magazine, the not inconsiderable sheaf of material from the pages of the *Monthly* includes poems, fiction, an essay on Shelley, a satire entitled "My Friend the Humanitarian Poet," and an editorial on the future of the Harvard Union.

Further, there is something of a natural flow between the *Monthly* and the *Dial*. Not only did Thayer achieve positions of great influence at both publications, but it is also true that a good number of the staff of the Harvard magazine ended up working at or for the *Dial*. Gilbert Seldes, Cuthbert Wright, Lincoln MacVeagh, John Dos Passos, and, of course, Cummings were all contemporaries of Thayer who would publish in or work for both magazines. Another Harvard acquaintance was Alan Seeger, author of "I Have a Rendezvous with Death," who died in the Great War.

Moore was right in describing Thayer as "categorically formal." His early poems in the *Harvard Monthly* are uniformly conventional in structure. The first to appear is "Midnight," in the November 1909 issue.[4] The sonnet discusses one of his favorite subjects, the night stars, and in the poem Thayer expresses the urge to journey into the sky, to "navigate that jewel-sprinkled sward," and, in a final rhetorical question, asks "what marvel, and what recompense supreme" might be enjoyed by the star traveler. (Another Worcester native, Robert H. Goddard, known as the "Father of the Rocket Age," had just been graduated from Worcester Polytechnic Institute that year and was to have a similar if more practical urge to reach the heavens through the creation of the first liquid-fueled rocket.)

In Thayer's next published undergraduate poem, "Clouds,"[5] another sonnet, seemingly inspired by Shelleyan odes, he is again gazing heavenward. He sees the clouds as "unwieldy galleons" sailing through the skies and wonders where they came from and where they might be going:

> What captain guides you on what enterprise?
> What restless soldier or what zealous priest
> Leads you upon what distant-reaching quest?

This poem begins and ends with a series of rhetorical questions such as these, which perhaps betray in Thayer some uncertainty in how he should approach his subject.

In 1911, he produced just one published poem, "Abode," which appeared in November's *Harvard Monthly*.[6] In this poem, Thayer's subject is morning (one wonders if the title should have been "Aubade").

> The glad, green meadows of morning
> Are bright with the breath of the flowers,
> And the gold-eyed lilies are scorning
> The bounds of their virginal bowers;
>
> They are small, white thoughts that are yearning
> Up from the vibrant sod;
> They are small white flames that are burning
> Up to the feet of God.

In this pastoral idyll, the lilies, bursting with life, are eager to worship God. And yet the interest of the speaker is not so much in nature as in the intended recipient of the apostrophe, whom we finally meet in the final quatrain:

> O shake out the dreams from thine hair, Love,
> Look forth on the lily-white lea,—
> Though thy star-scattered dreams may be fair, Love,
> Yet arise to the dawn and to me!

For all its Romanticism and excessively poetic and archaic diction, this poem seems more down-to-earth than the previous two. Rather than straining to understand the mysteries of distant phenomena such as clouds and stars, these lines stick to an admittedly idealistic description of the earth and its floral productions and finally touch on the image of a young woman waking from sleep, an image that would certainly be attractive to a twenty-one-year-old male who may still have been a virgin at this time.

The following January, Thayer published "Chronicle of the Monk Peter,"[7] a piece of fiction set in some remote chivalric realm wherein a young man, Edmund, elopes with the young woman his father had planned to marry. This tale of romance is tiresomely executed, to my taste, and is perhaps most interesting for its proto-Freudian theme of a man marrying the woman who was to have been his mother.

The following month there appeared "Vale,"[8] which again takes up the metaphor of flowers:

> Our hearts grew up together
> Like roses abloom on the lea,
> In pleasant, sun-blithe weather,
> Beside a sun-blithe sea.

But the roses are uprooted and replanted in "separate, sea-bound closes," bringing to mind the islands of isolation that haunt the poetry of Matthew Arnold. But while Arnold (sometimes) saw love as a power that could overcome this separation, Thayer simply celebrates the sadness:

> I pray we may weep hereafter
> In the lonely, latter years,
> For where there may be no laughter
> It is well that there be some tears.

"Ad Amicam Meum" also eulogizes some unearthly beauty, and in the final stanza, Thayer prays that he could lie forever beneath the eyes of his beloved, "For

then the stars might not dissever / Me from paradise."[9] This was as much romantic nonsense as at least one budding critic could take, and in an anonymous review of the *Monthly* in the school newspaper, the *Crimson*, a writer noted crossly,
"I do not believe that Schofield Thayer's 'Amica' exists in his imagination, much
less in his experience; she is only a creature of his vocabulary."[10] He may well have
been right. One wonders if the title gave Cummings the idea for his "Puella Mea."

In May 1912, Thayer published "Still the Old Songs," Villonesque with its
refrain, "Where are the flowers of other springs?"[11] In July, there appeared "An
Adieu," a poem that begins as a lightsome lyric, ("Sunlight on the meadow /
And sunlight on the lea / Sunlight in your laughter") but suddenly grows omi-
nous with the entrance of "[a] dark god at my shoulder." The final stanza is
ambiguous, if not incomprehensible:

> But laughter is an old god,
> A stronger god than he!
> And I am but a mortal—
> He comes for me.[12]

So laughter is a stronger god than the dark god that suddenly shows in the second quatrain. And the poet, being a mere mortal, is the quarry of some god. But
it is not immediately apparent which of these deities is coming for the poet, the
god of laughter or the "strange, cold" god of darkness. It may be that Thayer's
poor control of his prosody is distorting the meaning of the poem here, or it
may be that we should see the dash as a sudden breaking off of the thought as
the poet realizes that the dark god has come not to quell the lovely laughter of
the woman but to carry away the poet. The title is, after all, "An Adieu."

Also in the July edition there appeared "My Friend the Humanitarian Poet,"[13]
a heavy-handed satire that seems to be defending the idea of poetry as an art of
grace and decorum, not, as the essay puts it, the "union of gutter and palace."

This satire rather belaboringly paints the portrait of the contemporary poet
as someone who has ditched the ideas of beauty and an aesthetic for the reason
that art must reflect the human, and, since the human is imperfect, any attempts
to put beauty or symmetry into art are ill-advised.

In March 1913, Thayer published yet another sonnet, "On the Sudden Taking
Away of My Love."[14]

> The sky has been so very blue today
> I could not dream that aught might come to thee:
> Drinking the dawn, I had forgot that He
> Might deem it best to take my love away.

The day is so beautiful that thoughts of sudden death are far from the poet's mind, but something—a lover arising early to leave the poet alone in bed?—has caused him to consider this possibility. The poet, using his favorite device of the rhetorical question, imagines his love in the next world: "And dost thou then in happier gardens stray?" But, at the opening of the sestet, the poet sets about correcting himself:

> And hast thou then forgotten me so soon?
> Ah, no! I wrong thee with the thought,—for thou
> Hast quitted heaven, voyaged past the moon;
> Rebel to glory, thou art with me now.
> For what was there in paradise for thee?
> Thou lov'dst not heaven; thou rememb'rdst me.

The poet is speaking directly to his lover, who has returned to him after an unexpected and unavoidable separation. In an almost Donnean conceit, he sees this as her being momentarily transported to heaven, where she suddenly realizes what has happened and then, like Lucifer ("Rebel to glory"), returns to the one who loves her. The poet is joyous that she has chosen their love over heaven.

The April 1913 issue of the *Harvard Monthly* was largely devoted to essays celebrating the publication of George Santayana's *Winds of Doctrine*. Thayer's contribution to the issue was an essay on Santayana's "Shelley: Or the Poetic Value of Revolutionary Principles."[15]

In the May 1913 issue, Thayer published his longest poem up to that point, "A Portrait."[16] The quatrains describe a lover:

> My love is white as hawthorn blossoms
> That burst and foam in May,
> And there betwixt the billowing branches
> Her eyes let in the day.

All in all, the poem is more competent and better crafted than much of his previous work. His diction still tends to the archaic, and the metaphors of flowers and of a bird are a touch tired, but there is a confidence in the lines. Cummings, who was also writing for magazine by this time, compliments Thayer on the second stanza:

> Her body is a reed so slender,
> Whereon God's lips do blow,
> And in each petty human motion
> The great hymns come and go.

The lines also suggest the coda of the poem, which beatifies the beloved in images that link together the holy and the profane:

> All foolish things my youth has gathered
> In all his wandering years
> Will I cast forth from my heart's chapel
> And cleanse the walls with tears.
>
> And in that gloom shall hang her likeness,
> A radiant image there,
> And at her feet my soul—a taper—
> Shall seek her glittering hair.

Idolatry, certainly, but this worship of beauty was at the heart of Thayer's aesthetic. But there are two images here of the sacred and secular mixed: the woman is transubstantiated into a sacred object of art (shades of Browning's "My Last Duchess"?) and of veneration; and her lover becomes a monk whose worship is not through physical love but through holy offices. One is reminded of the young boy in Joyce's short story "Araby," who views the girl he longs for through a lens of Catholic imagery, since that is all the imaginative equipment he has with which to try to understand his new feelings.

"On a Gothic Tapestry Portraying the Holy Land" appeared in the June 1913 issue of the magazine.[17]

> Ascalon, Gaza, Sidon, and Tyre,
> Lordly turret and priestly spire;
> The cold glad face of the smiting sea,
> And many a good flag flaunting free.
> The dry brown sand where the paynims fly,
> The wet red sand where the paynims die,
> And over it all God's own blue sky!

It should be no surprise, perhaps, that Thayer should eventually find himself writing this kind of ekphrastic verse. His interest in art had been growing steadily and may well have been further stoked by his new friendship with Cummings, an avid painter and drawer. Also, it makes sense that Thayer, as a dyed-in-the-wool aesthete, should find something more real, more emotional, even, in a work of art than in a relationship with another human.

Thayer's final piece for the *Harvard Monthly* was "Anapaests," a poem about the earth and all of humanity existing as a kind of perpetual hymn to God.[18] We see here a repetition of images from his earlier poems, perhaps bespeaking a breakdown of creativity or Thayer's having reached a dead end in the neo-Romantic plot in which he had chosen to work. In the first stanza, he reuses the nautical image from "Clouds" when he talks of the world being "a golden galley / On a sea of ultimate blue." And the second stanza from "Abode," "They are small white thoughts . . . Up to the feet of God," has been reworked in "Anapaests":

> For life is an eagle winging
> Up from the vibrant sod,
> For life is a song that is singing
> Sweet to God!

Thayer's verse published in the *Dial* demonstrated the same love for form and convention that it had in the *Harvard Monthly*. Only one of the poems published in the New York magazine is in free verse—"Dawn from a Railway Day-Coach," which seems to be Thayer's one and only exercise in impressionistic imagist modernism:

> The nickeled orb Apollo
> Brays.
> The disarticulated limbs of life
> Assemble.
> And Time walks.
>
> Across lymphatic fields
> Thin shadows are spun out
> Tubercular.
> The heavens adulterate
> Crows blond.
>
> And the immediate noise
> Of myriad such planets
> Wandering derelict,
> Like leagues on leagues of tolerantly-winding whales
> Not easily to be not,
> Against insensible light
> Sickens.[19]

In this poem, the natural world here is overtaken by the mechanistic one. The sun is a "nickeled orb," and with a new morning life puts itself together to face the day like a robot reconnecting its own limbs. Further, the world in the poem that has so far not been touched by technology is described almost as being a medical condition, its fields being "lymphatic" and the shadows (of clouds?) "tubercular." The narrator sees a universe full of planets all scrupulously obeying the laws of science. It is a frighteningly mechanistic and Newtonian explanation of reality, and even in the metaphor of the cosmos as an elongated pod of migrating whales, the most important thing about the creatures is not their beauty or natural majesty but their dumb persistence ("tolerantly-winding") and the simple fact of their being ("Not easily to be not"—a double negative that is almost Cummingsesque). This vision of the universe the narrator finds sickening.

A poem published one month earlier, "Counsel to a Young Man," tackles a similar existentialist sentiment of an uncaring universe.[20]

> Clasp not the ankle of the cursive moon
> Nor agitate the stars with your despair:
> They know you not; and singularly soon
> Their beauty shall not be your nightly care.

The narrator advises the young man not to waste his time by responding to the world with anger or dismay but to stoically face suffering and pain by becoming like the passionless stone of which the planets themselves are made:

> Join not with dogs in barking a dead moon,
> Increase not mountainous rivers with your grief,
> Granite and dumb, outface the raucous noon.
> Granite and dumb, hold yet yourself in fief.

This stoicism defends the person (against despair, perhaps?) and yet is not the *whole* person. The narrator advises that the young man "[a]ssert the heart" and not be overly concerned with materialism ("count not loss or gain / In other metal than the heart allows"). He goes on to say that the suffering of the human being is a natural thing so long as those sufferings are of the heart. But the heart, even though it may have undergone an existential assertion of its importance, must accept its own fate, also, and eventually die. And when it does, no matter how one has struggled to achieve in this world ("Though multitudinously you prove your worth"), the fact of death must be faced honestly: "When death confronts you, you will not reply."

Thayer also tried his hand at more songlike poems, including "Chanson Banale."[21] (Many of Thayer's poems have French titles, perhaps as a dig at Watson for his excessive use of French material in the *Dial*.) This piece, reminiscent of Blake's "Poison Tree," tells of the poet giving his "jocund" lover a cake that immediately removes her happiness and causes her to describe to him a vision of a world gone bad "[b]eneath the broken skies." It ends:

> I sit and answer the dull women
> Who carry on this world,
> And in a corner of my sorrow
> My Dearest Love lies furled.

The cake may represent sustenance, but more likely (and perhaps subconsciously) it stands for Thayer's wealth and the poisonous effect his riches could have on just about any relationship. Among his personal papers are many IOUs that were never repaid (he was in the habit of crossing out with pen or pencil debts that were repaid). One of his notes reads, "E.E. [Cummings?] borrowed money. It will be a test of his character whether he pays me back."[22] There is no other reference to this particular loan.

"The Poet Takes Leave"[23] is a poem in Alexandrine couplets in which Thayer avows his companionship with the stars and the sea, two images of, if not eternity, then at least a longevity far beyond the human. The images crop up frequently in Thayer's poetry, almost always as symbols of purity and quietude. In the stars he sees a force so far away that it may never be tampered with by man, and he believes that they will outlast the age of the humans on Earth: "They shall live unsullied when man dies; / And all his evil with him." Thayer also lays claim to the sea, to which he was attracted throughout his life, even though it has been marred by the power of technology and will no doubt be subject to more insults:

> The sea is also mine. Across his heart they ride
> And shall tomorrow curb his inmost pulse and tide,
> And turn his salt to sweetness.

And yet the poet believes that there is an essence of the ocean that can never be changed, something almost human (the sea has a "heart"), something that will obstinately rebuff the efforts to sweeten its salty roughness, something that connects man to the creature that once decided to move from water to mud to the land: "He is ribbed and coarse and true. / And party to that salt-good scheme whereof hearts firstly grew."

"Chevaux de Bois"[24] (Wooden horses) carries an echo of Eliot's "The Hollow Men," which appeared in the *Dial* eleven months before Thayer's poem. Thayer satirizes those who "clutch for Gods" and "huddle after Fools" and who torture their own logic into arguing that they have chosen their own fate.

So let us dance only in rings
Since we are links in noble things!

However, some of the horses, trapped in their endless circling, understand that the only true act of free will they can perform is that of suicide:

And some whose wits were very bright
Have had the thought to drown by night.

Ingenious trick! To snap the pin
And watch the whole Great Tent cave in!

"On a Crucifix"[25] is a four-part poem celebrating Christ's triumph over the Roman empire. It ends with the poet wishing that he could be as close to Christ as was the cross. But the poem is not convincing. It is stuffed with repetition and rhetorical apostrophes and seems, in the end, insincere, or at least ill-conceived.

And yet Thayer's turning toward religion as his mental condition worsened did result in some fine verse. The two-part poem "Jesus Again" begins in a dream in which Jesus transforms the narrator into a tree:

And I was mighty like a tree
Which roots in heaven gloriously.

Its branches being firm in air
Twinkled about the sunlight there,

And twisted into noble fault . . . [26]

The narrator sees both the physical and spiritual magnificence of existence, in which a natural object (the tree) may in fact be planted in another world, rooted in heaven. This gives it a strength that can seem to defy physical law (its branches, though heavy, are thrust into the air, where they also twinkle, paradoxically, with the lightness of sunlight.)

More to the point, the tree has been made by Jesus from the essence of the narrator, and since, of course, a tree is the very thing upon which Christ was crucified, what Thayer suggests here is that Jesus himself gave humanity the ability to kill its redeemer. Indeed, being "twisted" in "noble fault" may mean that humanity actually has no option but to take part in the execution of the savior. The Old English "The Dream of the Rood" comes to mind.

In the second part of the poem, Thayer approaches Christ more familiarly: "Ah Jesus of the lonely smile, / Lord of the Heart." Yet here also Jesus can only be reached in dream rather than in reality, and the speaker of the poem is frustrated in his attempt to separate the man from the myth:

> I have not found the luxury to beguile
> Your white drained self from that which is proud dreams.

Christ is described as a shuttle (a metaphor taken from the textile factories of Thayer's father, perhaps) that moves too subtly in the heart for a mere human to perceive its actions, let alone touch it: "I cannot clasp you, for you would depart / If I were I, and you but naked you."

There is in the poem both a desire to be close to the figure of Jesus and a profound sadness arising from the thought of the nearness to such suffering. And yet, Jesus is so unreachable that only in dreams can humans achieve anything close to a physical union.

> In dreams we have accosted your proud eyes
> And touched your feet, incredulous at our lips,
> But in dream's blasphemy the beauty cries
> And we are not the loin-cloth on your hips.

There is a more homoerotic loneliness in this stanza that seems stronger than the spiritual urge for union with Jesus.

The final couplet demonstrates a resignation to the separation of the earthly and the spiritual, an image in which the two interplay without ever intermingling:

> We are the dust wherein your shuttle plies;
> We are the stars, and you but light, and skies.

In the brief song "And Love Said, Let There Be Rain," Thayer treats the subject taken up so famously in the *Dial* by his old rival, T. S. Eliot—drought.[27]

> Twist me not laurel from the mountains
>   Nor break me heather from the plains,
> For I have sat by Love's dry fountains
>   And now it wholly rains.

But this poem has none of the apocalyptic doom of "The Waste Land." Indeed, the poem is drenched in rain ("the downpour of disaster / In liquid drops is turned") almost to the point of comedy. Rain is a common symbol of God's grace, and here we find the narrator, ironically seated at the "dry fountains" of Love, all but drowning in the inundation from above. And in the final quatrain there is a taste of that thing so rare in Thayer's tortured and unhappy mind—serenity.

My heart has learned that every sorrow
   Though at the quick it dig and stay,
Shall liquefy in a tomorrow
   Whereof He Pours the day.

"On an Old Painting of Portsmouth Harbor," probably written after Thayer's decision to move to Europe more or less permanently, examines the rootlessness of Thayer's life.[28] The poem's conceit is of the narrator coming across the painting while in Europe. The picture triggers images of a childhood spent in and around the sea, whose waters were "[u]ngenerous to fledgling limbs." He speaks of the importance of place, of how all things are marked by the land that nurtures them, and that trying to transplant culture to an inhospitable region is self-defeating. He says of European ships approaching Portsmouth:

Though all those ships be smooth like apples
And packed inside with Gothic worth,
Chuck to the gills with Gothic chapels—
Shall that then give us Gothic Earth?

He expands this notion somewhat, seeing an unnaturalness in his own purchases of European art:

There is no sense in buying pictures
And swimming them across the sea:
The sun and moon have laid old strictures
On what a continent shall be.

That is, what is created in one place cannot be readily translated to another without there resulting an anomaly of some kind. He then begins to scold himself for his nostalgia. He advises himself to "[g]ive over the ridiculous battle" of mentally re-creating a sentimental scene from childhood and to let his new home embrace him.

The heart of Europe shall accept you
And hold you closelier for your pain . . .
. . . .
You shall sit down, and almost wonder
If you are not come home at last.
You shall sit down, and almost sunder
The pain that ties you to your past.

So in Europe, the wanderer will "almost" find something like a home. He will "almost" rid himself of the pains he has carried for so long. So even though the new homeland may embrace him, the healing will never be quite complete. No matter how much he may wish to be European or to achieve that transnationalism that many Progressives yearned for in this era, a part of his history is elsewhere, and thus he will never be complete. "I shall not be a whole hereafter, / Because I was a boy not here."

The final realization of the writer is that he is a virtual nomad, a traveler vainly in search of a cultural home. Always disdainful of his own country, never wholly satisfied with other countries and cities he tried to adopt, Thayer seems to see in this poem that his only true homeland is not land at all but rather the sea upon which he sailed his beloved sailboats as a boy and which had carried him so often between the New World and the Old.

> I have no home, unless it be
> The tortured excellence of the sea.

"On an Old Painting" is probably Thayer's best poem, harking back as it does to the ekphrastic experiment "On a Gothic Tapestry" from his Harvard years. It is more rhetorically restrained than his other work and seems to forcefully connect with real rather than "literary" sentiments.

Thayer lacked a sense of place or rootedness. This may have arisen because of his transnational view of the world, his sense of having the existential ability to take on another heritage. Of course, this act of self-creation would have been eased by the fact of his great wealth, which ensured that his transitions between cultures were largely free of the discomforts felt by other immigrants.

"I Walk, Understandingly" is a curious work by any standard.[29] It is a walk-poem, a genre that allows the poet to define reality by what he chooses to describe while at the same time giving him a kind of performance space. Every work of art is the vision of its creator, but the walk-poem celebrates this subjectivity by making the poet as much his subject as what is described. In "I Walk," the poet takes his "torn umbrella" on a walk, carrying with him "simple bread." He walks past houses that he sees as "occurring now and then." Of course, the houses are permanent, but for the walking narrator they "occur," as if events, precisely at the moment he passes them. We have jumped, briefly, into a more magical world in which buildings appear and vanish, but then we are immediately pulled back to reality by scenes of everyday activity, beauty, and squalor. The narrator sees women washing clothes, lakes in which scenery is reflected, and road ruts full of "shabby water." The moment of magic has produced water in three conditions, but none is the right one. The narrator continues walking.

He enters a wood "gravely"—a strange choice of adverb considering the lightsome, even flighty, tone of the piece throughout. There he passes sights of the natural world—trees, ferns, a deer, a surprised rabbit, an oak tree "clasping the great sun," and a "purple serpent." He walks on toward the sea, and as he nears it he sees the dramatic effects of coastal weather in the "trees with all their branches / Wrung one disastrous way." The poet twice notes the lack of noise:

> I open by the startling silence
> Of the immortal sea,
> And bowing in that barren silence
> The beach-grass is grave friends with me.

Because of the syntax of this final sentence, the action of "bowing" may be performed by either the narrator or the wind-blown grass. Either way, this is the end of the poem, and the speaker and the lowly grass become "grave" friends, "grave" perhaps in the sense of being sober and serious because each thrives only in this cold, silent, erosive environment, or "grave" perhaps because the two will, like all living things, share death.

The last poem Thayer published in the magazine was "Wherefore" in the October 1927 issue.[30] Thayer had been hospitalized by this time, although we don't know when the poem was written. Its thirty-two lines comprise a single sentence, which begins:

> Because my passion was deep and sad
> Because no peace of the world I had,
>
> Because the waves were clean and sound,
> Because it was good to hear them pound.

The relative simplicity of the language, the lack of his usual arcane vocabulary, the unstilted syntax, all suggest an emotional and intellectual authenticity in the poem that is not always present in Thayer's verse. After the introduction he moves quickly to his beloved sea. The narrator is standing on a "desert beach," where he imagines sailors whose hearts are "good" and "stiff like their own oars' wood." He watches boats putting out to sea, hearing "the sacred thole-pin's creak" and "stern heels on the braces squeak." The boat is "rowing out toward night" but the narrator is not aboard. He is left alone on the beach with his only companions the night sky and the ocean.

> Therefore I stood looking out to sea
> Till the Great Stars came and stood with me.

NOTES

Abbreviations

The numbers following each abbreviation in the endnotes refer to the collection number, which is used by institutions with multiple collections, followed by the box and folder numbers. So, for example, BDT 34.4.1 would refer to an item in a specific Dial/Thayer collection (34) at the Beinecke Library (there are two such collections there) contained in box 4, folder 1. In instances where material is undated or not sorted usefully inside a box, I give only the box number, as in BDT 34.54 (collection 34, box 54).

Some research institutions use names rather than numbers for their collections. In this case, I have provided the name and the box and folder numbers. For example, NJP 10.1 would refer to an item in the Nicholas Joost Papers that may be found in box 10, folder 1.

·

BAG Alyse Gregory Papers at the Beinecke Library.

BDT Dial/Scofield Thayer Papers at the Beinecke Library.

BF Presidents' Files, Albert C. Barnes Correspondence. The Barnes Foundation Archives. All letters from the Barnes Foundation Archives, Merion, Pa., are excerpted and reprinted with permission.

HL E. E. Cummings Papers at the Houghton Library, Harvard. (Call numbers are given for items in the Cummings manuscript collection, e.g., bMS Am 1892.10.)

JSW James Sibley Watson/The Dial Papers at the Berg Collection, New York Public Library.

LB Louise Bryant Papers in the Sterling Memorial Library, Yale University.

NJP Nicholas Joost Papers, Georgetown University Library, Special Collections Research Center.

WAM Largely uncatalogued papers in boxes at the Worcester Art Museum. When identifying information, such as a box number, is available, I include it in the endnotes.

Chapter 1. An Intellectual Sewer

1. "Johansen Tells What Is Wrong with Modern Artists," *Worcester (Mass.) Sunday Telegram*, July 20, 1924.

2. Gay, *Modernism*, 10–17 and passim.

3. Williams, *Autobiography*, 74.

4. "Soulful Spectrism Nothing but a Hoax," *New York Times Magazine*, June 2, 1918, 11.

5. BDT 34.28.746.

6. Ibid.

7. "Comment," *Dial* 78, no. 5 (May 1925): 441.

8. BDT 95.2.38.

9. Joost, *Scofield Thayer*, 235.

Chapter 2. Homes of Virtue

1. Washburn, *Industrial Worcester*, 161, 77, 201.

2. Edward D. Thayer, Filling Detector for Looms, U.S. Patent 1,018,218, filed July 12, 1906, and issued February 20, 1912.

3. Franklin Pierce Rice, *Worcester of Eighteen Hundred and Ninety-Eight* (Worcester: Blanchard, 1899), 96-97.

4. Ibid.

5. Nutt, *History of Worcester*, 3:131.

6. Ibid.

7. BDT 34.6.

8. NJP, September 15, 1921.

9. BDT 95.2.38.

10. BDT 95.2.37.

11. BDT 34.53.1509.

12. BDT 95.1.31.

13. BDT 34.56.

14. Ibid.

15. BDT 95.2.37.

16. BDT 95.2.36.

17. BDT 95.2.37.

18. BDT 95.2.36.

19. BDT 34.53.1507.

20. BDT 34.59.1610.

21. BDT 34.60.1634.

22. BDT 34.60.1628.

23. Lynne St. Germaine (Bancroft School Alumni and Development Office) to the author, e-mail, September 9, 2009.

24. BDT 95.2.37.

25. Ibid.

26. BDT 34.56.

27. Marjorie Clary to Nicholas Joost, NJP, 1.20.

28. BDT 34.56.

29. BDT 95.2.38.

30. Ibid.

31. BDT 34.53.1508; my emphasis.

32. BDT 34.53.1507.

33. BDT 95.2.37.

34. BDT 95.2.38.

35. "Life Work Is Closed," *Worcester Telegram*, July 18, 1907.

36. BDT 95.2.38; my emphasis.

37. Ibid.

38. BDT 34.53.1507.

39. Diane Pierce-Williams (Milton Academy archivist) to the author, e-mail, September 11, 2012.

Chapter 3. Harvard

1. BDT 34.53.1508.

2. BDT 34.62.1678.

3. Ibid.

4. Ibid.

5. Eliot, *Letters*, xx.

6. Ibid., xxn13.

7. BDT 95.2.49.

8. BDT 34.56.

9. BDT 34.30.782.

10. Sawyer-Lauçanno, *E. E. Cummings*, 79.

11. Ibid., 80.

12. BDT 34.56.

13. BDT 34.54.

14. BDT 34.56.

15. BDT 95.2.37.

16. BDT 95.1.31.

17. BDT 34.56.

18. Watson, *Edge of the Woods*, 89.

19. BDT 34.56.

20. BDT 34.53.1506.

21. Watson, *Edge of the Woods*, 92.

Chapter 4. Oxford during the War

1. BDT 34.53.1509.

2. BDT 34.42.1186–1211.

3. Ibid.

4. Matthew, "Edward VIII," *Oxford Dictionary of National Biography*, www.oxforddnb.com/view/printable/31061.

5. Langstaff, *Oxford, 1914*, 61–62.

6. BDT 34.42.1191.

7. Ibid.

8. BDT 34.56.

9. BDT 34.42.1191.

10. Ibid.

11. Langstaff, *Oxford, 1914*, 37.

12. BDT 34.42.1193.

13. Robin Darwall-Smith to the author, e-mail, April 26, 2006.

14. Langstaff, *Oxford, 1914*, 100.

15. BDT 34.42.1196.

16. Eliot, *Letters*, 75.

17. BDT 34.59.1519.

18. BDT 34.42.1194.

19. Seymour-Jones, *Painted Shadow*, 29.

20. BDT 34.56.

21. BDT 34.31.812.

22. Ibid.

23. Ibid.

24. BDT 34.78.2014.

25. Langstaff, *Oxford, 1914*, 36.

26. BDT 34.42.1196.

27. Santayana, *Soliloquies in England*, 1.

28. Ibid., 104.

29. BDT 34.32.849.

30. BDT 34.32.851.

31. BDT 34.32.854.

32. BDT 34.82.852.

33. BDT 34.32.853.

34. BDT 34.42.1198.

35. Ibid.

36. Ibid.

37. BDT 34.42.1186–1211.

38. BDT 95.1.32.

39. BDT 34.42.1186–1211.

40. BDT 34.56.

41. BDT 34.6.

Chapter 5. The Chicago Experiment

1. BDT 34.32.855. The quote is perhaps from F. S. Flint's poem "Hallucination."

2. Eliot, *Letters*, 112.

3. BDT 34.56.

4. WAM, large box 4, unpublished, typed interview of Henry McBride by Nicholas Joost.

5. Ibid.

6. BDT 34.78.2008.

7. BDT 34.42.1203.

8. Ibid.

9. Ibid.

10. Ibid.

11. Ibid.

12. Ibid.

13. Ibid.

14. BDT 34.54.

15. BDT 95.3.59.

16. BDT 34.42.1203.

17. Ibid.

18. "Miss Orr's Marriage," *Troy (N.Y.) Northern Budget*, June 25, 1916.

19. Ibid.

20. BDT 34.147.1333.

21. BDT 34.54.

22. Ibid.

Chapter 6. Lady of the Sonnets

Source of first epigraph: bMS Am 1892.10 (198).

1. NJP 1.20.

2. BDT 34.77.1993.

3. "Orr-Thayer Engagement," *New York Times*, April 14, 1916.

4. BDT 34.28.733.

5. BDT 34.32.848.

6. BDT 34.78.2016.

7. BDT 34.54.

8. BDT 95.2.36.

9. Carr, *Dos Passos*, 103.

10. BDT 34.56.

11. Ibid.

12. Watson, *Edge of the Woods*, 83.

13. Sawyer-Lauçanno, *E. E. Cummings*, 86.

14. Eliot, *Letters*, 137.

15. BDT 34.31.813.

16. BDT 34.30.783.

17. BDT 95.2.37.

18. Ibid.

19. BDT 34.54.

20. BDT 34.42.1204.

21. Ibid.

22. BDT 34.54.

23. BDT 34.30.782–94.

24. BDT 34.42.1205.

25. ST to Florence Thayer, October 7, 1916, BDT 95.1.13.

26. BDT 34.54.

27. Receipts, September 18, 1916, BDT 34.47.1331.

28. BDT 34.77.1331.

29. BDT 34.30.793.

30. BDT 34.30.784.

31. BDT 34.54.

32. BDT 34.56.

33. Ibid.

34. BDT 34.53.1506.

35. BDT 95.1.32.

36. BDT 34.56.

37. Sawyer-Lauçanno, *E. E. Cummings*, 140.

38. BDT 95.1.33.

39. BDT 95.2.38.

40. BDT 34.79.2037.

41. BDT 34.56.

42. Ibid.

43. Ibid.

44. Ibid.

45. BDT 95.2.37.

46. BDT 95.1.32.

47. BDT 95.2.38.

48. BDT 34.56.

49. BDT 34.54.

50. Ibid.

51. Sutton, ed., *Pound, Thayer, Watson*, 288.

52. BDT 34.56.

53. Ibid.

54. BDT 34.42.1208.

55. Watson, *Edge of the Woods*; BDT 34.42.1203.

56. BDT 34.56.

57. BDT 95.2.38.

58. BDT 34.56.

59. BDT 34.53.1508.

60. BDT 34.56.

61. Ibid.

62. BDT 95.2.36.

63. BDT 34.56.

64. BDT 34.53.1507.

65. BDT 95.2.37.

66. BDT 95.1.32.

67. BDT 95.2.36.

68. BDT 34.56.

69. BDT 34.47.1326.

70. BDT 34.42.1208.

71. BDT 95.2.37.

Chapter 7. Death of the Prophet

1. Abrahams, *Lyrical Left*, 23–24.

2. Dos Passos, *1919*, 81.

3. Joost, *Years of Transition*, 153.

4. Bourne, "Clipped Wings," 358.

5. Gregory, *Day Is Gone*, 153.

6. Bourne, *Letters*, 424.

7. BDT 34.47.1325.

8. Ibid.

9. BDT 34.54.

10. BDT 34.56.

11. Ibid.

12. BDT 34.34.920.

13. BDT 34.52.1493.

14. Ibid., 153.

15. Ibid., 154.

16. BDT 34.42.1186–1211.

17. Sawyer-Lauçanno, *E. E. Cummings*, 135.

18. BDT 34.79.2052.

19. Eliot, *Letters*, 236.

20. BDT 34.28.745.

21. BAG 163.10.154.

22. BDT 34.42.1186–1211.

23. Stearns, *Street I Know*, 168.

24. BDT 34.42.1186–1211.

25. Peltier, *Alyse Gregory*, 9–10.

26. Gregory, *Day Is Gone*, 166.

27. Rosenfeld, "Randolph Bourne," 559.

28. BDT 34.42.1186–1211.

29. Joost, *Years of Transition*, 239.

30. BDT 95.1.33.

31. BDT 34.54.

32. Gregory, *Day Is Gone*, 136.

33. BDT 34.55.

Chapter 8. To the Center of Things

1. Jorgensen and Jorgensen, *Thorstein Veblen*, 160.

2. Helen Morat to Albert C. Barnes, November 1918, Presidents' Files, Albert C. Barnes Correspondence, The Barnes Foundation Archives, Merion, Pa.

3. Ibid.

4. Ibid.

5. Ibid.

6. Watson, *Edge of the Woods*, 91.

7. Moore, *Selected Letters*, 135.

8. HL bMS Am 1892 (545).

9. Sawyer-Lauçanno, *E. E. Cummings*, 139.

10. Cummings, *Selected Letters*, 57.

11. Graves, *Brothers Powys*, 153.

12. BDT 34.48.1356.

13. Joost, *Years of Transition*, 166.

14. Scofield Thayer, "James Joyce," *Dial* 65, no. 773 (September 19, 1918): 201.

15. Cummings, *Selected Letters*, 63.

16. Sawyer-Lauçanno, *E. E. Cummings*, 162–63.

17. Anonymous, "Casual Comment," *Dial* 67, no. 802 (July 12–November 29, 1919): 46.

18. BDT 34.41.1185.

19. BDT 95.2.37.

Chapter 9. Starting with a Bang

1. S. Anderson, *Letters*, 51.

2. Carr, *Dos Passos*, 170.

3. BDT 34.28.730.

4. Eliot, *Letters*, 359.

5. Pound, *Selected Letters*, 154.

6. BDT 34.54.

7. Carr, *Dos Passos*, 170.

8. Albert C. Barnes to Scofield Thayer, January 16, 1920, Presidents' Files, Albert C. Barnes Correspondence, The Barnes Foundation Archives, Merion, Pa.

9. Cummings, *Selected Letters*, 71.

10. BDT 34.55.

11. BDT 95.2.37.

12. BDT 95.2.39.

13. BDT 34.53.1506.

14. BDT 34.55.

15. BDT 95.2.39.

16. Ibid.

17. BDT 34.55.

18. Ibid.

19. BDT 95.2.38.

20. BDT 95.2.39.

21. Ibid.

22. Ibid.

23. BDT 34.55.

24. BDT 95.2.39.

25. Ibid.

26. BDT 95.2.38.

27. BDT 95.2.39.

28. BDT 34.68.1839.

29. BDT 95.2.39.

30. Lynn, *Hemingway,* 241.

31. Lawrence, *Collected Letters,* 59.

32. BDT 34.54.

33. Pound, *Pound/Joyce,* 166.

34. Cummings, *Selected Letters,* 68.

35. Scofield Thayer, "Comment," *Dial* 68, no. 3 (March 1920): 408.

36. Stewart Mitchell Papers, Boston Athenaeum, LA 459 MSS.

37. Sutton, ed., *Pound, Thayer, Watson,* 30.

38. JSW, 940511.

39. Boyd, "Adult or Infantile Censorship?," 381.

40. Sumner, "Truth about Literary Lynchings," 63.

Chapter 10. Manhattan Love Stories

1. BDT 34.42.1186–1211.

2. BDT 95.2.37.

3. BDT 34.53.1509.

4. BDT 95.1.31.

5. BDT 34.53.1508.

6. BDT 95.2.37.

7. Gregory, *Day Is Gone,* 177.

8. Ibid, 178.

9. Graves, *Brothers Powys,* 153.

10. Gregory, *Day Is Gone,* 178.

11. Ibid.

12. Ibid.

13. LB 1840.7.103.

14. Ibid.

15. LB 1840.1.7.

16. LB 1840.7.103.

17. Ibid.

18. Ibid.

19. Ibid.

20. Ibid.

21. LB 1840.1.7.

22. BDT 34.29.774

23. Beam, *Gracefully Insane,* 162.

Chapter 11. Anti-Epithalamion

1. Moore, *Selected Letters*, 143.
2. Beach, *Shakespeare and Company*, 25.
3. Bryher, *Heart to Artemis*, 201.
4. Moore, *Selected Letters*, 144.
5. "'Heiress' Writer Weds Village Poet," *New York Times*, March 12, 1921, 11.
6. Williams, *Selected Letters*, 51.
7. Moore, *Selected Letters*, 152.
8. Sutton, ed., *Pound, Thayer, Watson*, 214.
9. Eliot, *Letters*, 449.
10. BDT 34.31.809.
11. BDT 34.56.

Chapter 12. To the Great Master

Epigraph source: BDT 95.2.38.
1. Thayer, "Comment," *Dial* 70, no. 1 (January 1921): 122.
2. BDT 34.47.1322.
3. BDT 34.54.
4. BDT 34.30.791.
5. M. Anderson, *My Thirty Years' War*, 220.
6. Marianne Moore to J. W. Moore, October 17, 1920, in Moore, *Selected Letters*, 135.
7. LB 1840.1.7.103.
8. Ibid.
9. BDT 34.28.736.
10. Ibid.
11. BDT 34.30.799.
12. Jay, ed., *Selected Correspondence of Burke and Cowley*, 88. The misspelling of "Cummins" appears in the original letter.
13. BDT 34.32.860, trans. Brisson.
14. Ibid.
15. Ibid.
16. Santayana, *Letters*, 6:170.
17. Ibid, 6:173.
18. Ibid.
19. BAG 163.51.880.
20. BDT 34.33.868–90.
21. Ibid.
22. BDT 34.28.736.
23. BDT 34.47.1322.
24. BAG 163.38.660.
25. Background on Vienna is taken from Gruber, *Red Vienna*.
26. BDT 34.31.812–13.
27. January 8, 1922, BDT 163.38.660.
28. BAG 163.38.660.

Chapter 13. Assessing the Modern

Epigraph source: NJP 3.6.

1. Pound, *Letters*, 235.
2. Eliot, *Letters*, 623.
3. Ibid, 472.
4. Ibid, 502.
5. BDT 34.31.810.
6. Eliot, *Letters*, 507.
7. BDT 34.31.808–11.
8. BDT 34.31.810.
9. Joost, *Scofield Thayer and "The Dial,"* 160.
10. NJP 3.17.
11. BDT 34.54.
12. BAG 163.38.661.
13. BDT 95.2.36.
14. BDT 34.54.
15. Ibid.
16. BDT 95.2.38. The final quote is from the epilogue of Marlowe's *Doctor Faustus*.
17. BDT 34.54.
18. Ibid.
19. BDT 95.1.33. The verse referred to is probably Hulme's walk-poem "Autumn."
20. BDT 34.54.
21. Ibid.
22. Ibid.
23. BDT 34.33.868–90.
24. BDT 95.2.39.
25. BDT 34.55.
26. BDT 34.55.
27. Ibid.
28. Ibid.
29. BDT 95.2.39.
30. BAG 163.38.661.
31. BDT 34.56.
32. BDT 95.2.39.
33. Ibid.
34. Ibid.
35. BDT 34.56.
36. BDT 34.53.1506.
37. BDT 34.55.
38. Ibid.
39. Ibid.
40. Scofield Thayer, "James Joyce," *Dial* 65, no. 773 (September 19, 1918): 201.
41. Unwerth, *Freud's Requiem*, 203.

42. BDT 34.54.

43. Joost, *Years of Transition*, 165.

44. BDT 34.32.863.

45. BDT 34.54.

46. BDT 34.53.1509.

Chapter 14. A Millionaire in Red Vienna

1. NJP 3.6.

2. BAG 163.38.661.

3. NJP 3.6.

4. JSW 940511.

5. Joost, *Scofield Thayer and "The Dial,"* 214.

6. JSW 940511.

7. NJP 3.6.

8. BAG 163.38.660.

9. Jay, ed., *Selected Correspondence of Burke and Cowley*, 79.

10. McBride, *Eye on the Modern Century*, 85.

11. Albert C. Barnes to Thomas Craven, 3 July 1923, Presidents' Files, Albert C. Barnes Correspondence, Barnes Foundation Archives, Merion, Pa.

12. WAM Box 15.

13. Gregory, *Day Is Gone*, 140.

14. BDT 34.54.

15. NJP 3.3.

16. NJP 3.4.

17. Ibid.

18. BAG 163.38.661.

19. NJP 3.6.

20. BDT 95.1.33.

21. BAG 163.38.661.

Chapter 15. Teuton versus Francophile

1. BAG 163.38.662.

2. Sawyer-Lauçanno, *E. E. Cummings*, 222.

3. Moore, *Selected Letters*, 202.

4. BAG 163.38.662.

5. Dial/Scofield Thayer Papers, Beinecke Library, Yale University, as qtd. in Sutton, ed., *Pound, Thayer, Watson*, 261.

6. Gregory, *Day Is Gone*, 203.

7. Sutton, ed., *Pound, Thayer, Watson*, 264.

8. BDT 34.29.763–67.

9. BAG 163.38.661.

10. BDT 34.53.1506.

11. BDT 34.54.

12. Ibid.

13. BDT 34.32.854.

14. BDT 34.54.

15. BDT 4.54.

16. BDT 34.54.

17. BDT 34.29.763–67.

18. BAG 163.38.662.

19. BDT 34.29.763–67.

20. NJP Papers, 3.6.

21. Ibid.

22. Ibid.

23. Ibid.

24. BAG 163.38.662.

25. BDT 34.3.891.

26. BDT 33.43.892.

27. BDT 34.33.892.

28. BDT 33.891–95, trans. Dollenmayer.

Chapter 16. Barnes in Eruption

Epigraph source: Albert C. Barnes to Thomas Craven, April 18, 1923, Presidents' Files, Albert C. Barnes Correspondence, Barnes Foundation Archives, Merion, Pa.

1. McBride, *Flow of Art*, 435.

2. Albert C. Barnes to Stewart Mitchell, January 22, 1920, Presidents' Files, Albert C. Barnes Correspondence, Barnes Foundation Archives, Merion, Pa.

3. Albert C. Barnes to Thomas Craven, May 27, 1921, Presidents' Files, Albert C. Barnes Correspondence, Barnes Foundation Archives, Merion, Pa.

4. Albert C. Barnes to Thomas Craven, March 1923, Presidents' Files, Albert C. Barnes Correspondence, Barnes Foundation Archives, Merion, Pa.

5. Thomas Craven to Albert C. Barnes, April 15, 1923, Presidents' Files, Albert C. Barnes Correspondence, Barnes Foundation Archives, Merion, Pa.

6. Albert C. Barnes to Thomas Craven, July 3, 1923, Presidents' Files, Albert C. Barnes Correspondence, Barnes Foundation Archives, Merion, Pa.

7. Albert C. Barnes to Scofield Thayer, September 20, 1923, Presidents' Files, Albert C. Barnes Correspondence, Barnes Foundation Archives, Merion, Pa.

8. Dial/Scofield Thayer Papers, Beinecke Library, Yale University, as qtd. in Sutton, ed., *Pound, Thayer, Watson*, 271.

9. Albert C. Barnes to Scofield Thayer, July 3, 1923, Presidents' Files, Albert C. Barnes Correspondence, Barnes Foundation Archives, Merion, Pa.

10. Ibid.

11. Ibid.

12. Craven, "Progress of Painting," 581.

13. Albert C. Barnes to Scofield Thayer, August 1923, Presidents' Files, Albert C. Barnes Correspondence, Barnes Foundation Archives, Merion, Pa.

14. Albert C. Barnes to Scofield Thayer, September 8, 1923, Presidents' Files, Albert C. Barnes Correspondence, Barnes Foundation Archives, Merion, Pa.

15. Scofield Thayer to Albert C. Barnes, November 19, 1923, Presidents' Files, Albert C. Barnes Correspondence, Barnes Foundation Archives, Merion, Pa.

16. Albert C. Barnes to Scofield Thayer, December 3, 1923, Presidents' Files, Albert C. Barnes Correspondence, Barnes Foundation Archives, Merion, Pa.

17. Sutton, ed., *Pound, Thayer, Watson*, 29.

18. Craven, "Psychology and Common Sense," 236.

19. Ibid., 242.

20. Albert C. Barnes to Scofield Thayer, February 28, 1924, Presidents' Files, Albert C. Barnes Correspondence, Barnes Foundation Archives, Merion, Pa.

21. Albert C. Barnes to *The Dial*, March 7, 1924, Presidents' Files, Albert C. Barnes Correspondence, Barnes Foundation Archives, Merion, Pa.

22. Alyse Gregory to Albert C. Barnes, March 8, 1924, Presidents' Files, Albert C. Barnes Correspondence, Barnes Foundation Archives, Merion, Pa.

23. Albert C. Barnes to *The Dial*, March 27, 1924, Presidents' Files, Albert C. Barnes Correspondence, Barnes Foundation Archives, Merion, Pa.

24. Albert C. Barnes to Leo Stein, n.d., Presidents' Files, Albert C. Barnes Correspondence, Barnes Foundation Archives, Merion, Pa.

25. Albert C. Barnes to Leo Stein, August 12, 1924, Presidents' Files, Albert C. Barnes Correspondence, Barnes Foundation Archives, Merion, Pa.

26. WAM, Box 17.

Chapter 17. Feuds Galore

Epigraph source: BDT 95.1.31.

1. BDT 34.33.891–95, trans. Dollenmayer.

2. Sutton, ed., *Pound, Thayer, Watson*, 296.

3. BDT 34.54.

4. BDT 95.2.36.

5. BDT 34.33.891–95.

6. Hemingway, *Selected Letters*, 111.

7. *New York Times Magazine*, January 27, 1924, 10.

8. BDT 34.29.769.

9. *Dial* 76, no. 3 (March 1924): 292.

10. Murry, *Discoveries*, 308.

11. Scofield Thayer, "Comment," *Dial* 76, no. 4 (April 1924): 574.

12. BDT 34.54.

13. "Notes on Pablo Picasso," *New Republic*, April 23, 1924.

14. Qtd. in Sutton, ed., *Pound, Thayer, Watson*, 14.

15. BDT 34.30.801.

16. *Dial* 77, no. 2 (August 1924): 177.

17. *Dial* 77, no. 4 (October 1924): 353.

18. Albert C. Barnes to Leo Stein, 12 August 1924, Presidents' Files, Albert C. Barnes Correspondence, Barnes Foundation Archives, Merion, Pa.

19. BDT 34.30.791.

20. BDT 34.30.795.

21. BDT 32.29.772.

22. WAM Box 16.

23. Sutton, ed., *Pound, Thayer, Watson*, 295.

24. Sawyer-Lauçanno, *E. E. Cummings*, 237.

25. Kennedy, *Dreams in the Mirror*, 148.

26. Sawyer-Lauçanno, *E. E. Cummings*, 238.

27. Administration of the Estate of Scofield Thayer, Mountain Dearborn LLC, Worcester, Mass., 4.

28. Kennedy, *Dreams in the Mirror*, 248.

29. Ibid., 177.

30. Jay, ed., *Selected Correspondence of Burke and Cowley*, 158.

31. Gregory, *Day Is Gone*, 208.

32. Ibid., 210.

33. Ibid., 211.

34. Ibid.

35. BAG 163.38.660.

36. Powys, *Verdict of Bridlegoose*, 165.

37. Powys, *Llewelyn Powys*, ed. Hopkins, 60.

38. Powys, *Letters*, introduction by Louis Wilkinson, ed., 22.

39. Sutton, ed., *Pound, Thayer, Watson*, 288.

40. Gregory, *Cry of a Gull*, 21.

41. BDT 34.30.791.

42. WAM Box 16.

43. BDT 34.29.773.

44. WAM Box 17.

45. BDT 34.33.891–95, trans. Dollenmayer.

Chapter 18. Annus Belli

1. WAM Box 18.

2. *Dial* 78, no. 5 (May 1925): 399.

3. BDT 343.39.1105–6.

4. WAM Box 18.

5. Williams, *I Wanted to Write a Poem*, 163.

6. BDT 34.30.798.

7. Ibid.

8. BDT 34.33.891–95, trans. Dollenmayer.

9. Ibid.

10. Ibid.

11. Powys, *Letters*, 120.

12. Stewart Mitchell Papers, Boston Athenaeum, L459 mss.

13. BDT 34.28.736.

14. BDT 34.30.798.

15. Ibid.

16. Ibid.

17. BDT 34.37.1039.

18. Ibid.

19. Ibid.

20. WAM Box 18.

21. WAM Box 17.

22. WAM Box 18.

23. BDT 34.1.2.

24. Wilson, *Letters on Literature and Politics*, 126.

25. BDT 34.4.136–42.

26. BAG 163.38.664.

27. Sutton, ed., *Pound, Thayer, Watson*, 305.

28. Ibid., 305.

29. BDT 163.38.664.

30. Albert C. Barnes to Scofield Thayer, 3 December 1923, Presidents' Files, Albert C. Barnes Correspondence, The Barnes Foundation Archives, Merion, Pa.

31. BDT 163.55.942.

32. Sutton, ed., *Pound, Thayer, Watson*, 307.

33. BDT 34.30.798.

34. BDT 34.33.891–95, trans. Dollenmayer.

35. Joost, *Scofield Thayer and "The Dial,"* 92.

36. Ibid.

Chapter 19. Freudless in Vienna

1. Stewart Mitchell Papers, Boston Athenaeum, L459 mss.

2. HL bMS Am1892.545.

3. Qtd. in Sutton, ed., *Pound, Thayer, Watson*, 307.

4. Ibid.

5. JSW 940512.

6. Knox, *Oscar Wilde in the 1990s*, 13.

7. Sutton, ed., *Pound, Thayer, Watson*, 308.

8. BAG 163.38.664.

9. Ibid.

10. Ibid.

11. Ibid.

12. BAG 163.38.665.

13. BDT 34.32.860, trans. Brisson.

14. BDT 34.32.860, trans. Dollenmayer.

15. Ibid.

16. BDT 34.32.860, trans. Brisson.

17. BDT 34.38.665.

18. BAG 163.38.665.

19. Ibid.

20. Marianne Moore Collection, Rosenbach Museum and Library, Philadelphia, as qtd. in Sutton, ed., *Pound, Thayer, Watson*, 313.

Chapter 20. Return of the Prodigal

1. Moore, *Selected Letters*, 212.
2. BDT 34.41.1183.
3. Moore, *Selected Letters*, 121.
4. Sutton, ed., *Pound, Thayer, Watson*, 318.
5. Marianne Moore Collection, general correspondence (series 5), Rosenbach Museum and Library, as qtd. in Sutton, ed., *Pound, Thayer, Watson*, 318.
6. BAG 163.38.665.
7. Ibid.
8. Ibid.
9. BAG 163.54.936.
10. BDT 44.1237–45.
11. NJP 3.6.
12. Powys, "Recollections of Thomas Hardy," 425–34.
13. BDT 163.38.665.
14. Moore, *Selected Letters*, 224.
15. BDT 34.29.763–67.
16. All cables found in BAG 163.38.666.
17. Ibid.
18. Sutton, ed., *Pound, Thayer, Watson*, 317.
19. Ibid.
20. Moore, *Selected Letters*, 226.
21. LB MS 1840.7.103.
22. BDT 95.1.11.
23. BAG 163.54.936.
24. Marek, *Women Editing Modernism*, 150.
25. Moore, *Complete Prose*, 124.
26. Sutton, ed., *Pound, Thayer, Watson*, 314.
27. Fisher, *Hart Crane*, 268.
28. Witemeyer, ed., *Pound/Williams*, 86.
29. Molesworth, *Marianne Moore*, 431.
30. BDT 34.1.12.
31. Ibid.
32. Ibid.
33. Ibid.
34. Ibid.
35. Ibid.
36. Ibid.
37. Ibid.
38. Ibid.
39. Ibid.

40. Moore, *Selected Letters*, 230.

41. BAG 163.38.666.

42. BDT 95.1.32.

43. BDT 95.1.33.

44. BDT 95.2.36.

45. Ibid.

46. BDT 95.1.31.

47. BDT 95.1.33.

48. Ibid.

49. BDT 34.55.

50. BDT 95.2.36.

51. Ibid.

52. BDT 95.2.37.

53. BDT 95.2.36.

54. BDT 95.2.39.

55. BDT 95.2.36.

56. BDT 95.2.39.

57. BDT 34.30.795.

58. HL bMS Am 1892.7 (198).

Chapter 21. The Death of the *Dial*

1. Joost, *Scofield Thayer and "The Dial,"* 246.

2. *Dial* 83, no. 4 (October 1927): 343–46.

3. BDT 34.1.4.

4. *Dial* 83, no. 6 (December 1927): 534.

5. Qtd. in Hoffman, Allen, and Ulrich, *Little Magazine*, 205.

6. Witemeyer, ed., *Pound/Williams*, 89.

7. Ibid., 91.

8. BDT 95.1.12.

9. BDT 34.1.6.

10. Qtd. in Moore, *Selected Letters*, 243.

11. Ibid., 245.

12. Ibid.

13. Ibid., 215f.

14. Riding and Graves, *Survey of Modernist Poetry*.

Chapter 22. Thayer in Eclipse

1. Ezra Pound, "Small Magazines," *English Journal* 19, no. 9 (November 1930): 689.

2. Hoffman, Allen, and Ulrich, *Little Magazine*, 205.

3. Ibid., 197–98.

4. Ibid., 200.

5. Sammons, "The Dial File," 200.

6. NJP 1.51.

7. Joost, *Scofield Thayer and "The Dial,"* 271n2.

8. Hoffman, Allen, and Ulrich, *Little Magazine*, 200.

9. WAM Box 4.

10. McBride, *Flow of Art*, 434.

11. Ivan Sandrof, "Worcester's Famed Editor and the Genius of Taste," *Worcester Telegram*, December [?], 1964.

12. Richard Poirier, "Table of Contents Was a Roster of Greatness," *New York Times Book Review*, January 31, 1965.

13. Nicholas Joost, "Letter to the Editor," *New York Times Book Review*, March 7, 1965, 40.

14. Richard Poirier, "A Reply," *New York Times Book Review*, March 7, 1965, 41.

15. NJP 1.51.

16. Ibid.

17. NJP 1.20.

18. Ibid.

19. Ibid.

20. Probate and Family Court Department, Worcester Division, Massachusetts Court system.

21. Molesworth, *Marianne Moore*, 425.

22. Margaret Coughlin, phone interview with the author, Worcester, Mass., June 8, 2012.

23. Ibid.

24. BDT 34.53.1506.

25. "Dr. Clark Arrested in Alienation Suit," *New York Times*, April 21, 1927, 12.

26. BDT 95.2.39.

27. Ibid.

28. Arnold, *Works*, 4:185.

Chapter 23. Postmortem

1. WAM Thayer Papers.

2. Administration of the Estate of Scofield Thayer, p. 4, Mountain Dearborn LLC, Worcester, Mass.

3. BDT 95.2.38.

4. BDT 34.53.1508.

5. BDT 34.53.1509.

6. BDT 34.53.1506.

7. BDT 34.53.1507.

8. BDT 34.56.

9. BDT 34.53.1506.

10. BDT 34.54.

11. "Briefer Mention" *Dial* 73, no. 5 (November 1922): 581.

12. Administration of the Estate of Scofield Thayer, Charles B. Swartwood, Worcester, Mass., unpublished.

13. Peter P. Donker, "Museum Losing Dial Art," *Worcester (Mass.) Telegram*, August 11, 1982, 1.

14. Peter P. Donker, "Thayer Estate Battle Is Continuing," *Worcester (Mass.) Telegram*, August 31, 1983.

15. Gary V. Murray, "Judge Rules Thayer Collection Need Not Be Always on View," *Worcester (Mass.) Evening Gazette*, December 14, 1983, 1.

16. BDT 34.55.

17. Ibid.

18. Thayer Annual Account, Worcester Probate Court, January 5, 1937.

19. *La doleur* (1902 or 1903), Metropolitan Museum of Art, Bequest of Scofield Thayer, www.metmuseum.org/Collections/search-the-collections/210003565.

20. Sutton, ed., *Pound, Thayer, Watson, and "The Dial,"* xxv.

21. BDT 34.54.

God, Stars, and Sea

1. BDT 34.67.1801.

2. Hoffman, Allen, and Ulrich, *Little Magazine*, 200.

3. Joost, *Scofield Thayer and "The Dial,"* 87.

4. *Harvard Monthly*, November 1909, 84.

5. Ibid., March 1910, 69.

6. Ibid., November 1911, 110.

7. Ibid., January 1912, 133.

8. Ibid., February 1912, 174.

9. Ibid., March 1910, 69.

10. *Crimson*, April 10, 1912.

11. *Harvard Monthly*, May 1912, 108.

12. Ibid.

13. Ibid., July 1912, 207.

14. Ibid., March 1913, 22.

15. Ibid., April 1913, 62.

16. Ibid., May 1913, 92.

17. Ibid., June 1913, 141.

18. Ibid., July 1913, 170.

19. *Dial* 79, no. 2 (August 1925): 117.

20. Ibid. 79, no. 1 (July 1925): 21.

21. Ibid. 79, no. 4 (October 1925): 310.

22. BDT 95.2.37.

23. *Dial* 79, no. 6 (December 1925): 467.

24. Ibid. 80, no. 2 (February 1926): 113.

25. Ibid. 80, no. 4 (April 1926): 267.

26. Ibid. 81, no. 1 (July 1926): 60.

27. Ibid. 83, no. 1 (July 1927): 46.

26. Ibid. 80, no. 6 (June 1926): 464.

27. Ibid. 81, no. 2 (August 1926): 148.

28. Ibid. 83, no. 4 (October 1927): 283.

29. Ibid. 81, no. 2 (August 1926): 148.

30. Ibid. 83, no. 4 (October 1927): 283–84.

BIBLIOGRAPHY

Archives and Collections

Barnes Foundation Archives, Merion, Pa.

Louise Bryant Papers in the Sterling Memorial Library, Yale University, New Haven, Conn.

E. E. (Edward Estlin) Cummings Papers, Houghton Library, Harvard University, Cambridge, Mass.

Dial Collection Papers, Worcester Art Museum Archives, Worcester, Mass.

Dial/Scofield Thayer Papers, Beinecke Rare Book and Manuscript Library, Yale University, New Haven, Conn.

Alyse Gregory Papers, Beinecke Rare Book and Manuscript Library, Yale University, New Haven, Conn.

Nicholas Joost Papers, Georgetown University Library, Special Collections Research Center, Washington, D.C.

Stewart Mitchell Papers, Boston Athenaeum, Boston, Mass.

James Sibley Watson/The Dial Papers, The Berg Collection, New York Public Library, New York, N.Y.

Primary and Secondary Sources

Abrahams, Edward. *The Lyrical Left*. Charlottesville: University Press of Virginia, 1986.

Ackroyd, Peter. *T. S. Eliot: A Life*. New York: Simon and Schuster, 1984.

Ahearn, Barry, ed. *Pound/Cummings: The Correspondence of Ezra Pound and E. E. Cummings*. Ann Arbor: University of Michigan Press, 1996.

Anderson, Margaret. *My Thirty Years' War*. New York: Horizon Press, 1969.

Anderson, Sherwood. *The Letters of Sherwood Anderson*. Edited by Howard Mumford Jones. New York: Little, Brown, 1969.

Arnold, Matthew. *The Works of Matthew Arnold*. 15 vols. London: Macmillan, 1903.

Beach, Sylvia. *Shakespeare and Company*. Lincoln: University of Nebraska Press, 1991.

Beam, Alex. *Gracefully Insane: The Rise and Fall of America's Premier Mental Hospital*. New York: Public Affairs, 2001.

Birnbaum, Martin. *The Last Romantic*. New York: Twayne, 1960.

Blake, Casey Nelson. *Beloved Community: The Cultural Criticism of Randolph Bourne, Van Wyck Brooks, Waldo Frank, and Lewis Mumford*. Chapel Hill: University of North Carolina Press, 1990.

Bourne, Randolph. "An Autobiographic Chapter." *Dial* 68 (January 1920): 1.

———. "Clipped Wings." *Dial* 64 (April 11, 1918): 358.

———. "Conscience and Intelligence in War." *Dial* 63 (September 13, 1917): 183.

———. *History of a Literary Radical and Other Essays by Randolph Bourne*. Edited by Van Wyck Brooks. New York: Biblo and Tannen, 1969.

———. *The History of a Literary Radical and Other Papers*. New York: Russell, 1956.

———.*The Letters of Randolph Bourne: A Comprehensive Edition*. Edited by Eric J. Sandeen. Troy: Whiston, 1981.

———. "Traps for the Unwary." *Dial* 64 (March 28, 1918): 277.

———. *War and the Intellectuals: Essays by Randolph Bourne 1915–1919*. Edited by Carl Resek. New York: Harper and Row, 1964.

———. "A War Diary." In *War and the Intellectuals*. New York: Harper and Row, 1964.

Boyd, Ernest. "Adult or Infantile Censorship?" *Dial* 70 (April 1921): 381.

Braddock, Jeremy. "Neurotic Cities: Barnes in Philadelphia." *Art Journal* 63, no. 4 (2004): 46–61.

Brooks, Charles F. "The 'Old-Fashioned' Winter of 1917–18." *Geographical Review* 5, no. 5 (1918): 405–14. www.jstor.org/stable/207470.

Brooks, Van Wyck. *Days of the Phoenix*. New York: Dutton, 1957.

———, ed. *History of a Literary Radical and Other Essays by Randolph Bourne*. New York: Biblo and Tannen, 1969.

———. *Scenes and Portraits*. New York: Dutton, 1954.

Brown, Gaye L. *"The Dial": Arts and Letters in the 1920s*. Worcester, Mass.: Worcester Art Museum, 1981.

Bryher. *The Heart to Artemis: A Writer's Memoirs*. New York: Harcourt, Brace and World, 1962.

Buermeyer, Laurence. "Communication: Mr Craven's Reply." *Dial* 76 (April 1924): 380.

———. "Some Popular Fallacies in Aesthetics." *Dial* 76 (February 1924): 107.

Bush, Ronald. "In Pursuit of Wilde Possum: Reflections on Eliot, Modernism, and the Nineties." *Modernism/modernity* 11, no. 3 (September 2004): 469–85.

Callaghan, Morley. *That Summer in Paris*. Toronto: Macmillan, 1963.

Callard, D. A. *"Pretty Good for a Woman": The Enigmas of Evelyn Scott*. New York: Norton, 1985.

Carr, Virginia Spencer. *Dos Passos: A Life*. Garden City: Doubleday, 1984.

Clayton, Bruce. *Forgotten Prophet: The Life of Randolph Bourne*. Baton Rouge: Louisiana State University, 1984.

Colum, Mary. *Life and the Dream*. Chester Springs, Pa.: Dufour Editions, 1966.

Crane, Hart. *The Letters of Hart Crane*. Edited by Brom Weber. Berkeley: University of California Press, 1965.

Craven, Thomas Jewell. "A Good Teacher." *Dial* 68 (April 1920): 500.

———. "Mr. Roger Fry and the Artistic Vision." *Dial* 71 (July 1921): 101.

———. "The Progress of Painting." *Dial* 74 (April 1923): 357.

———. "Psychology and Common Sense." *Dial* 76 (March 1924): 236.

Cummings, E. E.. *Selected Letters of E. E. Cummings.* Edited by F. W. Dupee and George Stade. New York: Harcourt, Brace and World, 1969.

Dabney, Lewis M. *Edmund Wilson: A Life in Literature.* New York: Farrar, 2005.

Deming, Robert H., ed. *James Joyce: The Critical Heritage.* New York: Barnes and Noble, 1970.

Donnelly, Honoria Murphy. *Sara and Gerald: Villa America and After.* With Richard N. Billings. New York: Times Books, 1982.

Dos Passos, John. *The Best of Times.* New York: New American Library, 1966.

———. *1919.* New York: Harcourt Brace, 1932.

Eliot, T. S. *The Letters of T. S. Eliot.* Edited by Valerie Eliot. San Diego: Harcourt Brace Jovanovich, 1988.

Ellman, Richard. *Oscar Wilde.* New York: Knopf, 1988.

Elwin, Malcom. *The Life of Llewelyn Powys.* London: John Lane, 1946.

Filler, Louis. *Randolph Bourne.* Washington, D.C.: American Council on Public Affairs, 1943.

Fisher, Clive. *Hart Crane.* New Haven: Yale University Press, 2002.

Freud, Sigmund. *A General Introduction to Psychoanalysis.* New York: Boni and Liveright, 1920.

Gallup, Donald C. *Pigeons on the Granite: Memoirs of a Yale Librarian.* New Haven: Yale University, 1988.

Gay, Peter. *Modernism: The Lure of Heresy.* New York: Norton, 2008.

Glassco, John. *Memoirs of Montparnasse.* Toronto: Oxford University Press, 1970.

Graves, Robert Perceval. *The Brothers Powys.* New York: Scribner's, 1983.

Gregory, Alyse. *The Cry of a Gull.* Dulverton, UK: Ark Press, 1973.

———. *The Day Is Gone.* New York: Dutton, 1948.

Gruber, Helmet. *Red Vienna: Experiment in Working-Class Culture.* New York: Oxford University Press, 1991.

Hale, Nathan G., Jr. *Freud and the Americans: The Beginnings of Psychoanalysis in the United States.* New York: Oxford University Press, 1971.

Hanscombe, Gillian, and Virginia L. Smyers. *Writing for Their Lives: The Modernist Women, 1910–1940.* Boston: Northeastern University Press, 1987.

Hemingway, Ernest. *Ernest Hemingway: Selected Letters.* Edited by Carlos Baker. New York: Scribner, 1981.

Hoffman, Frederick J., Charles Allen, and Carolyn F. Ulrich. *The Little Magazine: A History and a Bibliography.* Princeton, N.J.: Princeton University Press, 1947.

Holt, Guy, ed. *Jurgen and the Law.* New York: McBride, 1923.

Hoopes, James. *Van Wyck Brooks: In Search of American Culture.* Amherst: University of Massachusetts Press, 1977.

Jay, Paul, ed. *The Selected Correspondence of Kenneth Burke and Malcolm Cowley, 1915–1981.* New York: Viking, 1988.

Joost, Nicholas. *Scofield Thayer and "The Dial."* Carbondale: Southern Illinois University Press, 1964.

———. *Years of Transition: "The Dial" 1912–1920.* Barre, Mass.: Barre, 1967.

Jorgensen, Elizabeth Watkins, and Henry Irvin Jorgenson. *Thorstein Veblen, Victorian Firebrand.* Armonk, N.Y.: Sharpe, 1999.

Kammen, Michael. *The Lively Arts: Gilbert Seldes and the Transformation of Cultural Studies in the United States.* New York: Oxford University Press, 1996.

Kempf, Edward J. *Psychopathology.* St. Louis: Mosby, 1921.

Kennedy, Richard S. *Dreams in the Mirror.* London: Norton, 1994.

Knox, Melissa. *Oscar Wilde in the 1990s: The Critic as Creator.* Rochester, N.Y.: Camden House, 2001.

Koelsch, William A. *Clark University 1887–1987.* Worcester, Mass.: Clark University, 1987.

Langstaff, J. Brett. *Oxford, 1914.* New York: Vantage Press, 1965.

Lawrence, D. H. *The Collected Letters of D. H. Lawrence.* Edited by Harry T. Moore. New York: Viking, 1987.

Lewis, Wyndham. *Blasting and Bombardiering.* Berkeley: University of California Press, 1967.

Lovett, Robert Morss. *All Our Years.* New York: Viking, 1948.

Lynn, Kenneth Schuyler. *Hemingway.* New York: Simon and Schuster, 1987.

Marek, Jayne E. *Women Editing Modernism: "Little" Magazines and Literary History.* Lexington: University Press of Kentucky, 1995.

Mariana, Paul. *William Carlos Williams: A New World Naked.* New York: McGraw-Hill, 1981.

Matthew, H.G.C. "Edward VIII [*later* Prince Edward, duke of Windsor] (1894–1972)." In *Oxford Dictionary of National Biography.* New York: Oxford University Press, 2004. www.oxforddnb.com/view/printable/31061.

McAlmon, Robert, and Kay Boyle. *Being Geniuses Together.* New York: Doubleday, 1968.

McBride, Henry. *An Eye on the Modern Century: Selected Letters of Henry McBride.* Edited by Steven Watson and Catherine Morris. New Haven: Yale University Press, 2000.

———. *The Flow of Art.* New York: Athenaeum, 1975.

Miller, Donald L. *Lewis Mumford: A Life.* New York: Weidenfeld and Nicolson, 1989.

Molesworth, Charles. *Marianne Moore: A Literary Life.* New York: Athenaeum, 1990.

Moore, Marianne. *The Complete Prose of Marianne Moore.* Edited by Patricia C. Willis. New York: Penguin, 1987.

———. *Marianne Moore: Letters to Hildegarde Watson 1933–1964.* Edited by Cyrus Hoy. *University of Rochester Library Bulletin* 29, no. 2 (Summer 1976).

———. *Selected Letters of Marianne Moore.* Edited by Bonnie Costello, Celeste Goodridge, and Cristanne Miller. New York: Knopf, 1997.

Moreau, John Adam. *Randolph Bourne: Legend and Reality.* Washington, D.C.: Public Affairs, 1966.

Mumford, Lewis. *My Works and Days: A Personal Chronicle.* New York: Harcourt, 1979.

Murry, John Middleton. *Discoveries: Essays in Literary Criticism.* London: Collins Sons, 1924.

Norman, Charles. *Ezra Pound.* New York: Macmillan, 1960.

———. *The Magic-Maker: E. E. Cummings.* New York: Macmillan, 1958.

Nutt, Charles. *History of Worcester and Its People.* 4 vols. New York: Lewis Historical Publishing, 1919.

Peltier, Jacqueline. *Alyse Gregory: A Woman at Her Window.* London: Cecil Wolfe, 1999.

Pound, Ezra. *The Letters of Ezra Pound.* Edited by D. D. Paige. New York: Harcourt, 1950.

———. *Pound/Joyce: The Letters of Ezra Pound to James Joyce, with Pound's Essays on Joyce.* Edited by Forrest Read. New York: New Directions, 1967.

———. *Pound/The Little Review: The Letters of Ezra Pound to Margaret Anderson: The Little Review Correspondence*. Edited by Thomas L. Scott, Melvin J. Friedman, and Jackson R. Bryer. New York: New Directions, 1988.

Powys, Llewelyn. *The Letters of Llewelyn Powys*. Edited by Louis Wilkinson. London: John Lane, 1943.

———. *Llewelyn Powys: A Selection from His Writings*. Edited by Kenneth Hopkins. New York: Horizon Press, 1961.

———. "Recollections of Thomas Hardy." *Virginia Quarterly Review* 15, no. 3 (1939): 425–34. www.vqronline.org/articles/1939/summer/powys-recollections-thomas/.

———. *So Wild a Thing*. Edited by Malcom Elwin. Somerset: Ark Press, 1973.

———. *The Verdict of Bridlegoose*. New York: Harcourt, 1926.

Rabaté, Jean-Michel. *1913: The Cradle of Modernism*. Malden, Mass.: Blackwell, 2007.

Rainey, Lawrence. *Institutions of Modernism: Literary Elites and Public Culture*. New Haven: Yale University Press, 1998.

Richardson, John. "Rediscovering an Early Modern Vision: The Dial Collection Recalls the Life and Times of Scofield Thayer." *House and Garden*, February 1987, 158–63, 215–16.

Riding, Laura, and Robert Graves. *A Survey of Modernist Poetry*. New York: Haskell House, 1969.

Rosenfeld, Paul. "Randolph Bourne." *Dial* 75 (December 1923): 545.

Sammons, Christa. "The Dial File." *Yale University Library Gazette*, October 1987.

Santayana, George. *The Letters of George Santayana*. Edited by William G. Holzberger. 8 vols. Cambridge: MIT Press, 2001.

———. *Soliloquies in England*. New York: Scribner's Sons, 1922.

Sawyer-Lauçanno, Christopher. *E. E. Cummings: A Biography*. Naperville, Ill.: Sourcebooks, 2004.

Seymour-Jones, Carole. *Painted Shadow*. New York: Doubleday, 2002.

Smoller, Sanford J. *Adrift among Geniuses*. University Park: Pennsylvania State University Press, 1975.

Stearns, Harold E. *The Street I Know*. New York: Furman, 1935.

Sullivan, Kevin. *Oscar Wilde*. New York: Columbia University Press, 1972.

Sumner, John S. "The Truth about Literary Lynchings." *Dial* 71 (July 1921): 63.

Sutton, Walter, ed. *Pound, Thayer, Watson, and "The Dial": A Story in Letters*. Gainesville: University Press of Florida, 1994.

True, Michael D. "The Achievement of an American Literary Radical: A Bibliography of the Writings of Randolph Silliman Bourne (1886–1918)." *Bulletin of the New York Public Library* 69, no. 8 (1965): 523–36.

———. "Randolph Bourne—Fifty Years Later." *Papers on Language and Literature* 3, no. 1 (1967): 86.

Tulloch, Donald, ed. *Songs and Poems of the Great World War*. Worcester, Mass.: Davis Press, 1915.

Unwerth, Matthew von. *Freud's Requiem: Mourning, Memory, and the Invisible History of a Summer Walk*. New York: Riverhead Books, 2005.

Vaill, Amanda. *Everybody Was So Young*. New York: Houghton Mifflin, 1998.

Vanderham, Paul. *James Joyce and Censorship: The Trials of "Ulysses."* New York: New York University Press, 1998.

Washburn, Charles G. *Industrial Worcester*. Worcester, Mass.: Davis Press, 1917.

Wasserstrom, William. *The Time of "The Dial."* Syracuse: Syracuse University Press, 1963.

Watson, Hildegarde Lasell. *The Edge of the Woods: A Memoir*. Rochester, N.Y.: Watson, 1979.

Whipple, Robert. "Administration of the Estate of Scofield Thayer." Unpublished manuscript, Fletcher, Tilton and Whipple, Worcester, Mass.

Wilhelm, J. J. *Ezra Pound in London and Paris*. University Park: Pennsylvania State University, 1990.

Williams, William Carlos. *I Wanted to Write a Poem: The Autobiography of the Works of a Poet*. Edited by Edith Heal. New York: New Directions, 1978.

———. *The Selected Letters of William Carlos Williams*. Edited by John C. Thirlwall. New York: New Directions, 1957.

Wilson, Edmund. *Edmund Wilson: Letters on Literature and Politics 1912–1972*. Edited by Elena Wilson. New York: Farrar, Straus and Giroux, 1977.

———. *The Twenties*. New York: Farrar, Straus and Giroux, 1975.

Witemeyer, Hugh, ed. *Pound/Williams: Selected Letters of Ezra Pound and William Carlos Williams*. New York: New Directions, 1996.

Worcester City Council. "Ceremonies at the Laying of the Corner-Stone of the New City Hall in Worcester, September 12, 1896, and at the Dedication of the Building, April 28, 1898, with an Account of the Semi-Centennial Celebration of the Incorporation of Worcester as a City, June 20–24." Worcester, Mass.: F. S. Blanchard, 1898.

Zeigler, Philip. *King Edward VIII*. New York: Knopf, 1991.

Zilboorg, Caroline. *Richard Aldington and H.D.: The Later Years in Letters*. Manchester, UK: Manchester University Press, 1996.

INDEX

Page numbers in italics refer to illustrations.

James Dempsey is an instructor in the Humanities and Arts Department at Worcester Polytechnic Institute, where he teaches writing and literature.